What people are saying about ...

D0395217

Survive or Thrive

"Jimmy Dodd writes not as a mere theorist but as a seasoned practitioner of his subject: pastors. Jimmy has twice been my pastor. He baptized my oldest daughter. He mentored me in my earliest years of ministry and has since served me and countless other pastors with a listening ear, an understanding heart, the wisest counsel, and the deepest encouragement for what Paul Tripp has called God's most 'dangerous calling.' If you are a pastor, desire to be a pastor, or want to understand and be a source of strength to your pastor, this is the book for you."

Scott Sauls, senior pastor of Christ
Presbyterian Church, Nashville, and
author of *Jesus outside the Lines*

"Even though ministry leaders are surrounded by people, leadership can be a lonely journey. The external pressures to perform and achieve and the internal struggles of the heart can sap a leader's passion and strength. It is crucial that leaders guard their hearts, and that is impossible to do alone. This book is a treasure trove of wise and practical advice for protecting and nurturing the heart of any leader. While serving as Compassion's president, for years I was fed by the ministry of Jimmy Dodd. I love that his warmth and humor come through in these, his down-to-earth written words. Let them guide you toward living in joyful authenticity."

Dr. Wess Stafford, president emeritus
of Compassion International

"Okay, let's be clear about Jimmy Dodd's book. It's a mess! It raises as many questions as it answers. It will make readers shake their heads in disagreement and shed tears of frustration. It details failure as graphically as any victory. It manages to crush every easy answer to pastoral effectiveness—and that's the point! We learn that the gospel that heals the broken and messed-up lives that pastors are called to help might just help pastors too. Jimmy points us to relationships that will help funnel the grace pastors need—if their humility will allow it."

Bryan Chapell, pastor of Grace
Presbyterian Church, Peoria

"I don't know anyone more qualified to expose and address the most critical issues pastors and church leaders are facing today than Jimmy Dodd. For decades Dodd has been sharing his life-changing 'six relationships' message with thousands of pastors and ministry leaders across a broad spectrum of ethnic groups and denominations. This gospel-centered message of hope and healing, deeply rooted in the relentless love of God in Christ, is finally being published. I highly recommend it."

Dr. Steve Childers, associate professor of
practical theology at Reformed Theological
Seminary, Orlando, and president
and CEO of Pathway Learning

"There's a special calling on the heart of anyone serving as a pastor, but that doesn't mean pastors aren't human. They need supportive relationships as much as anyone else does. The insights Jimmy Dodd shares in this book will help you as a pastor identify those areas in your life that need to be shored up, and they will give you practical guidance for reaching out to others."

Jim Daly, president of Focus on the Family

"The truth is that sometimes we as pastors have to just survive. But survival is a place to visit. The place where we want to live is in thriving. In this biblical and practical book, Jimmy has shown us the way to not just endure but also *enjoy* our ministry."

Darrin Patrick, lead pastor of The Journey,
St. Louis, vice president of Acts 29, and
chaplain to the St. Louis Cardinals

"Spiritual leaders are not immune to struggle. In fact, loneliness and relational dryness are common for those who take on the mantle of leading the people of God. Jimmy knows firsthand the challenges leaders face, and he is a sought-after authority in pastoral soul care. Spiritual leaders, whether pastor, nonprofit leader, or board chair, will benefit from these timeless truths."

Dr. Doug Nuenke, US president
of The Navigators

"As I began reading *Survive or Thrive*, I assumed it would be a good book to give my pastor friends in times of crisis. Having now read what Jimmy wrote, I have found it to be a book I personally needed to read. What incredible insights! This book will hit the target of every pastor's heart—and will certainly be the instrument God will use to rescue many a pastor who is convinced there is no hope."

Randy Pope, pastor of Perimeter Church

"*Survive or Thrive* is a must-read for any pastor, church board member, or leader who would like to see their organization flourish under leadership who has broken free of the life-condemning chains of pride, fear, and the demand for perfection. Jimmy Dodd's writing style, combined with his own transparency, is both winsome and effective as he explains the normalcy in some of the personal and vocational struggles facing Christian leaders today. At Peacemaker Ministries we see the catastrophic impact and consequences that come from leading in a vacuum. Jimmy Dodd has written what I believe is a God-ordained prescription for preventing most of those failures. This book will be on the top of our suggested reading list for clients and supporters."

Dale Pyne, CEO of
Peacemaker Ministries

"The emotional and spiritual health of a pastor affects the life of a congregation more than any other factor. As goes the health of the shepherd, so goes the health of the flock. I was a pastor in four churches over three decades. Now as a church consultant for the last ten years, I've concluded that shepherds are more needy than sheep. That's why every pastor needs a pastor. *Survive or Thrive* is a book for pastors written by a pastor's pastor, Jimmy Dodd. It has been honed from four decades of doing pastoral work and fifteen years with PastorServe Ministries. This book is the culmination of Jimmy's investment in pastors. He understands the world of a pastor, speaks our language (humorously and insightfully), and wraps his big arms around you through the pages of this book. Let Jimmy Dodd pastor you through this book and teach you how to thrive, not just survive, as a pastor. Your congregation will thank you."

Jim Tomberlin, pastor, author, church consultant, and founder of MultiSite Solutions

"Jimmy Dodd has effectively come alongside pastors for years through his wonderful organization, PastorServe. Now within this book you can receive the same coaching, cheering on, and practical insight he gives in person. He teaches pastors how to acknowledge their brokenness, embrace their weaknesses, and become outstanding leaders in their ministry and personal life. This book is affirming, enjoyable, practical, and challenging all at the same time."

Jim Burns, president of HomeWord and author of *Getting Ready for Marriage* and *Pass It On*

"You simply can't have a healthy church or youth ministry without a healthy pastor providing leadership. Unfortunately many of us in ministry reach out to others only after we've tried to figure it out on our own, and sometimes it's too late to change course. We need relationships before a crisis hits because relationships are preventative medicine, and Jimmy Dodd has identified six that each of us needs in order to thrive. His work at PastorServe has given him unprecedented access to the most sacred spaces in the lives of ministers in their darkest moments. Learn from the best, and begin moving from daily survival to growth."

Mark Matlock, executive director of Youth Specialties

"As a pastor and spiritual leader, you need relationships, people you can trust who are there for *you*. You are there for others; now Jimmy Dodd defines who you need and when you need them. Sometimes you need a coach, sometimes a trainer, maybe a counselor, definitely a friend, certainly a mentor, and like it or not, even a boss. Jimmy Dodd hits the bull's-eye with this book. Now you have a guide to help you find the right people to serve you."

Floyd McClung, founder of All
Nations, Cape Town

"Many pastors I meet operate under the false premise that they need to be superheroes. Jimmy reminds us that this is not only wrong but dangerous. This book will help you see the six key relationships every pastor *must* have in his life. These relationships will help you as a pastor not only survive but thrive! It's a must-read!"

Patrick O'Connell, president
of NewThing Network

"This is a great and necessary book written by one of the most gifted guys I know. Jimmy Dodd is supremely relational, is loved and respected everywhere he goes, and has personally worked through a complex and painful ministry crisis. Ironically, people in Christian ministry find themselves in a vocation with one of the lowest job-satisfaction ratings, and we don't share healthy relationships with one another. More often than not, we are isolated and alone. If this describes you, you need this book and the wise, godly people of PastorServe!"

Gary Kinnaman, former senior pastor, author
of *Leaders That Last*, and pastor to pastors

"There is a certain language that spiritual shepherds speak. For pastors, this language is honed by unseen acts of leadership, personal sacrifice, congregational comprehension and misunderstanding, feeling overwhelmed, fatigue, and bouts of emotional and spiritual dryness. Jimmy Dodd knows 'pastor speak.' Better still, he has experienced and knows the full suite of 'pastor think,' 'pastor feel,' and best of all 'pastor thrive.' Lots of practical advice in this volume from a successful practitioner and consultant to those called to one of the most demanding of journeys."

Steve Haas, chief catalyst of
World Vision United States

"As a loan officer who deals almost exclusively with churches, I see the strength and sustainability of church leadership as important as the financial strength of a church. It is our experience that the most damaging event a church can experience is the moral failure of leadership. When we see that a church is connected to and consults with PastorServe, our concern in this area of the underwriting process lessens significantly. As church leaders, you *must* protect the integrity of your church and remain above reproach. *Survive or Thrive* provides you with the armor needed to do so."

Jim Lehman, senior vice president of
Central Bank of the Midwest

"After working in full-time ministry for over forty years, I am no stranger to the relational challenges that exist alongside the rewards. Pastor Jimmy Dodd candidly addresses these challenges in *Survive or Thrive*, reminding every pastor that their relationship choices matter! Emphasizing the importance of biblical community, Pastor Dodd provides practical insight to fulfilling the relational needs that many pastors place on the back burner. His wise words prove to be a worthwhile read!"

Dr. Joe White, president of Kanakuk Ministries

"I've known Jimmy Dodd for thirty-four years. He has consistently loved Jesus and the church all of those years. The wisdom he has gained in ministry comes through in his new book, *Survive or Thrive*, in such a way that every pastor can benefit and thrive as they make the most of the complex, yet high call of shepherding God's people."

Jerry Root, PhD, associate professor at Wheaton College and author of *The Sacrament of Evangelism*

"This is an important book. Rooted in gospel grace, Jimmy Dodd addresses the biggest challenges facing today's pastorate. This book is filled with real-life stories, heart-wrenching honesty, and challenging insight, and Dodd's love for pastors is evident throughout. Every pastor who has the privilege of serving God's church needs to read *Survive or Thrive*!"

Rob Bentz, author of *The Unfinished Church* and pastor of Woodmen Valley Chapel, Colorado Springs

"Oftentimes the most transformational realities come to us in the form of things we have always sensed but never fully articulated and, therefore, never completely understood. That's the potential of *Survive or Thrive*. Reading this book will reveal great truths in service of a life of freedom devoted to God's glory. It will also introduce you to a man well traveled in the role of each of these six relationships. My prayer for readers of this book is that many will embrace the freedom of the gospel of God's scandalous grace. And that God will create communities of wise Christians who embrace their weaknesses, the reality of their needs, and the beauty of the diverse community of relationships God has designed us to need!"

Kevin Cawley, preaching pastor and directional leader of Redeemer Fellowship, Kansas City

"Jimmy Dodd is a pastor's pastor, and that calling comes through on every page of *Survive or Thrive*. I've known Jimmy for three decades, and his credibility to write such a book comes from years in ministry alongside pastors. He's familiar with the explosions of the battlefield, the dryness of the desert, the replenishment of the oasis, and the joy of the harvest. He is also fluent in the grace that strengthens us. His practical wisdom and shepherd's heart permeate each chapter, and I am excited about many more pastors being able to experience the encouragement of having Jimmy come alongside them through his writing."

Matt Heard, author of *Life with a Capital L*

"Pastors struggle with burning out, bumming out, and failing out of ministry. When they fail morally, our company often gets to look at the problem through the lens of litigation. We're coming to realize that helping pastors thrive in ministry is a form of risk management we've neglected for far too long. Jimmy Dodd and PastorServe are standing in the gap. If this important and insightful book helps prevent even one pastor's moral failure, the kingdom value is immeasurable."

Hugh White, MDiv, CPCU, vice president of
Strategic Relationships, Brotherhood Mutual

"Spiritual Lone Rangers preaching their silver bullets and riding out into the badlands armed with only a reference Bible to lasso souls for the kingdom are as fictional and futile as the Lone Ranger himself. It has always taken a posse to do the Lord's work—even for the greatest of apostles. Jimmy Dodd profiles the posse that we all need in his tried and true *Survive or Thrive.* Jimmy's devotion to biblical principles and candor make for an exhilarating and life-saving read."

R. Kent Hughes, senior pastor emeritus
of College Church, Wheaton, and visiting
professor of pastoral ministry at Westminster
Theological Seminary, Philadelphia

"John Lennon called the Beach Boys' 'In My Room' one of the greatest songs ever written. In the song, Brian Wilson talks about his room as his safe place where he can reflect, dream, pray, and 'tell his secrets.' Brian's room may have saved his life, but he constantly struggled because he did not have a support group to draw strength from. Jimmy Dodd's *Survive or Thrive* provides both a safe place for pastors as well as keys to success in the forms of insight, instruction, and encouragement to pastors. Jimmy Dodd and PastorServe are wonderful gifts to all pastors and their churches."

Bill Johnson, president of Prepare-Enrich

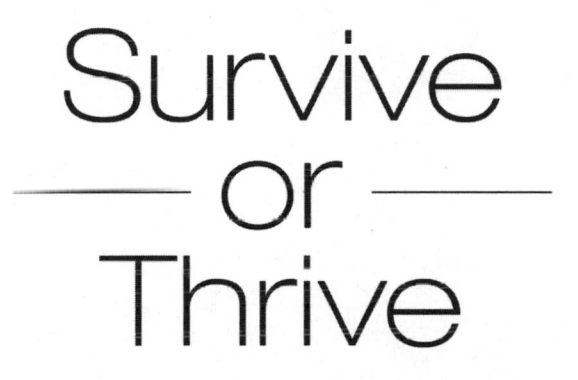

Survive
— or —
Thrive

Jimmy Dodd

Survive
— or —
Thrive

6 Relationships Every Pastor Needs

A
PastorServe
— RESOURCE —

David C Cook®
transforming lives together

SURVIVE OR THRIVE
Published by David C Cook
4050 Lee Vance View
Colorado Springs, CO 80918 U.S.A.

David C Cook Distribution Canada
55 Woodslee Avenue, Paris, Ontario, Canada N3L 3E5

David C Cook U.K., Kingsway Communications
Eastbourne, East Sussex BN23 6NT, England

The graphic circle C logo is a registered trademark of David C Cook.

The website addresses recommended throughout this book are offered as a
resource to you. These websites are not intended in any way to be or imply an
endorsement on the part of David C Cook, nor do we vouch for their content.

All Scripture quotations are taken from The Holy Bible, English Standard
Version® (ESV®), copyright © 2001 by Crossway, a publishing ministry
of Good News Publishers. Used by permission. All rights reserved. The
author has added italics to Scripture quotations for emphasis.
Maturity Gap Index © 2015 PastorServe.

Some names have been changed to protect the privacy
of the individuals mentioned in this book.

LCCN 2015944606
ISBN 978-1-4347-0919-6
eISBN 978-1-4347-0963-9

© 2015 Jimmy Dodd
Published in association with the literary agency of Wolgemuth & Associates, Inc.

The Team: Alex Field, Jamie Chavez, Amy Konyndyk, Nick
Lee, Jack Campbell, Susan Murdock, Karen Athen
Cover Design: FaceOut Studio, Tim Green
Cover Photo: Getty; Shutterstock

Printed in the United States of America
First Edition 2015

1 2 3 4 5 6 7 8 9 10

071015

To my son, Mark Dodd. I could not be more proud of you for following the call of our heavenly Father. I am incredibly thankful to the Lord for blessing me with a son who is committed to living out the gospel. As you pastor God's people, may the words of this book reflect your life and your ministry. I love being your dad.

Contents

Preface

Just this past week, PastorServe advised a Texas pastor as he wrote a letter of resignation to his congregation. His resignation revolved around secrets. A brief excerpt follows:

> It's with the deepest sense of regret and sadness that I am resigning as your lead pastor. I'm not currently qualified due to sin in my life that I unfortunately allowed to take root and grow. I didn't listen when it was obvious that God was trying to get my attention. I have violated many people's trust. I embarked down a road of keeping secrets. As one who has tried to follow Christ I'm not sure what is worse, the sin itself or the secret life of hiding. There are so many lessons, so much to say, and so much to learn.

The powerful core of the letter of resignation—"I embarked down a road of keeping secrets … *I'm not sure what is worse, the sin itself or the secret life of hiding*"—is heartbreaking. Countless pastors have left the church because they arrogantly walked a road of keeping secrets, convincing themselves they would walk alone rather than face being fired.

Conversations with the pastor revealed a typical story, which I have heard on numerous occasions. I walked through the six relationships with the pastor, who then responded, "Professionally, we are a staff-led independent church, so I don't have a boss. I don't regularly receive training, primarily because I am the trainer and I have never had a ministry coach. Personally, I have never been to counseling; I lost touch with my mentor a decade ago, and if I were completely honest, I don't have one single friend."

We see this truth revealed again and again: When the six relationships are absent, a pastor is on the verge of a crumbling cliff. If nothing changes, he or she will certainly fall. The question is not if but when.

God created people with an intrinsic need for relationship. *And I'll be one of your first.* Thank you for journeying with me. I count it a privilege to walk with you as a friend, a mentor, a counselor, a trainer, and a coach.

Let me acknowledge, then, that I struggled to find ways in the book to convey my acceptance of females in the role of pastor. I am grateful the Lord has called women who love the Lord Jesus and preach the gospel to serve as pastors. At PastorServe, we have a female pastor who is a critical part of our team. We serve a wide variety of denominations, many of which unreservedly ordain women. That said, ordained clergy in the United States are overwhelmingly male.

How to be inclusive then? In the majority of cases, I defaulted to the masculine pronoun when speaking of pastors and I most commonly refer to "wives" when talking about the pastor's spouse. I've used some sports analogies, which may appeal more to men, but that's my perspective. This is not intended to slight female pastors or male spouses. I apologize for any unnecessary roadblocks I have placed in the paths of female pastors reading this book.

I have worked to make this book as readable in the townships of Johannesburg, South Africa, as in suburban United States. Despite my best efforts, there will be some illustrations and sections more easily understood by an American audience. I pray that this book will read as easily in the urban core as in suburban or rural contexts. PastorServe is committed to serving as a multicultural ministry. From the outset, our staff has included white, African American, and Hispanic pastors, and we have a desire to add additional ethnic pastors to the PastorServe team. We have pastors serving the urban core, the suburbs, and rural communities. We are committed to serving the whole church.

Finally, it's important to me you know that 100 percent of the proceeds of this book are being poured back into PastorServe in order that every pastor would have a safe place to go to have access to equipping and care for the challenges and crises they face. Because every pastor needs a pastor.

Jimmy Dodd
Kansas City
April 2015

Introduction
Front Stage and Back Stage

I'm outraged! Well, I'm a *little* outraged. Okay, I honestly wish there was a whole lot more outrage. Let me explain.

I am a big sports fan. Just in the past couple of weeks, I have suffered through two major officiating gaffes that likely cost two of my favorite teams certain victories. The days following the blown calls were filled with every sports reporter and even the president of the United States expressing outrage at the horrific calls. There was genuine anger. One of the referees who made the decisive call that cost a team a critical victory reported that, in the following days, he had received multiple death threats. In less than twenty-four hours, frustrated exasperation had morphed into frenzied rage.

As I closely followed the news reports, stoking my personal fire of sports outrage, I was unexpectedly reminded that I am outraged over games being played by grown-up boys who are being paid millions of dollars. I was outraged that a referee, doing his very best, made a bad decision that just happened to be witnessed by millions across the planet. I was—and am—outraged over trivial, insignificant, irrelevant, increasingly small things.

I am seldom outraged over the things that outrage God. Worse, I am all too often apathetic over the things that demand godly outrage. I should be outraged that more than twenty-seven million people are living in slavery. I should be outraged that sexual trafficking targets children as young as five years old. I need to feel outrage that two billion people live in extreme poverty. I need to be outraged that twenty-one thousand children under the age of five die each day from preventable causes. I should be outraged that roughly six million children per year under the age of five die from hunger. That's one every five seconds.

Allow me to bring this outrage a little closer to your vocational home.

I need to experience outrage that more than half of those who are called to the pastoral ministry leave within the first five years. I should be angered that the majority of pastors believe there is no place to confidentially process their disappointment. I should be outraged that pastors suffer in silence feeling as if there is no safe place for them to turn. I want to experience heightened outrage that an overwhelming majority of pastors do not feel they were adequately trained to face the challenges that await them in the local church.

Front Stage and Back Stage

I am a fan of the fine arts. And while my male insecurities want me to assure you that I am a bigger fan of sports, I openly confess that I have long enjoyed everything from film to poetry to the musical theater. In fact, I enjoy attending a Broadway musical as much as a college basketball game. I remember attending my first musical on Broadway at the tender age of eight. My family (Mom, Dad, and my older brother, Kenny) enjoyed front row seats for *Man of La Mancha*.

I can't honestly say that hearing Don Quixote sing "The Impossible Dream" changed my life, but it was a splendid introduction to the musical stage. Since then, I have been blessed to witness some of the finest Broadway productions.

If you have ever had the opportunity to tour a fine arts theater, you know that there are two distinctive sections—the front stage and the back stage. The front stage includes the lobby, the auditorium, and the stage itself. These are the areas of the theater that are visible to the general public. Tremendous attention is paid to these spaces. The back stage is a different story. Accessible only to employees of the theater, the area is out of public view. It's where you store the props, wardrobe, and sets. The back stage houses the dressing rooms and the makeup tables. The back stage is where the production invisibly takes shape before it is presented to the public.

On one particular occasion I was asked to emcee an event that was to take place at a gorgeous theater. This particular venue had hosted some of the great musicals over many decades. As a much younger man, I'd seen Yul Brynner on this very stage starring in *The King and I*. Naturally, while I was excited to host the event and work with some incredibly gifted musicians, I was perhaps even more excited to see the inner workings of an iconic theater. I arrived the night before the event for a brief rehearsal. And what I saw that night the human language has yet to invent words to describe.

The back stage of the theater was a muddled, chaotic mess! It appeared to be in complete disarray. The back stage was filthy, dingy, dark, grimy, foreboding, and downright nasty. Tiny quarantined corners separated by sheets served as makeshift dressing areas. Costumes dangled on hooks everywhere! The light board looked like a five-year-old had scribbled all over it with a Sharpie. It was difficult to walk without tripping, as every inch of available space seemed to be littered with props and pieces of scenery. My high school had more space to stage performances. I simply couldn't believe it. And I was walking around with the back stage lights on! Imagine navigating this minefield in the back stage darkness of a production. How could a personality as large as Yul Brynner perform amid such disorder? The tiny back stage in no way reflected the massive lighted sign in front of the theater. I struggled to process this lack of congruence. I had been to performance after performance in this theater. From my seat in the audience, the theater was pristine. The stage was magnificent! And now, my idealistic perception of the theater had been permanently crushed by the dissonance between the front stage and the back stage.

The front stage–back stage image goes far beyond the material space of a theater. It's the same in my home. Physically, we have front stage areas, namely the living room and kitchen, and back stage areas, which would include the garage, basement office, and storage area. If anyone wants a tour of our house, we are definitely skipping the back stage! And there is another form of front stage and back stage in the Dodd household. If you come to my home, I want you to meet my family. I want you to hear about how my children are growing in their walk with the Lord Jesus. I want you to hear about how they are using their gifts and their passions to advance God's kingdom agenda. However, I will likely not talk with you about the conflict that dominated our kitchen only hours before. I won't share our bank account information with you. There are a number of "Dodd family back stage issues" I don't want you to see.

The same applies to any church, any ministry, any educational institution, or any business. Naturally, we long to make an extraordinary first impression. If I am the president of a private liberal arts college and you visit my campus, I am not going to lead off our discussion with the fact that we are currently running a deficit and the board of trustees is considering eliminating five majors. I won't mention the foundation issues recently discovered beneath the freshman dorm that will result in next year's freshman class living in temporary student housing. I will focus on the positives, doing everything I can to present a first-class public persona.

In the case of the church, the front stage is what the congregation perceives on Sunday morning. We hope they see an organized, healthy, vibrant church led by competent, gifted, unified individuals. Meanwhile, in reality, the back stage of a church can be a place of chaos, conflict, miscommunication, and personal agendas where the staff struggle with the same mundane sins that plague the average believer. The back stage can be filled with contentious ministry meetings, argumentative staff gatherings, and combative board meetings.

My wife, Sally, and I were privileged to plant a church in Kansas City. And in our church, while my giftedness was pushed to the front stage for all to see, my character was pushed to the back stage, where no one would ever truly see what lay beneath. My front stage was one of smiles, confidence, and togetherness while my back stage was one of envy, jealousy, anger, pride, defensiveness, arrogance … (it's a long list). While some caught a peek of my back stage, it was commonly dismissed because of what I offered on the front stage. While I clearly had issues that were crying out for attention, who wants to rock the

boat when I was leading a growing church? Like an immature athlete who consistently leads the team to victory, my back stage issues
were ignored as long as the front stage persona was one of church
growth and financial stability. Ignored that is, until, through a series
of painful events that I would never trade for anything, the gospel
of Jesus Christ marvelously destroyed the emotionally thick curtain
that separated the front stage from the back.

We Can't Fire You!

For close to two decades, I have shared the six-relationship message
with thousands of pastors and ministry leaders. Additionally, I have
had the privilege of sharing this message with business leaders, teachers, athletes, musicians, coaches, medical personnel, and a host of
other individuals. While this book is targeted to pastors and ministry
leaders, everyone can benefit from the six relationships.

The factors that contribute to the downfall of so many pastors
are most closely paralleled in college athletic coaches. Like pastors,
college coaches commonly feel as if they have no place to go to be
100 percent honest. They certainly wouldn't share their struggles
with the team. In this day of social media, a private confession to a
team can instantly become a very public embarrassment. No mother
wants to send her son to play for (and be mentored by) a coach who
is struggling with moral issues.

Similarly, many business leaders have sought me out in order to
process the loneliness of leading multimillion-dollar corporations.
So, while you may not be a pastor or in full-time vocational ministry,
there is a good chance the principles set forth in this book will apply

directly to you. I encourage you to read this book in the context of your particular vocation.

I am privileged to write from extensive life experience. In 1999, the Lord directed Sally and me to resign from our church and launch the ministry of PastorServe. Filled with fear, we stepped away from the beloved church we had planted to follow a call that was undeniable—that of pastoring pastors. Since that time, by God's gracious hand, PastorServe has grown to be widely recognized as one of the leading ministries of its kind. The PastorServe team serves pastors from every denomination, every race, and every geographic location. We have served thousands of churches and tens of thousands of pastors. We consult with male and female pastors, pastoral spouses, and ministry leadership. We have worked closely with church boards as well as denominational leadership. The reason why we have experienced exponential growth is really quite simple. PastorServe is a gospel-centered, confidential ministry that provides care, coaching, and crisis support to pastors in America and around the world. We provide training and counseling, and we are friends to thousands of pastors.

But we are no one's boss. That's the key. We hold no autonomous authority. We have zero positional authority. The only authority we carry at PastorServe is imputed authority. We have only as much influence as we are given. *We can't fire you.* We are outsiders. And we wouldn't have it any other way.

Many pastors confide in me that they are merely surviving. They feel incompetent to do what they are expected to do—week after week. They labor to lead in areas in which they were never trained. For many, the thought of thriving in ministry is a distant, unachievable dream. And yet, I know the Lord has called every pastor and ministry leader to experience the joy of thriving in ministry! Hear me, thriving is not defined by numbers or accomplishments. Pastors who are thriving are not necessarily those who are well known, respected by peers, or financially secure. Thriving has nothing to do with whether a church meets in a grade school, an open-air hut, or a 500,000-square-foot megachurch. Personally, I know thriving pastors who lead seemingly insignificant churches and I know surviving pastors who are regarded as international spiritual superstars. Thriving has everything to do with the heart of a leader.

Acknowledging Brokenness

Let me be clear. I am not the hero of this book. In fact, as you will read, in many ways I have lived as the antagonist to the protagonist, Jesus. This book is not intended to serve as a checklist to high-performance living. Anyone who thinks that filling the six relationships alone will lead to pastoral thriving will be sorely disappointed. The six relationships are not a system that will fix your life. This is not a guide to ministry leadership behavior modification. There is no formula to guarantee you ministry success—as success is defined by culture. This book is not your hope. While there are helpful insights contained in the following pages, Jesus is your only hope. The beginning point of this journey is to acknowledge brokenness and your constant, consistent, daily need for a savior. For many in pastoral ministry and ministry leadership, the starting point is simply to acknowledge need. And yet, many find it difficult to acknowledge the need for anything, let alone six relationships. We need to reframe and reculture pastoral ministry, allowing pastors to acknowledge weakness, embrace brokenness, and reject isolation.

I write with the full understanding that there is nothing new under the sun. I don't claim to have a novel approach to pastoral ministry. This book is not the "Six Secrets." While I write with nearly four decades of pastoral ministry experience, I certainly don't believe that I have cracked the pastoral crisis code. While I would like to tell you that this book is a chronicle of personal pastoral success, in reality the majority of insights contained in the following pages have been gleaned through repeated failure. Furthermore, in no way do I believe this is the definitive book on pastoral ministry. Far better works precede this book, and I anticipate superior books to follow. I do wholeheartedly believe that this book will contribute to and advance the conversation, though.

I invite you to journey with me from surviving to thriving. While you may be tempted to skip to section 2 and jump into the six relationships, I strongly encourage you to start at the beginning to learn how and why pastors and ministry leaders have buried themselves in relational survival mode. Before we detail how to begin to tear down the curtain and reveal our back stage brokenness, let's be clear on the factors that initially led to the construction of the isolationist curtain. Let's be clear on what has driven pastors deeper and deeper into the well-worn ruts of shame and fear. Let's understand why culture has driven a wedge between our private and public lives—which only adds to the front stage–back stage curtain. It's important to understand root causes behind the dark hole of secrets and pretending. And finally, as we will discuss in section 3, our greatest confidence that transforms hope to certainty is that the isolationist curtain has been ultimately destroyed by the life, death, and resurrection of the Lord Jesus Christ.

I encourage you to read this book in the context of community. A gathering of local pastors coming together to discuss this book would be ideal. A church staff or a ministry staff would greatly benefit from processing this material together, as a team. The questions at the conclusion of each chapter will serve as a guide for discussion.

Let's get started.

Survive

The Heart of the Problem—How Did We Arrive Here?

I couldn't make this conversation up if I tried.

Recently, I was attending an event at the invitation of a PastorServe board member. As I stood in a noisy, crowded room, I strained to engage in conversations above the deafening roar of the crowd. It was one of those times when each sentence requires you to lean in toward the ear of the listener and speak at a level just below a shout. I met one gentleman who introduced himself as a vice president of a local bank. Then, in a piercing voice, he asked me about my occupation. I loudly responded that I was privileged to serve on the PastorServe team. I went on to explain how PastorServe works around the country serving pastors. He nodded enthusiastically as I went on to describe our work in greater detail. And then, the following exact conversation took place.

"That's amazing work. You must feel deeply satisfied helping so many farmers. So what is your favorite crop?"

After a lengthy period of silence, I replied, "I'm sorry, did you just ask me about my favorite crop?"

"Yes, you said that you work with farmers to help them produce the very best yield from their crop."

Another long pause; then I said, "I work with PastorServe, a ministry serving pastors and churches across the country." Then the miscommunication struck me. "We serve pastors—not pastures."

"Oh," he said, now laughing. "I thought you said 'Pasture Serve.' I thought you traveled across the country helping farmers with their pastures."

Communication. Even in a quiet room, it's a challenge. Too often, miscommunication feels like the standard. Misunderstandings, assumptions, body language, tone of voice, defensiveness, and assigning motives all make it challenging to effectively connect and convey ideas. It's no surprise that communication issues remain at the center of the majority of church conflicts.

Chapter 1

What Drives Us Back Stage?

I admit it; I love sports. While my wife remains unconvinced that this is a God-given gift, I can engage in a respectable conversation about most any sport. Recently, my attention was drawn to an amazing young athlete who quarterbacks a highly ranked college football team. A remarkable physical specimen, on the football field he is a natural, a superstar. National sportswriters describe him as a once-in-a-generation player, and he consistently executes above and beyond expectations on the field of play.

However, few were surprised when it was revealed that this star football player was in trouble—again. While the fan base appreciated his leading the university to consecutive conference titles, they most reluctantly acknowledged that his superior athletic ability had a dark side, commonly known as extreme immaturity bordering on sheer idiocy. Time and time again his outrageous off-field decisions resulted in a call to the local authorities followed by a meeting with the athletic director, a negative headline in the local sports page, a brief suspension, and embarrassment for every alumni and fan of the university. And yet, when memory of the wrongdoing (or in some cases, crime) faded, he was enthusiastically welcomed back, because we like to say we are all about second chances—and because the team couldn't win without him.

Why is it that when the talent and skill level are off the charts, we are more tolerant of glaring immaturity, even scandalous behavior? What causes us to turn a blind eye to deep character issues when the benefits of talent bring so many positives? *Yes, I know he confessed to spousal abuse, but we just won the Super Bowl!*

Going a bit deeper, why do we apply words such as *amazing*, *incredible*, and *remarkable* to people when we know absolutely nothing about their personal lives? "Our quarterback is an amazing person." "That singer is incredible." "That actress is the absolute best." "I am in love with that author." "She is the most remarkable designer." I get it. It feels only natural to praise those whom we admire on the front stage of public performance despite the fact that we know nothing about their back stage private personas. I'm not judging people who use such words. I have used similar expressions on countless occasions. My favorite professional football team, the Green Bay Packers, has been led by a number of quarterbacks I have described as incredible, amazing, and at times, faultless. I was fortunate to be present when my favorite college team, the Kansas Jayhawks basketball team, won their fifth national championship. That night in San Antonio, I struggled to find adequate superlatives to describe every member of the championship team, including the players, coaches, team managers, ball boys, and bus driver. In moments like these, we magnify natural gifts and abilities while minimizing character flaws.

When we apply adoring, descriptive, character-based words to people we essentially know nothing about, we are naively feeding a monster. We are adding fabric to the curtain separating the front stage from the back stage. We are driving a wedge even deeper between the public and the private. We are affirming that what takes place in the private sector (off the field) has no impact on the public sector (on the field). We are applauding the front stage performance while we turn a blind eye to embarrassing back stage behavior. And, well fed, this monster can lead to behavior for which there is little to no explanation.

Similar Problems in the Church

We have a mounting epidemic in the church. We have far too many amazing, wonderful, incredible pastors.

I recently attended a leadership conference with a number of fellow pastors. Following a particularly powerful message from a well-known speaker, a friend leaned over to me and said (actually he gushed), "Wow! What a message! I love that guy! He is incredible! I can't believe how someone that young can be that mature! That was life changing!" Words typically used to describe elite athletes and Hollywood celebrities were now being enthusiastically applied to this well-known Christian speaker.

It's harmless, common, everyday language, right? In the case of the conference speaker, clearly my friend was deeply touched by a particular message. Thank the Lord! And yet, it's this common, everyday, seemingly innocent language of adulation (bordering on idolatrous worship) that pushes leaders down a dangerous road of secrets, deception, fraud, and lies. What I want to say to people (and sometimes I do) is that while I can appreciate their admiration of the speaker, they have selected the wrong words to describe the person delivering the message. What my friend at the conference meant is that the message delivered by the speaker was insightful, powerful, even life transformational. He was thankful to the Lord for gifting a speaker with the incredible ability to so clearly deliver a message. I considered asking, "Have you ever met the speaker? Do you know anything about his marriage, his parenting, his temperament, his walk with the Lord, or his personal habits? Do you know how he treats his staff? Do you know how he handles money? Is his life characterized by humility? Is he a man of prayer?" Far too often we link giftedness, talent, and skill with maturity and character. And it is this mistake that contributes to multitudes of pastors shrinking into a life of hiding, deception, fear, and fraud. I should know. This is my story.

Gripped by Fear

My wife and I had the privilege of serving on the pastoral teams of thriving churches in Wheaton, Illinois; Lexington, Massachusetts; and Greenville, South Carolina. In the early '90s, my wife and I returned to our beloved home state of Kansas to plant a church in the Kansas City suburbs.

While challenges confronted us at every turn, the church grew. If you looked at the church from an outside perspective, you would have seen a young, vibrant, healthy, growing, influential church being led by a youthful, energetic, passionate pastoral team. An outstanding children's program, engaging worship, faithful expositional preaching, exceptional small groups, and a commitment to missional living and generosity were pillars of the church. From day one, the church dedicated 40 percent of all its resources to needs outside the local congregation. We were engaged with the urban core of Kansas City, the poor, the prisoner, and the sick. The congregation included a healthy mixture of mature believers and new Christians. Not surprisingly, people enthusiastically invited their friends to be a part of this new church.

The front stage looked good—*really good*—from a seat in the middle of the theater. However, a look into the back stage of the church would have revealed a young lead pastor whose life was dominated by insecurity, defensiveness, envy, and above all, fear. And it was these things that Satan used to twist my heart into knots even as I led an outstanding church. Before I continue the story, I believe it's important to briefly review the most common tools used by Satan in his attempt to destroy the lives of believers.

The Limitations of Satan

The Screwtape Letters is a classic Christian apologetic novel written by C. S. Lewis in 1942. In his satirical work, Lewis recounts letters from a senior demon, Screwtape, to a junior demon, Wormwood, who also happens to be his nephew, regarding how to bring down a client—a new believer in Jesus. It takes a little time to get used to the structure of the letters. God the Father is referred to as "The Enemy" and "The Evil One." "The Bad News" is the gospel of Jesus Christ. Satan is referred to as his infernal majesty.

We must be reminded that Satan has a limited toolbox. While he unquestionably possesses power, his power is strictly limited by God the Father, who has Satan on a short leash, meaning that Satan can do nothing to thwart the ultimate purposes of

God. While Satan certainly possesses power, unlike God he is not omnipotent. Similarly, unlike God the Father, Satan cannot be all places at all times. He is not omnipresent. And while Satan is aware of many things, he is far from omniscient. For example, Satan cannot hear the prayers of believers. Unlike God the Father, he does not know everything. Whereas God is a creator, Satan is a destroyer. He does nothing new, as he can only do unoriginal ideas or designs (or undo original ideas or designs). Everything that Satan does is a cheap counterfeit of the original. Satan is a $5 Tijuana Rolex, a worthless, cheap imitation of the original. He is a bogus, back-alley phony. Do not give him more credit than he deserves!

When teaching on spiritual warfare, I regularly engage the audience in a simple game of opposites. Answer the following simple questions: What is the opposite of up? How about the opposite of over? Not too hard, huh? The opposite of large? Do you know the opposite of in? Any ten-year-old could easily answer any of these questions. Let's go on. What is the opposite of light? What is the opposite of good? What is the opposite of love? Finally, what is the opposite of God? Okay, pencils down. Let's check your work. (Does anyone else still get a nervous tic when you hear those words?)

I can set your mind at ease by affirming the opposite of up is indeed down. And despite what your college philosophy professor taught, the opposite of over is under, the opposite of large is small, and the opposite of in is indeed out. It was this brilliance that allowed you to escape third grade relatively unscathed. Nonetheless, the opposite of light is *not* dark and the opposite of good is definitely *not* bad. Furthermore, the opposite of love is far from hate and the opposite of God is certainly *not* Satan. In fact, the words *light, good, love*, and *God* have no opposite. *Pure, beauty*, and *truth* are just a few more of the many other words that have no opposite.

Let's begin with light. Light and darkness do not share equal properties. Light will always push back darkness, but darkness will never overwhelm light. Darkness is not the opposite of light; rather, it is the absence of light. Similarly, bad is the absence of good. As my friend Jerry Root would say, bad is to good as bread mold is to bread. While love has no opposite, the closest word would be *indifference*. Stated another way, hate is nowhere as hateful as love is loving. Bad is not as bad as good is good. Why is this so important? Simply for this primary reason. *Satan is not the opposite of God.* God is good (Psalm 136:1), God is beautiful (Psalm 27:4), God is light (1 John 1:5), and God is love (1 John 4:7–8). Satan is none of these attributes. I am amazed at the number of believers who for some unknown reason are convinced that Satan is God's archenemy, reverse equal. Again, Satan is extremely limited in his ability to attack believers. And yet, his primary tool in his toolbox is spawning confusion, chaos, and devastation in the lives of countless believers.

The primary tool that Satan regularly pulls out of his toolbox is that of lies. Without equal, Satan is the world's greatest liar. He lives to whisper lies into the ears of believers. Even more, he loves to plant lies into the hearts of pastors and ministry leaders. And while I was leading a growing church, Satan whispered lies into my adoration-loving ears, numerous lies that I believed for many years.

Some of Satan's most frequently whispered and often believed lies include:

- God may forgive you, but you can never forgive yourself.
- If people really knew you, they wouldn't like you. Therefore, don't allow anyone to really get to know you.
- You have no choice but to give in to this temptation.
- Because of the amount of time you labor, you deserve an occasional shortcut. No one will know or care if you cut a few ethical corners.
- Never trust anyone. No one is safe. Keep your secrets to yourself.
- For all you do for the Lord and for this church, you deserve to indulge in this particular sin.
- You are the only person struggling with this particular sin. Your friends don't struggle with this sin. No one does. You are the only one.
- This sin is the only way to fill the void in your life. Nothing else will numb your pain.
- This sin has not fulfilled you in the past. In fact, this sin has always left a void, but this time is different. This time you will be fulfilled.
- God is supremely disappointed in you. He expected so much more from you. You need to work your tail off to make God proud of you.

- You can handle this just one more time. Nothing bad will happen to you.
- You have what you have because you are an amazing person who has worked hard. You deserve everything you have.
- God is mad at you. In fact, God is downright furious with you.

In my case, I believed that if people knew the real Jimmy Dodd, they wouldn't like the real Jimmy Dodd. And so, posing, pretending, hiding, and deceiving characterized my life. I might allow you to get to know 90 percent of my story, but the final 10 percent was reserved for only me. I worked hard to be perceived as being whole (as opposed to broken) and competent (as opposed to clueless). What made this all the more severe was that in the midst of my commitment not to allow anyone into the dark recesses of my heart, I was hearing inflated words of affirmation and adoration from those around me. This fed the pride monster that steeled my determination not to allow anyone inside where they would get their first glimpse of the real me.

Over the course of my ministry with PastorServe, I have heard a frighteningly similar story from literally thousands of pastors. Most pastors and ministry leaders fear letting anyone inside. In fact, I believe the above paragraph describes the majority of pastors in America and around the world. I have heard a similar description from pastors in Europe, Asia, Africa, South America, and the Middle East.

In my personal life, the curtain between the front stage and the back stage was thick. The discontinuity between perception and reality was frightening. What people saw on the front stage only convinced me to do more to hide the back stage realities of brokenness.

The Deception of Giftedness

We all know stories of gifted pastors and ministry leaders who live life largely unchallenged. Gifted Christian leaders with substantial maturity issues continue to lead. Believers turn a blind eye. Church leadership charged with guarding the biblical integrity of the church ignores the obvious. We know the end is coming, but we continue to justify their leadership while ignoring their lack of integrity because of the results of their ministry. But church growth, people committing their lives to follow Jesus, and the poor being served do not justify ungodly leadership.

When a leader possesses unusually keen insight, prodigious quantities of knowledge, the ability to communicate in everyday language, and an unbridled passion for leadership, we place him or her in a special category of giftedness. The more exclusive the category of giftedness, the more reluctant people will be to challenge their leadership. *The irony is that exactly the opposite is required.* The higher the giftedness of an individual, the greater the need for accountability. Or, stated another way, the greater the talent of an individual, the greater the need for corresponding character (much more on this in chapter 2).

Why do some leaders possessing off-the-chart giftedness live a life of off-the-chart immaturity? Let's face it; most people are not comfortable challenging supremely gifted individuals who are leading growing churches and ministries. And it's fun to be friends with gifted people. We are flattered when someone we consider to be famous remembers our name.

I remember being pursued by a particular church to become the lead pastor. My wife and I gave a great deal of time to prayer, but we felt strongly that the Lord had not called us to leave Kansas City. When I called the chairman of the search committee to inform him that I would not be accepting the call, he informed me that (1) I had not heard correctly from the Lord. God did want me to come, and I was now living in disobedience. (2) He had forgotten to inform me of one of the perks of the lead pastor position. Because the general manager of the local NBA team attended this particular church, the lead pastor would also serve as the chaplain to the local NBA team. The chaplain position also came with a pair of complimentary front row season tickets. Was I sure that God wasn't calling me to leave Kansas City?

I'm embarrassed to say the "NBA twist" gave me pause. The thought of friendship with NBA players and rubbing shoulders with the rich and famous while sitting courtside was enticing. Why? Because I liked the thought of being linked to people who possessed rare athletic ability. And because of that fact alone, I would have been a terrible NBA chaplain. The only person qualified to serve as chaplain in any sport is the one who is not impressed by the players. In the end, despite the front row tickets, I turned down the position.

I Know I Don't Want to Be a Pastor

By 1998, my life was out of control and something desperately needed to change. It's exhausting to go through life pretending that you are better than you actually are, and I was exhausted. I finally admitted to myself that I was a prideful, arrogant leader whose life was largely controlled by fear. I came to the realization that my gifts exceeded my character and I desperately needed to close the gap. There was excruciating emotional pain as I came to grips with the depths of my self-deception. A great deal of my insecurity, egotism, and fear was revealed by the ridiculous hills I arrogantly declared I would die on.

There are times in life when we need a wake-up call. We desperately need a metaphorical slap in the face to awaken us to what we fail to perceive and to open our eyes to what lies right before us—but for some reason we are missing. I received that wake-up call in the fall of 1998. My son, Mark, who was eleven at the time, had spent a Saturday afternoon playing golf with my father-in-law, Roger. When they returned to the house, Roger asked if he could speak with me privately. This was an unusual request, as we discussed very few things that would warrant a private conversation. In many ways, Roger was the ideal father-in-law because he clearly understood boundaries. He didn't bombard me with advice on how to run my family, and he never told me how to run the church. Our conversations were generally limited to sports, the grandkids, and … sports. At the time of the conversation, Roger was not a believer, although the Lord would later save his soul in one of the most transformational salvations I have ever witnessed.

Roger and I stepped into the kitchen, and he proceeded to share with me words that immediately cut me to the core. I can confidently say that this was and remains the most painful, heartbreaking, demoralizing conversation in my life. And yet, this is the conversation the Lord used to open my eyes to my relational isolation, my out-of-control drive to find my approval in the affirmation of others, and my upside-down life priorities. I am grateful for the opportunity to record Roger's words to me in a book because, honestly, I can't share this story verbally. It's simply too painful. Even though it's been many years, tears immediately begin to flow and I find I can't get through the story. Here were Roger's words to me on that momentous 1998 Saturday fall afternoon.

"Jimmy, you know that I don't ever want to tell you how to run your life or how to run your church. But I had a conversation today with Mark, and I think you need to hear what he said. I casually asked Mark what he wanted to be when he grew up. There was a period of silence as Mark gave the question some thought, and then he responded. 'Grandpa, I really don't know what I want to be when I grow up.' Then a long pause. 'But … I know what I *don't* want to be. I *don't* want to be a pastor. Because when I grow up, I want to be able to spend time with my family.'"

More painful words have never been spoken to me. And yet, there simply aren't words to express how grateful I am that the Lord used that conversation to launch me on a journey that would eventually end at the foot of the cross. Today, my son, Mark, is a pastor in Austin, Texas. He is one of the most gifted ministers of grace I have ever encountered. God has given him a unique gifting in the area of evangelism. Thank Jesus for redeeming my family relationships.

Knowing Which Hills to Die On

When working with churches, I regularly teach about knowing which hills we should die on and which hills we should *not* die on. I ask people to extend their hands with their left hand closed and their right hand open. In our left hand, we place things that we will die for: Jesus Christ is God, the Bible is the inspired Word of God, Jesus is the only way to God the Father, we are saved by grace through faith, and so on. We close this hand. We will give our lives for these primary biblical truths. These are the hills on which we will sacrifice our lives. In our right hand, which is open, we place secondary issues, such as believer's baptism, form of church government, eschatology, the practice of spiritual gifts, style of worship, and other similar topics. For every topic I hold in my open right hand, there are smart people who love Jesus on both sides of the issue. Problems surface when we take something from the secondary right hand (a hill we should not die on) and place it in our primary left hand and declare that we will defend it to the death.

In my case, I had taken several issues from my open right hand and placed them in my closed left hand, declaring that these were worth defending to the death. I took the issue of baptism, the role of women in the church, the use of spiritual gifts, and a host of other secondary issues and proudly declared them to be primary issues. In the height of arrogance (and stupidity), I was convinced that, if given thirty minutes of your time, I could and would convince you of any of my arguments. We differ on the mode of baptism? Let me straighten you out. The role of women in the local church? Got twenty minutes? Nearly every view I held became a hill to die on.

To be clear, I fully expect thinking Christian leaders to maintain defendable positions on each topic they hold in their open right hand. Personally, I have strong views on nearly every position in my right hand. But to make these litmus-test issues over which we will break fellowship is a serious mistake. Just because a position is defendable doesn't mean we take every opportunity to defend it! In John 17, Jesus makes clear that unity in the truth testifies a life-giving message to the world. The unity of John 17 is not a call to uniformity. It is not organizational unity. We are not being called into one worldwide external church void of doctrinal distinctions. Jesus is not calling us to abandon denominations. We are not being called to set aside truth and sound doctrine for the sake of a superficial unity. Rather, Jesus is calling us to a tangible spiritual unity surrounding truths that we hold in our left hand. We are being called to a spiritual unity surrounding the gospel and the person of Jesus.

When I moved secondary issues from my open right hand into my closed left fist, I drove myself deeper into the dark hole of isolation. Arrogance, pride, and secondary doctrinal superiority wrapped in a cocoon of pretentiousness and fear only served to isolate me from my friends I so desperately needed. When I should have run to Jesus, my insecurity only increased my emotional remoteness in the back stage.

Believing the Gospel

In 1998, following my conversation with my father-in-law, I began to reach out to mentors and trusted leaders across the country. I shared my doubts, fears, and anxiety with men I trusted to speak hard truth to me. And they spoke the unfiltered gospel. The irony was that it was the same gospel I had believed for others and yet had never fully believed to be true for myself. One of the most significant transformations in my heart was that Satan's number one lie was crushed. People were getting to know me, the real me—and they liked me. The Lord began to melt my conceited shell of emotional seclusion. I slowly began moving secondary issues back into the proper perspective. I approached a number of my friends and apologized for my theological arrogance. And there was one friend in particular to whom I owed an enormous apology.

While my wife is unquestionably my very best friend, in terms of male friends, I am the type of guy who believes that you can have lots of buddies, many good friends, a handful of extremely close friends, and only one best friend. From my sophomore year of high school, Bruce has been my best friend. From sports to music, we did nearly everything together. We attended Wheaton College together. Together we took a year away from Wheaton and attended Kansas University, then later returned to Wheaton for our senior year. We worked summer jobs together at a Christian sports camp in the Ozark Mountains of Missouri. Bruce was the best man in my wedding and I was the best man in his. Around 1985, Bruce and I took different theological secondary paths. And for fifteen years, our friendship was severely strained. We never disagreed on primary doctrine. But we had numerous disagreements when it came to secondary issues. Unity became unachievable. While Bruce continued to unconditionally love me like a brother (he was always the bigger man), it became my quest to help him see the errors of his "shallow theology" (only because he disagreed with my theology). There were a number of tense conversations during which I drew a theological line in the sand. I convinced myself that I could not be the best friend to someone who did not share my doctrinal distinctives. I was trampling John 17 and the words of Jesus into the muck of immature superiority.

When, by God's grace, I grasped the truth of the gospel and began to comprehend the depths of my depravity, I knew I would need to approach Bruce with a sincere apology. Following the advice given by Ken Sande in his outstanding book *The Peacemaker: A Biblical Guide to Resolving Personal Conflict*, I owned my arrogance; I specifically admitted my sinful attitudes and actions; I acknowledged the hurt I had caused Bruce; and I committed to him that I would continue to allow the Lord to melt away my inclination to be a theological bully. Finally, I asked for his forgiveness. I may or may not have used a few other colorful words, such as, "Forgive me for being a jerk" (except I didn't use the word *jerk*). Not surprisingly, Bruce, who had more closely reflected Jesus throughout the fifteen tense years, immediately forgave me. It's been a long time since that moment, and honestly, I wept again as I wrote that last sentence. His forgiveness meant that much.

When Jesus freed me from the grasp of the isolationist monster, other exciting outcomes occurred. I experienced a newfound freedom not to be the hero. When someone approached me after a message with the words "You are so wonderful," "You are amazing," or anything similar, I would gently remind them that while I was grateful the Lord had used the message to minister to them, only Jesus is amazing, only Jesus is great, only Jesus is wonderful. I am a broken sinner standing before the throne of grace, just like them. That may sound a little ostentatious, but you need to understand that words of adulation were an idol in my twisted mind. The more elevating praise I heard on the front stage justified the sinking isolation on the back stage.

There were many more radical changes in my life that I will touch on in the following chapters. Astonishingly, the most immediate impact was a narrowing of the gap between my giftedness and my maturity. I was closing the Maturity Gap Index, as I will explain in the next chapter.

Questions for Reflection

Reality—What gifted leaders are you presently following while ignoring their immaturity deficits? Have you followed talent more than you have followed character? What leader can you place yourself under, perhaps in a mentoring relationship, who excels in godly character?

Rewind and Review—Why do we often praise people for their outward performance and turn a blind eye to their personal character? Have you ever seen this happen in the church?

Do you believe in second chances? Have you ever seen a pastor who was given a second chance? What impact was made because of this second chance in his personal life and his ministry life?

In your opinion, should pastors who fail in ministry be given a second chance? If not, why not? If so, why? If a pastor were given a second chance, what would that look like? Full reinstatement and ministry responsibilities and leadership, or something else? What are the mitigating factors?

Reflect—Review the list of lies that pastors often believe. Which of these have you found yourself believing at some time? What is the impact on your life, your marriage, your family, and the church when you believe those lies?

How many people know 100 percent of your story? What kinds of things do you do in ministry so that you will be perceived as being whole and competent? What do you do to keep any remaining percentage of your story hidden?

Why do you think some gifted leaders walk a road of personal destruction? What have you tried to do to avoid this possibility in your own ministry and life?

Remember—"I do not ask for these only, but also for those who will believe in me through their word, that they may all be one, just as you, Father, are in me, and I in you, that they also may be in us, so that the world may believe that you have sent me" (John 17:20–21).

How do these words of Jesus practically impact your life and ministry?

Respond—In your opinion, what makes something a primary issue? How can you tell when something is a secondary issue? Have you taken time to sort through primary and secondary issues in your own beliefs and ministry?

Has there ever been a time when making a secondary issue into a primary issue damaged a relationship? If so, what could you do to repair that relationship now? What keeps you from going to people you have hurt and asking them to forgive you?

Chapter 2

Closing the Front Stage–
Back Stage Gap

I received a call from Brad, a polite, quiet southern pastor who asked for a face-to-face meeting. I wondered why he requested a personal meeting, when we had just connected at a denominational gathering a couple of weeks earlier; he had been buoyant as he told me about the work the Lord was doing in his church. We met the following Tuesday morning at a local McDonald's. I immediately sensed that Brad was in trouble.

When any PastorServe team member meets with a pastor in crisis, we have found that of any counsel we can give, or any advice we might dispense, the following words are by far the most important thing we can say.

"First of all, I love you. There is absolutely nothing you could tell me today that will make me think less of you. It won't be a shock to me when you tell me you're broken because I already know you're broken; and I am too. Apart from Jesus, neither of us has an ounce of hope. I don't think that you are in deep weeds and I'm not. I *do* think you're in deep weeds and I'm right there with you. *I* need the grace of Jesus today as much as *you* need the grace of Jesus today. I know that there is a tendency to hold back as we talk today. I understand you may be reluctant to tell me everything in this initial meeting. You likely think that because you believe Satan's number one lie: *I can't tell him everything, because if he knew everything, he would reject me. He says he wants to be my friend now, but if he really knew me, he definitely wouldn't like me. He would stand up and walk out and tell me I have no business in pastoral ministry. There is no way I disclose everything. I'll share just the tip of the iceberg and see how he reacts."*

We continue, "I know you will disclose some things to me today. And just know that when you share an inch of your story, because I understand the tendency to hold back, I am going to assume it's closer to a mile. And let me tell you now; if it's a mile, we are going to love you, walk with you, care for you, and pastor you. We are *for* you. There is nothing you can share that will surprise us. At this point in our ministry, we have *heard it all*! So let's both confess our need for Jesus and our desperate daily need for His grace. From the outset, let's commit to honesty and full disclosure. What happens today is between us. I have a lot of weaknesses in life, but confidentiality is not one of them. Let's commit to not wasting each other's time. So tell me what's really going on."

While that may seem a bit lengthy, I can't count the number of times a pastor has emotionally melted on the floor after hearing simple words of gospel grace. Secrets carry devastating weight, and the anticipation of unburdening oneself from crushing secrets can emotionally overwhelm the spirit. I sensed Brad was ready to talk.

Beginning with his childhood, Brad began to share a dark story of a lifelong addiction to pornography. He shared how his obsession with pornography had led him into chat rooms where he had engaged in inappropriate conversations with women and, at times, men. He shared that remorse and shame were overwhelming him and he desperately needed to find relief.

The entire time Brad was sharing his story, my spirit was deeply troubled. While I don't claim to have the gift of discernment (the Lord seemed to give my portion to my wife, who has a double portion of discernment), I had an overwhelming sense that Brad was lying. When he finished his story, I asked him if he had told me everything. He assured me that he had not asked me to travel from Kansas City to make a halfhearted confession. But I couldn't shake the overpowering prompting of the Holy Spirit. So I said:

"Brad. I love you. I told you at the beginning of this meeting and it's still true now. As I said at the outset of our time together, the tendency is to share a little and see how I react. And yet, you have adamantly insisted that you have shared everything. I'm going to take a risk and just say what I feel. I think you're lying. You did not tell me everything. In fact, I don't even think you scratched the surface. But I'll say it again, I will walk with you no matter what your story."

It's worth noting that I have said something like this only a couple of times in several decades of ministry. It's rare that I will say to a pastor, "I'm calling you out on this"; though, I have occasionally used that line (and other, perhaps even more blunt ways of saying that line).

When I said the words "I think you're lying," I could see Brad's body physically tense up. I had barely finished when Brad stood up and, in a loud voice (in McDonald's) and with very colorful language, yelled that he was out of there. He had been told PastorServe was a place of grace and that was clearly wrong (again, said with very colorful language). He let me know that we would never speak again, and he stormed out of the restaurant. I drove back to the conference I was attending, spoke in the evening, returned to my hotel room, and waited for the call. It came around 10:30 p.m.

Brad was sobbing. Finally, through his tears he said these words: "Dude, I didn't know what to say. I'm sorry. You're right; there's more. There's a lot more. And if you are willing, can we try this again tomorrow, same time, same place?"

The next day we met at the same McDonald's. It was no surprise that some of the employees remembered us from the day before. I assured them there would be no outburst today. Brad sat down, and with not one word from me, he launched into his story. It was painfully dark. It was far more than chat rooms. He had acted out. He had engaged in wicked sinful behaviors. He had broken his covenant to his wife. When he finished his story (I was convinced he had shared everything), I repeated my commitment to love him, walk with him, and care for him. Brad broke down and said, "Thank you. You are one in a million."

I told him this was yet another lie of Satan. I was not one in a million, and in fact, I could prove it. I reminded him that we had a number of mutual friends attending the conference where I was speaking. I told him that the next day I would bring three of his good friends (who knew nothing of Brad's issues), and then Brad could share the exact same story he had just shared with me and we would together watch their reaction.

The next day—same McDonald's. A total of five men; and Brad again shared his story. And the reaction of the men was predictable. They told Brad that while they hated his sin, they loved him and were fully committed to walk with him through the deep valley ahead. By the end of the week, Brad had disclosed his story to twenty men. *Every man* committed himself to Brad. While it's a long story, let me just say that Brad resigned from his church, disclosed everything to his wife, and committed to living a new life characterized by gospel grace. After a six-month marital separation, months and months of three-times-a-week intensive counseling, both individual and together with his wife, Brad and his wife reconciled.

Nearly one year to the day after our initial McDonald's meeting, I flew to his hometown and presided over a ceremony in which Brad and his wife recommitted to each other. Brad didn't renew his vows to his wife, because his earlier vows had been destroyed and there was nothing left to renew. Standing in front of family and friends, surrounded by their four children, Brad made new vows to his wife and then vows to his children. There wasn't a dry eye anywhere. Now, five years removed from our initial McDonald's conversation, Brad is a counselor at a local halfway house, working with recently released convicts, most of whom are young men struggling with issues surrounding addiction. He has come out of the shadows of isolation and shame and entered into the freedom of Jesus. His life is a testimony to the grace of God, the victory of Jesus, and the love and care of men committed to walking with a brother.

Brad was living with an enormous gap between his front stage and his back stage. Brad possessed a number of pastoral gifts and justified his secret life by convincing himself that revealing his sin would be too difficult for those in his congregation. He hid his character deficiency, his immaturity, and his sin deep in the back stage. In other words, Brad had a dangerously large Maturity Gap Index.

The Maturity Gap Index

Let's face it; in the life of nearly every pastor, gifting exceeds maturity. And the gap between gifting and maturity is fertile ground for hiding, secrets, abuse, and a series of dangerous sinful behaviors.

Let's create a grid. At the bottom we will place a timeline based on age. The left side of the grid comprises two factors: character and giftedness.

Consider the case of Billy, an incredibly gifted young man in his midtwenties who believes God has called him into a leadership role within the local church. The talent and skill portion of the Maturity Gap Index is specific to one's chosen occupational field, so we will determine Billy's skill in the area of pastoral ministry. The maturity and character portion of the MGI is universal and applies to every arena of life.

Now let's plot two sets of data on the chart. The first set of data is Billy's giftedness or skill. This can be referred to as talent, natural ability, or aptitude. After observing Billy from a distance as he interacts with his spouse, his coworkers, and his close friends, you objectively determine that Billy is presently a 7.0 on a 10-point scale. Some would consider this to be the very low end of what management expert Jim Collins, in his book *Good to Great*, refers to as a "Level 5 Leader" (although Collins looks for a combination of sincere personal humility and passionate professional determination for a "True Level 5 Leader"). My dad would have said that Billy was a whiz-bang, cracker-jack, top-drawer, swell leader (surprisingly, my dad never wrote a business book that sold 2.5 million copies).

The 7.0 skill assessment was arrived at after conducting a rigorous PastorServe assessment, observing Billy (again, from a distance) preach, teach, lead a staff meeting, interact with coworkers, interact with congregational members, solve difficult problems, explain a difficult doctrine, share his faith with an unbeliever, and network with other pastors during a local pastors gathering. Though young, Billy has clearly got "it." This assessment is not based on potential.

It is based on the present demonstration of God-given ability. In other words, after an initial, surface-level, front stage assessment—using biblical language—you believe Billy to be a "five-talent" individual. Jesus told a puzzling parable about giftedness in the parable of the talents (Matthew 25:14–30). Clearly, in the time of Jesus, "talent" referred to a specific measure of money. It was as if the Master gave one servant fifty dollars, another twenty dollars, and the third ten dollars. In other words, the Master granted one servant greater opportunity with a fifty. This is a hard truth as everyone wants to think of themselves as a "fifty-dollar leader." I have never in my life asked a pastor to assess his giftedness and have him respond, "Basically, I'm about a one-talent, ten-dollar pastor." I doubt that conversation will ever come.

However, let's place the parable in a more accurate cultural context. A talent was actually a weighted measure, and one talent was generally thought to be worth twenty years' labor. Let's say the average American worker (my apologies to friends around the world) makes $40,000 per year. Five talents would be the equivalent of $4 million. This leads to a different reading of the parable. Even the one-talent guy was given $800,000, an enormous sum. Any of the three amounts would make one wealthy. The parable is a powerful affirmation of God's grace. What did each servant deserve? Nothing. What was each servant given? A fortune. So, while I do believe that some are naturally more gifted than others, we need to remember that every gift we are given is a gift of grace from a gracious heavenly Father.

With training, coaching, dedication, and consistent hard work, Billy can grow his giftedness from a 7.0 to an 8.5. In a very rare case, he may go beyond a 9.0. We can grow our skills, talents, and abilities, but only within the limits of boundaries set forth by the Lord Jesus. As hard as I worked on my basketball game as a kid, I wasn't going to be a 10 on the talent scale. Going from a "basketball 2" to a "basketball 4" was a significant accomplishment. I played against some players who were clearly 8s and 9s, as they would go on to be college and NBA stars. Talent and skill reside in a limited window, and Matthew 25 makes clear that we are to make the most of our potential in every opportunity. No one has ever started as a 1 on the talent scale and then twenty-five years later suddenly became a 10. That simply doesn't happen. If you are a 6.5 pastor, thank God for your God-given ability and commit to grow your giftedness to an 8. Don't waste time being bitter that you're not a 10. So let's assume the best and hope that Billy can grow to an 8.5 by the end of his lifetime.

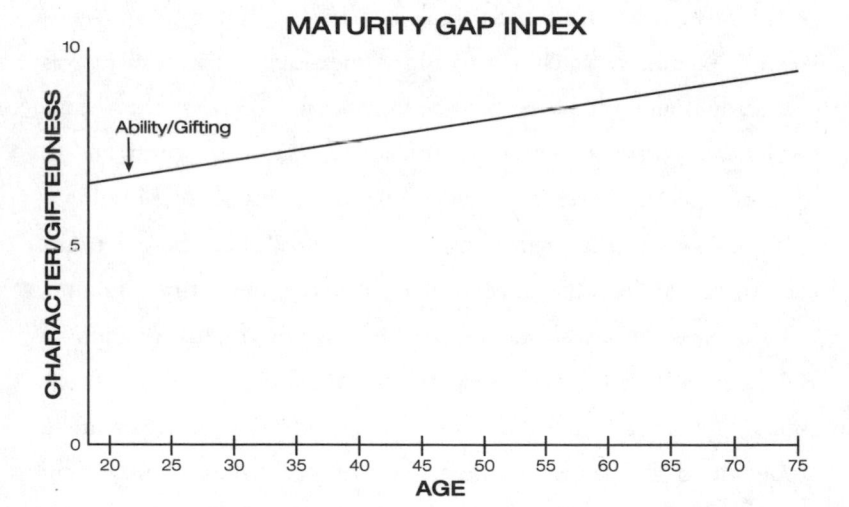

Maturity is a completely different matter. This is a different line on the scale. This line tracks the growth (or in some cases regression) of maturity and character over our life.

Unlike talent, maturity *can* grow from a 1.0 to a 10. I can meet someone who is twenty and profoundly immature, and then meet up with him again twenty years later, and he will have matured into a godly leader, known for his exceptional character. But while the talent and skill generally, with work, grow at a steady pace, the maturity and character growth is wildly varying. There is growth, but there are ups and downs, coming through painful seasons and challenging circumstances.

After conducting a maturity assessment, we concluded that Billy is a 2.5 on the maturity scale. This is not atypical for a young man in his midtwenties, but it does raise serious concerns if areas of immaturity are not addressed.

Whereas the talent and skill assessment can be objective, the maturity assessment is much more subjective, as it is deeply personal. The 2.5 maturity assessment was arrived at after observing Billy (in close proximity) interact with his spouse, staff, and congregants. However, significant weight was given to one-on-one conversations with his spouse, coworkers, and close friends. Finally, we determined which, if any, relationship roles Billy had filled in his pastoral ecosystem. In addition to his boss and friends, did Billy have a trainer, coach, counselor, or mentor? If yes, we asked him to describe the relationship. We concluded that Billy has a boss and some immature friends but no coach, no counselor, no mentor, and sporadic, minimal training. And yet, Billy is widely regarded as a gifted young pastor. People love Billy on the front stage. People don't know Billy back stage. Our assessment concluded that Billy presently has a Maturity Gap Index of 4.5. Any Maturity Gap Index over 4.0 is like a sea of yellow and red flags waving in the wind. If there is

not a well-defined plan that includes quickly filling out his relational
pastoral ecosystem, coupled with a willingness to grow, learn, and
receive correction, Billy will almost certainly crash, burn, and exit
the ministry. Sadly, we have seen this play out over and over again.
But there is hope! Billy can close his Maturity Gap Index. I am living
proof of the fact that by God's grace, it can be done.

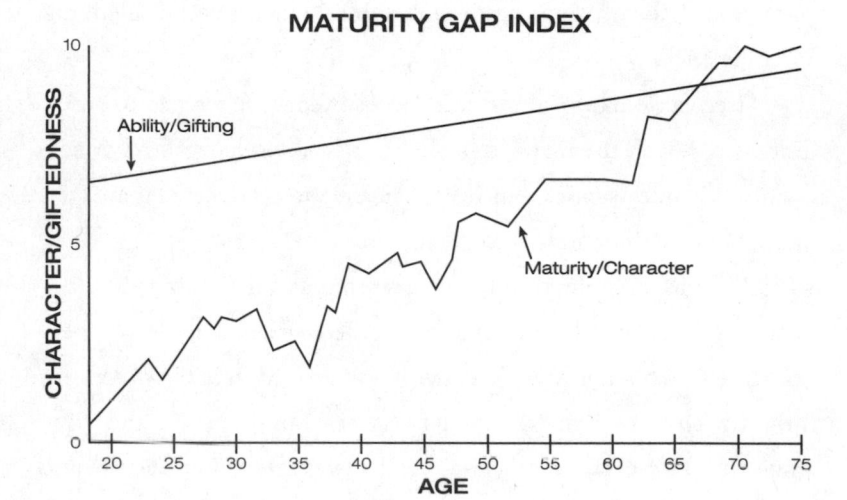

I know the argument commonly put forth at this point of the
MGI explanation. How can the MGI account for the apparent
injustice of penalizing someone just because they are particularly
gifted? If two pastors with the same maturity level are evaluated side
by side, and one pastor is clearly a level 5 leader while the other pastor, though gifted, is nothing close to level 5, how is it fair that the
supremely gifted pastor emerges with a significantly higher MGI? It's
a fair question. The resulting MGI is fair because of three key factors.

First, the pastor with a higher level of gifting will be presented
with more opportunity, more adoration, and more applause—all

potential dangers that can contribute to a sharp *decrease* in maturity. He or she *needs* to grow up quickly. There is no static MGI, as the failure to mature will only broaden the front stage–back stage gap. The MGI needs to be reduced (the pastor needs to grow up!) in order to maintain a realistic, level-headed perspective of both life and ministry.

Second, when a pastor has a higher level of gifting, the church will more naturally turn a blind eye to deficient issues of maturity and character. Why? Because of sin—there is no other explanation. We love to be around gifted, well-known rock stars, be it on the concert stage or in the pulpit. We want to be friends with the talented NFL quarterback, even if he is an unkind, ungracious, narcissistic jerk. The higher the talent and skill, the more intentional we must be to raise the level of character and maturity.

Third, leaders with a high MGI tend to either hide or abuse. They hide by pretending to be someone they are not. They hide by not allowing anyone back stage in their lives. Why would they? "If you want to hear me preach and teach three times a week, and if you like having a rock star for a pastor," they reason, "why would I tell you about my addiction to alcohol?" This front stage–back stage gap creates a deep, inner, personal struggle that can and often does lead to a breach in integrity. Pastors with a high MGI can abuse others by allowing the dark side of their gifting to become the predominant default of the gift. For example, if your gift is preaching, the gift can be abused by using your gift of speaking to manipulate others through words. If you have an intense passion for the Lord and His church, you may belittle others who do not share your passion. If you are an insightful leader, your dark side may be to correct in a situation before being invited to correct. If you are a visionary leader, as many pastors are, you may tend to place your style of leadership above other valuable styles of leadership.

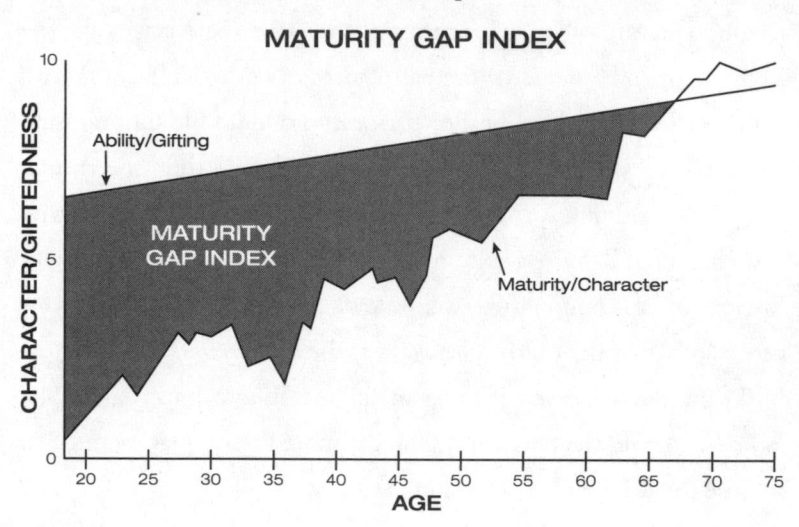

As detailed in the previous chapter, one of the contributing factors to low maturity and character development among pastors is that the church (dominated by the Western church) appears to be obsessed with the talent and skill of a pastor while turning a blind eye to glaring maturity and character deficiencies. Surprisingly, one place that understands the need to track both talent and skill as well as maturity and character is the National Football League Scouting Combine.

What Does the NFL Know That We Don't?

The NFL combine is an annual post–Super Bowl showcase in which potential pro football prospects are invited to Indianapolis for one week of assessment. While, naturally, there is football skill assessment at the combine (40-yard dash, vertical leap, broad jump, 225-pound bench press), the time and money dedicated to determining a player's off-the-field challenges are noteworthy. Each team is given the opportunity to spend a ridiculously short fifteen minutes of "alone time" with any prospect they so choose. In another life, I would like to advise NFL teams on the best questions to ask in those fifteen-minute interviews. I believe you can discern a maturity level in a short conversation when the right questions are asked.

Each year, there are several highly touted prospects who come carrying the baggage of off-field issues. The primary question being asked by every NFL team is this: Is this player worth the risk? Everyone invited to the NFL combine is somewhere between an 8.5 and 10 on the talent and skill portion of the index. This means it is not unusual for players attending the combine to have a Maturity Gap Index of 6.0, 7.0, and in some extreme cases, 8.0 and above. The higher the talent and skill, the higher the MGI a team is willing to gamble on. Every year, there are stories of players chosen by NFL teams who are paid millions of dollars (thus increasing the Maturity Gap Index) and then crash and exit the league. The same could be said about any sport, any business, any church.

I am privileged to be friends with several men leading banking institutions that make loans to churches ranging anywhere from $100,000 to $50 million. Competition among banks will not allow them to require a lead pastor assessment before making a loan, so they are risking a massive amount of money on the front stage of a church while they turn a blind eye to back stage issues. Each banker has told me they would love to have the MGI of the lead pastor and to consider this the leading criterion in a loan-evaluation process.

So the key is learning how to close the Maturity Gap Index. To narrow one's MGI, a pastor needs to come out of isolation and live and minister in community. A pastor needs a boss, trainer, coach, counselor, mentor, and friend consistently providing boundaries, speaking into his or her life.

Negative Maturity Gap Index

There is such a thing as a negative Maturity Gap Index. A negative MGI indicates that maturity exceeds gifting, and it is most often (if ever) reached by pastors in the later years of their career. These pastors developed the relationships necessary to effectively address maturity and character issues in their lives. If you have a negative MGI, I hope you will commit to pouring your life back into pastors in the midst of the MGI battle. We need you! We need you to fight to help close the gap between what the church sees on the front stage and what the pastor knows about the back stage.

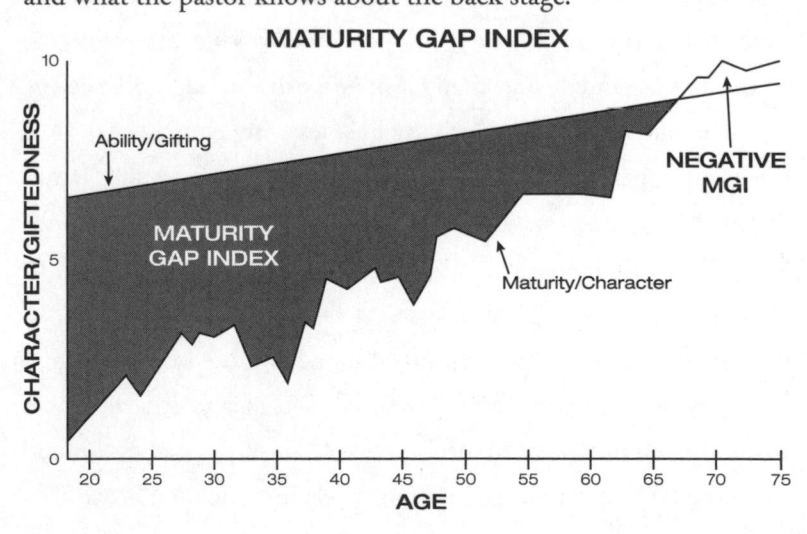

Questions for Reflection

Reality—Jimmy talked about beginning conversations with gospel foundations. When you start a conversation with someone whom you sense is in trouble, how do you usually start?

What do you do in a counseling situation when you sense someone is not telling you the whole truth? Do you confront it? If so, how? Do you let it slide? If so, why?

Rewind and Review—How comfortable are you hearing other people's sins, especially the darker kinds? Do you like hearing confessions or tend to avoid hearing them? If you enjoy hearing confessions, why is that? If you avoid hearing them, why is that? When someone begins to share their darker sins with you, what kinds of things go through your mind?

When Jimmy heard Brad's story, he brought other godly, loving men into the situation to hear the story too. Why was that a good idea?

When you are brought into a difficult situation, do you tend to try to handle it alone or do you involve others? Explain your reasoning.

Jimmy says the church is "obsessed with the talent and skill of a pastor while turning a blind eye to glaring maturity and character deficiencies." Why do you think that is? Do you believe this has always been the case? Looking through church history and back to the New Testament, do we see other leadership principles and models that seem contrary to our Western church standards?

What are some things that will help to lower the MGI of a pastor?

Reflect—Is there a particular skill for which you wish God had given you a higher gifting? If the Lord had given you a higher skill level, what difference would that make? Since He hasn't, what do you do about it?

Think about a leader you personally know who is far more talented than mature. What is happening as a result of this maturity gap?

When was the last time you told someone about God's grace for him or her? What was the situation? What happened when you shared with that person about God's grace?

Remember—In Matthew 25:14–30, Jesus gives us the parable of the talents. Remembering that even the man who was given one talent received an enormous sum of money, what does that say to you about God's grace to every believer?

Respond—In terms of your personal Maturity Gap Index, what steps can you take to narrow your MGI? What are you currently doing in your life to help you continue to grow in maturity?

Who do you know who has a negative MGI (maturity has surpassed the person's gifting)? What fruit do you see in that person's life? What could you do to spend more time with people who have negative MGIs? Why could that be beneficial to you right now?

Chapter 3

Created for Community

Though I live in Kansas, I have spent a great deal of my life in Colorado—in childhood hanging out with my cousins around Gunnison and Crested Butte, and more recently, I spent ten years commuting from Kansas City to Colorado as part of a teaching team at a great church in Colorado Springs. My family often vacations in Colorado, I still have relatives in Colorado, and I write for a publisher based in Colorado. So you ask, why don't you move to Colorado? And leave Kansas! Are you out of your mind!

While there are many things I love about the majestic beauty of Colorado, near the top of the list would be the trees. If your life were reflected by a particular kind of tree, what kind of tree would that be? It sounds like a question you would hear at the local tofu and granola lovers meeting (for the record, I like both tofu and granola), but bear with me.

If strength, independence, and longevity are hallmarks of what you are striving for, your life might be reflected by a giant redwood or a sequoia. Redwoods reach heights of 375 feet. Giant sequoias can live up to 3,000 years and have bark 3 feet thick. If you are struggling with pride, a trip to the Redwood National Parks in Northern California may remind you just how small you really are. Those valuing flexibility might choose a weeping willow, the ultimate testament to "bend but don't break." If variety is your life ambition, the palm tree may be your best descriptor, as the palm family contains more than 2,500 species! If you primarily find your affirmation in your offspring, the coco de mer palm tree produces a seed that can be as large as 20 inches in diameter and nearly 70 pounds! That's impressive! Others might want to be a pine tree, steadfastly enduring all four seasons of life. One of the world's great tree stories can be found in Bahrain: The Tree of Life is a solitary mesquite tree growing in the middle of a vast desert. If you struggle in the midst of a relational desert, the mesquite may be your tree.

Me? I would want my life to be reflected in an aspen tree, the strongest tree in the world. The aspen is a comparatively small tree and is most notable for its beautiful cream-colored bark, leaves that appear to shudder and quake in the slightest breeze, and beautiful fall colors. Aspens are most commonly found in cold winter and cool summer high-altitude regions. Yet the tree doesn't do well in a suburban yard, even in those conditions. The vast majority of solitary aspens do not survive.

But if they do, what started as a gardening dream quickly turns into a horticultural nightmare! Soon, aspen trees are growing all over the yard, in the neighbor's yard, underneath the driveway, and against the foundation. How could such a beautiful tree be such a big problem?

The "problem" of the aspen is actually the strength of the aspen. Aspen trees were never meant to be alone. They were designed to live in a grove—a community of aspen trees. These trees reproduce not only by seed but also because new shoots grow off existing roots. Every aspen grove starts with a mother tree, which arrives at the site by seed. As suckers shoot off the roots, a grove is formed. In reality, aspens are not *individual* trees—they share the same root system, which means an aspen grove is really one living plant. In fact, the largest living thing in the world is an aspen grove in central Utah. The interconnectedness of the aspen gives life and strength. What affects one aspen tree affects them all. In a forest fire, while every tree may burn down, the aspen root survives and quickly reestablishes itself. The aspen is the first to regrow.

What does this have to do with pastors? *Everything!*

Far too many pastors are redwoods, oaks, palms, mesquites, and pines. Too few pastors are aspens. In our ever-evolving world of technology, social networking, and self-protection, we live increasingly fragmented, isolated lives. And yet, no one was created for isolation. We were created for community. Deep in our hearts we all yearn for release from loneliness, inaccessibility, and isolation. We were fashioned by God for authentic relationships. We long for belonging. We yearn to be interconnected, interdependent aspens.

And it's not possible to thrive alone. The fires of life are inevitable. We cannot survive the pain and agony of this life apart from the body of Christ.

The deep, inner pull to community can be seen in many facets of life. Personally, I find it difficult if not impossible to fully enjoy a new piece of music until I share it with someone else. If I watch something on YouTube that makes me laugh uncontrollably (confession: often a Jimmy Fallon *Tonight Show* clip), I immediately want to share it with Sally. When she laughs at the video clip, my eyes light up and I experience a heightened level of enjoyment. Why? Because we are created for community.

Why has social media exploded to become a permanent part of culture? Because it is our shallow attempt to experience community. I say "shallow" because the majority of social media information is a false outward representation of a deep, inner loneliness. I know people who are living sad lives in miserable marriages with fractured family relationships—and yet, if you looked at their Facebook page and their staggering number of "likes," you would think they just received the Fun Family of the Year award. But we torpedo heart affiliation when we present inauthentic lives.

Why do so many believers resist authentic community? What is it about the local visible church that drives so many believers—who may live socially and intellectually connected lives—to live spiritually sequestered lives? And even more concerning, why do pastors live relationally disconnected lives? I have found that there are at least five factors that are battling against the need for community.

Five Factors Battling against Community

1. Friendship is a vital component of community.

Pastors long for soul-baring friendships and understand the need for friendships with nonbelievers. Many pastors are committed to friendships with those who have yet to trust Jesus primarily because they want to see that particular person come to Jesus. But this is a misplaced motivation for friendship, confusing primary longing and secondary motivation. We don't primarily connect with people because they might become Christians; we primarily connect with people because they have been created in the image of God. If we chiefly serve because we long for our friends to share our belief in the gospel grace of Jesus, we are using them, and if they reject Jesus, the friendship has no basis. However, if we serve others because they have been created in the image of God, the basis of our friendship cannot be destroyed.

Community is weakened when we form friendship around conditionally based behaviors that were not a part of God's original creation. The initial state of mankind was *not* that we were sinners in need of a savior, but that mankind was simply created in the image of God (Genesis 1:27). How can I love a radicalized Muslim who seems like he will never bow his knee to Jesus? I can love him because he is created in the image of God. What motivates me to love the homeless man who has not bathed in weeks? I can reach out and touch him because he is created in the image of God.

The primary foundation for community is that each and every person—man, woman, and child; Muslim, Jew, Hindu, Atheist, Buddhist, LGBT, Jehovah's Witness, Mormon, Church of Scientology; those struggling to survive day to day—*everyone* is created in the image of God and is therefore worthy of our respect, our love, and our service. Because God loved the world (John 3:16), we, too, should love the world. Because Jesus loved and prayed for His enemies (Matthew 5:43–45), so should we love and pray for our enemies. Because the love of Jesus is unselfish (1 Corinthians 13:4–8), so, too, our love should be unselfish. This is the basis of true community.

2. We have believed the lie of Satan when he convinces us to say, "If people knew my secrets, they wouldn't like me."

When we fail to share the deep complexities of our broken lives with a select few, we play the church game. We come to church, lonely. We put a smile on our face, sit through worship and community groups, and assure everyone that we are fine when they ask how we are doing. We don't bring our authentic life to church—our pain, brokenness, hopes, and even our joys!

There will always be those who argue that the risk is too high because the possibility of betrayal is always present. At PastorServe, we regularly deal with the pain of pastoral betrayal. We have been deeply disappointed on a number of occasions when a pastor has confessed a particular sin to his superiors (an offense we believe is worthy of discipline but not termination) only to be asked for his keys and immediately shown the door. But to live as followers of Jesus, we must take relational risks. While there are discerning and wise recommendations to help us in selecting those with whom we share our secrets, the fact remains: pastors need community, even in the face of potential ungraciousness.

Dietrich Bonhoeffer, the German pastor who was martyred for resisting the Nazi regime, wrote a classic on fellowship, *Life Together*. In it, he suggests, "Disillusionment with our local church is a good thing because it destroys our false expectations of perfection. The sooner we give up the illusion that a church must be perfect in order to love it, the sooner we quit pretending and start admitting we're all imperfect and need grace. This is the beginning of real community."

Unquestionably, there will be moments of ungrace in every community. And yet, these moments remind us that a kingdom awaits where there is no ungrace, no unkindness, and no sin.

3. The inevitability of pain drives many away from community.

Countless pastors have been heartlessly wounded in the church. And for that, my heart breaks. Over and over again I have heard pastors tell me they entered the pastoral ministry aware of spiritual warfare, aware they were being deployed to the front line of a cosmic battle. They fully expected to take Satan's arrows in the chest in the course of battle. But they did not expect to be shot in the back by their own people. They were shocked when those they had sacrificed so much to serve responded with disgust, anger, pettiness, resentment, even hatred. There is no wound as devastating and debilitating as that inflicted by those in whom we have placed our highest confidence and shared our personal lives. Statistics tell us that in the United States alone, more than fifteen thousand pastors are fired each year. The list of hurts is quite long: conflict, hurt, hypocrisy, neglect, pettiness, legalism, and other sins. Rather than being shocked and surprised, we must remember that the church is made up of real sinners, including ourselves. Because we're sinners, we hurt each other, sometimes intentionally and sometimes unintentionally. The question is not *if* we will be wounded in the church but *when* we will be wounded in the church.

A pastor was ministering at a growing, thriving Midwest church. Deeply loved by the congregation, he had served the people for ten years and was looking forward to many more years of ministry in their midst. During a particularly fruitful time of ministry, he reached out to me to share about a past sin that had bothered him (code for the Holy Spirit wouldn't leave him alone) for more than three decades: he had been emotionally involved with another woman while serving on the mission field. While there was no sex, they absolutely crossed emotional boundaries. At one point, his wife asked him if he was emotionally involved with the other woman, which he adamantly denied. Fast-forward thirty years; he couldn't shake the fact that he had lied to his wife. He sensed the urging of the Holy Spirit to tell his wife everything— which he did straightaway. They wisely entered into intensive counseling with an incredible commitment to honesty, their marriage, and the Lord Jesus. It brought healing and reconciliation to their marriage and was also evident by the pastor's enhanced understanding of the gospel.

Near the conclusion of their reconciliation, the wife encouraged her husband to confess the sin to the board of elders. "After all," she reasoned, "when you were hired ten years ago, the elders asked you if there was anything else that they should know about your life and you said no. That was a lie and you need to make it right."

This is where it's difficult to know where things will go in a local church. At this point I would have guessed the elders might do one of two things: They might thank him for his honestly and commit to a greater openness with one another. Worst case, they would discipline him for lying, placing him on a one- to two-month leave of absence, potentially with no salary. What I had not expected was that he would be immediately fired.

Many similar stories end here. Many wounded pastors permanently walk away from the local church dismayed, disillusioned, and disheartened. But this pastor allowed the pain of the firing to drive him into a deeper and fuller understanding of God's grace and mercy. He is now being used of the Lord to minister around the world in a variety of settings. Being treated ungraciously led him into a deeper understanding of grace.

4. Superficial, faux social media friendship creates a false sense of community.

I am momentarily encouraged when pastors assure me that they live in community as they have surrounded themselves with close friends. The encouragement is momentary because I want to explore the obvious question: What is their definition of a friend?

I have a "friend" who is materially blessed. He owns a burgeoning franchise that has opened successful stores in hundreds of malls across the country. He is widely recognized as an innovative pioneer in his particular field. Many years ago, I found myself included in a group email sent to his "Ten best friends in the entire world." Naturally, anyone would feel flattered to be included on such a list. Perhaps he doesn't know how to use the BCC email function, but his "ten best friends" included famous athletes (I doubt they appreciated their personal email addresses being displayed for commoners like me to see), well-known business leaders, and a couple of regular joes like me. Here is the tragedy of my inclusion on his "top ten" list: Over the course of our friendship, we have enjoyed a total of three meals together, but never alone. He always brought another friend along. We have spoken on the phone less than half a dozen times. We have not had face-to-face contact in several years. Over the past ten years I have spent more time with my neighbor's dog! Recently, during a phone conversation, I gently pushed back, asking him if I was really one of his ten best friends in the entire world. He passionately assured me that I was absolutely on his list. He went on to share how much I had meant to him over the past decade. I wanted to cry. If I am one of his ten best friends, he has told me that he has no real friends.

At its lowest level, social media has redefined friendship to mean casual awareness. I can "friend" you on Facebook although we have never met, let alone had a personal conversation. Our great-grandparents would shudder at our definition of friendship. To gain a richer, longer perspective on friendship, I encourage you to read classic novels that will assist in resetting our friendship compass to true north. Often the best friends are the ones you're born with. In Louisa May Alcott's *Little Women*, Meg, Jo, Beth, and Amy paint a memorable picture of sisterhood and friendship. The friendship between Tom Sawyer and Huckleberry Finn in *The Adventures of Tom Sawyer* by Mark Twain is a powerful portrait of how two very different lives can connect through friendship. Jane Austen masterfully crafts an insightful picture of friendship between Elizabeth and Charlotte in *Pride and Prejudice*. I have long loved the power of the friendship between Anne, Marilla, Matthew, Gilbert, and Diana in the Anne of Green Gables series by Lucy Maud Montgomery. I confess that I have shed more than a few tears reading about the friendship between Anne and Matthew (have I mentioned that I love sports?).

What is your definition of a friend? Don't allow shallow, unintentional friendship to pass as friendship. Invest your life in those whom you can truly refer to as friends.

5. Church growth (ministry growth) in many ways fights against authentic community.

Recently, I led a retreat for the executive team of a megachurch on the West Coast, during which it became clear there was a lot of tension in the room. What we eventually discovered was that each pastor had widely varying expectations of what it meant to serve as a member of a ministry team. Some viewed "team" as most closely defined by a family, some as healthy working relationships, others as close friends. While each pastor frequently referred to "team," the concept was distinctly different in the way different individuals believed it was to be executed. And thus was born the PastorServe *Team Scale*, which has proved to be one of the most effective tools used by our ministry.

The Team Scale: The Importance of Defining "Team"

An astute pastor understands the life cycle of the church. A church plant begins as a family. Soon, as the church grows, the team is often defined as close friends. As the staff begins to serve in specialized areas of ministry, the team is most commonly redefined as friends. And as the church continues to grow toward megachurch size, the staff often becomes a team of individuals working in their own area of ministry. A dysfunctional staff loses all desire for inner-staff relational connection. This is the typical life cycle of a church staff ministering together as a team. That said, I do believe it is possible for megachurches to operate between friends and close friends on the Team Scale. I also believe that it is possible for a small church staff to function at the level of working relationships.

Understanding that there will always be "family pockets" on a church staff, what is the overall desired level of relationship within your church? Do you hope your staff will always be defined as close friends? Are you content to serve together at the minimal level of friendship? Is your church so large that the staff is nothing more than a group of employed individuals working together as if running a spiritual assembly line? Are people joining your staff to become a part of a family, or are they joining solely because they are in need of a paycheck? How would you define your team in the world of sports? Are you an Olympic team, football team, baseball team, basketball team, or a tennis doubles team? If you are serving in a lead role, are you assuming a particular level of team that is not shared by the majority of your staff? Is the growth of your church ultimately impeding community? These are vitally important questions that every growing church must address!

"TEAM"

ABSENCE OF RELATIONSHIP	WORKING RELATIONSHIP	FRIENDS	CLOSE FRIENDS	FAMILY
Olympic team	Football team	Baseball team	Basketball team	Tennis doubles team
No community	Detached community	Cohort community	Connected community	Meshed community
Conflict does not impact team	Conflict influences team	Conflict impacts team	Conflict cripples team	Conflict abolishes team
No staff meeting	Executive staff meeting	Meetings are mostly business	Meetings are some business, some personal	Meetings are mostly personal

A team can be likened to a family. In this enmeshed level of team, the staff lives all of life together. When a church is birthed, it is commonly led by a smaller team of individuals or families who believe that God has uniquely called them to launch a church in a particular community. Commonly, a new church begins with a team functioning as a family. The church planting team is enmeshed, living life together as a family. Staff meetings are loosely organized and are dominated by personal sharing and team prayer. The team knows one another equally inside and outside of work. Community meals are shared, strategies are together formulated, and advancement is jointly celebrated. Team

members communicate multiple times throughout the day. The staff
vacations together. They are at the hospital to celebrate together when
a child is born. When a team member is in a car accident, after the
victim calls his spouse, the church staff is his next call. The team spends
significant time with one another. They know the names, birth dates,
and favorite hobbies of each other's spouses and children. Using the
sports genre, this team is similar to a tennis doubles team. Out of
necessity, the team engages in consistent, heightened communication.
If there is unresolved conflict, the relational tension can abolish the
entire team.

As the church grows and the staff expands, the heightened level
of family becomes both unrealistic and impossible to maintain. It is
this point when a staff moves into the level of close friends serving
together as ministry partners.

A team can be described as close friends serving together to
achieve a clearly defined goal. As a church grows, the staff numeri-
cally increases in order to meet the needs of the congregation. And as
the staff develops, a measure of closeness is sacrificed, as the logistical
challenge to maintain a family atmosphere becomes overwhelming if
not impossible. Although pockets of family remain, the overall staff
is generally defined as close friends. While they discuss church business in regularly scheduled staff meetings (which include the entire
team), a significant amount of time will be devoted to personally
"checking in" and team prayer.

In a team defined by close friend relationships, there are multiple annual proactive staff retreats. This includes a minimum of one
all-staff off-site overnight retreat as well as multiple all-staff one-day
local retreats. Additionally, there are four to six annual team-building

days that may involve activities such as challenge courses, a canoe
trip, bowling, or an outing to a sporting event. These days are specifically designed to bring the staff closer together by placing them in a
variety of environments.

At this level of team, the staff knows one another outside of
work and they enjoy hanging out together. If you have an extra
ticket for a sporting event, a fellow staff member will likely be one
of your first calls. The staff communicates daily; they spend a significant time with one another and know the names of each other's
spouses and children. Using the sports genre, the staff is likened
to a basketball team. Much larger than a tennis doubles team, but
the staff must mesh and work well together. As close friends, every
decision directly impacts every other member of the team. If any
team member fails to function on the level of ministry partner,
the strained relationship will have a direct negative impact on the
entire team.

As the congregation surpasses the five-hundred mark and the
staff continues to expand, the natural tendency is to move on the
Team Scale from close friends into the realm of friendship.

Third, a team can be defined as joining together with friends to
achieve a clearly described goal. We may not live all of life together,
but we are friends. We communicate, spend time with one another,
and know the names of each other's spouses. A measure of closeness
is sacrificed as the logistical challenge to maintain a close friendship
with each staff member becomes logistically impossible. While pockets of family and close friends are scattered throughout the team, the
overall staff is generally defined as friends who are laboring together
in the service of the Lord.

As a church breaks through the seven-hundred and one-thousand barriers, an executive leadership team is often created to make major decisions. Team members (even those in support roles) who have served on the staff from the beginning but are now excluded from executive decisions will have a difficult time being left out of the decision-making process. For the first time in the life of the church, staff meetings are predominantly given over to business (communicating decisions rather than making decisions) with minimal time devoted to personal sharing and corporate prayer.

In this level of team, the staff knows one another predominately inside of work. The staff communicates as needed; they spend a minimal amount of time with one another and may or may not know the names of each other's spouses. Using the sports genre, they are more like a baseball team. Much larger than a basketball team, the team will regularly cross paths, though they may have significantly different areas of ministry. One team member may be a pitcher and another may be the first baseman, but they will, by necessity, spend significant time together. If a conflict exists within the team, the relational tension will, at a minimum, indirectly impact the entire team. Worst case, an inner-team conflict can potentially cripple a team.

In a team defined by friend relationships, it is unlikely that there will be an all-staff off site overnight retreat, as cost and logistics provide a convenient justification. If the entire staff participates in one annual team-building day, that is viewed as success!

As the church becomes a megachurch (surpassing two thousand regular attendees) and the staff continues to expand, the natural tendency is to move on the Team Scale from friends into the realm of a working relationship. If nothing is done to proactively combat the slide away from community, this is the natural church default position.

In a megachurch, team is commonly defined as working relationships, much like a football team. I once asked a friend who played in the NFL to give me some insight into a particular star running back. His answer surprised me. "I couldn't tell you," he said. "We've never spoken to one another." When I gently reminded him that they were part of the same team, he responded, "I play defense; he plays offense. There is little to no occasion for our paths to cross. Clearly, we hold different values, so it's not like we hang out after practice. I go home to my family and he goes ... somewhere." Each respects the job the other is doing and would do anything in their power to make the other more effective, but it remains a detached working relationship. There are teams within the teams. The offense, defense, and special teams are separate entities, which together make up the whole. In a megachurch it is not uncommon to have a worship team, children's team, youth team, missions and mercy ministry team, and a number of additional ministry teams, each of which comprises several pastors. Some ministry teams may seldom if ever cross paths, and yet they are a distinct part of the whole staff.

In a team defined by working relationships, there may be multiple proactive staff retreats, but they take place within specific teams within the team. The worship team may have an overnight getaway, but it is limited to those who are a part of worship. Off-site overnight retreats are designed exclusively for the executive team.

Because an executive team makes the majority of decisions, staff meetings rarely bring the entire team together. When staff gatherings do occur (commonly once a month), while there may be teaching from a lead pastor, there will seldom be discussion, as there simply isn't time to delve into personal disclosure. If some members of the team are not friends, it generally does not affect the overall performance of the team. In fact, a conflict among the team is often minimalized, as the sheer size of the team diminishes its impact on the team as a whole.

Finally, teams can and do function despite a complete absence of relationship. At this point, the term "team" becomes loosely defined. In the sports genre, this would be likened to an Olympic team. Other than the opening and closing ceremonies and a visit to the White House, there is no occasion for the entire team to cross paths. There are teams within teams within teams. For example, the volleyball team is a specialized unit within the Olympic team. Within this specialized team, the volleyball team actually consists of four separate teams: men's and women's indoor volleyball and men's and women's beach volleyball. There is unquestionably no reason for a member of the women's volleyball team to connect with a member of the men's equestrian team (if they are connecting, that is a problem of a different kind!). Most athletes don't know one another, and they have no desire to know one another, as they have neither reason nor occasion to spend time together outside of their individual team environments. Yet each person is identified as a unified member of the Olympic team.

In the everyday world, the phrase "I didn't take this position because I needed friends; I took this position because I needed a job" is typical of this level of team. It is a purely silo approach to ministry. An executive team or an overseeing board makes all major decisions, as it would be logistically impossible for each member of the team to register an opinion. There is no staff engagement outside of the work environment. The thought of organizing a staff outing is repulsive to many, as they have zero desire to relationally connect with the majority of their fellow employees. Staff meetings never bring the entire team together. If members of the team are embroiled in conflict, it will not affect the overall performance of the team. A simple resignation removes a staff member from the team with no impact on the rest of the church staff.

Defining the Desired Level of Team

I have walked through the Team Scale with a number of church and ministry staffs. I have yet to find any single church (no matter how large) or ministry (no matter how massive) that wishes their staff functioned at a level beyond the friendship line. In nearly every team assessment, if the church is a minimum of five years old and has achieved consistent growth over the first five years, the staff, or in some cases the executive team, will identify that their desire is for their staff to function just above the friends level. While they encourage family pockets within the team, they are realistic and know that they can't continue to grow as a church and maintain the close friends level of team.

The challenge becomes to maintain the desired level of team knowing that, if left untouched, the Team Scale naturally moves toward working relationships. The Team Scale does not naturally move toward family. And if a team is accurately described by the Olympic team paradigm, something has likely gone wrong.

I have found that while many *lead pastors* and leadership teams assume their staff is functioning at a level between a basketball team and a baseball team, many *staff members* report that the team level is actually that of a football team. Lead pastors commonly overestimate the functioning level of their staff as a team. Superficial assumptions and limited assessments are dangerous tools in the hands of a myopic lead pastor.

First and foremost, do a staff assessment to discern the present level of team within your staff. In an environment of grace and trust, this can be an excellent staff discussion. In many church contexts, pastors may want to allow for anonymous responses, as the truth may be too painful for staff members to share openly.

Second, depending on the present state of the team, the staff, lead pastor, or executive team must agree on the desired level of team. Realistically, where on the Team Scale do you desire your church staff to function? While your first tendency might be to plot a point on the Team Scale between close friends and family, take a moment and ask yourself: (1) Is this what is truly desired, and (2) are changes that need to be instituted to reach that level realistic?

Third, once you have agreed on a desired level on the Team Scale, devise a detailed plan to achieve and maintain the desired level of team. As stated earlier, I do believe it is possible for megachurches to operate above a friend level on the Team Scale. Appoint a relational creative to a special team, and task them with the responsibility to devise an intentional plan to achieve and maintain the desired level of team. I am intrigued by Fortune 500 corporations that go to great lengths to maintain a friendship level of team. Google, for example, is a great example of a massive staff doing everything they can to fight against detached community. Take time to investigate large corporations who are going the extra mile to achieve genuine community.

You might want to start with Four Seasons Hotels and Resorts, St. Jude Children's Research Hospital, and the Boston Consulting Group.

Living Life in Community

Jesus chose twelve disciples that they might be with Him (Mark 3:14). In his classic work *The Training of the Twelve*, A. B. Bruce reminds us of the need to pour our lives into those around us in order that they might be equipped to do the work of the local church (Ephesians 4). The wonderfully sublime subtitle of the book is *Passages Out of the Gospels Exhibiting the Twelve Disciples of Jesus Under Discipline for the Apostleship*. Bruce goes to great lengths, even in 1871, to correct the perception that the church is simply something that people attend. His theme is that as the body of Christ, we are called by Jesus to live life committed to one another. The early church worshipped, lived, and studied in community; and Bruce concludes that it's not possible to be freestanding, isolated entities. It's not possible to survive without each other.

Worshipping in Community

Psalm 95 is regularly used as a call to worship, particularly the first seven verses:

> Oh come, let us sing to the LORD;
> > let us make a joyful noise to the rock of our
> > > salvation!

Let us come into his presence with thanksgiving;
> let us make a joyful noise to him with songs of
> praise!
For the LORD is a great God,
> and a great King above all gods.
In his hand are the depths of the earth;
> the heights of the mountains are his also.
The sea is his, for he made it,
> and his hands formed the dry land.

Oh come, let us worship and bow down;
> let us kneel before the LORD, our Maker!
For he is our God,
> and we are the people of his pasture,
> and the sheep of his hand.

Look over the psalm again. There are no fewer than ten references in the first seven verses pointing to community. "Let *us* sing to the LORD; let *us* make a joyful noise to the rock of *our* salvation! Let *us* come into his presence … let *us* make a joyful noise to him…. Oh come, let *us* worship and bow down; let *us* kneel before the LORD, *our* Maker! For he is *our* God, and *we are the people of his pasture, and the sheep of his hand*."

The Lord's Prayer is another example of community. Jesus instructs His disciples to pray "Our Father" as opposed to "My Father." The prayer goes on, "Give *us* this day *our* daily bread. Forgive *us our* debts as *we* forgive *our* debtors. Lead *us* not into temptation but deliver *us* from evil." The entire prayer rests in the context of community. We are called to live in community, to worship in community, and to minister in community. Because sin flourishes in isolation, community is one of the cosmic antidotes to human depravity, the primary answer being Jesus. We have not been created by God to live lives characterized by loneliness, remoteness, and isolation. We have been created for community—and for family.

The Family of God

We have been welcomed into the family of God in every conceivable manner. I am blessed to be a part of a marvelous family. My wife, Sally, and I were blessed with three biological children: Mark, Megan, and Sarah joined our family via blood. Later, our family increased to welcome Paige and Allie into our family through adoption. When Mark married Holly, we joyfully welcomed her into our family via marriage. Blood, adoption, and marriage are the only three ways to join a family.

How secure are we in the family of God? We have been grafted into the family of God through the shed blood of Jesus (Colossians 1:19–20). We have been welcomed into the family of God through the miracle of adoption (Romans 8:15–17). Finally, we have entered into the family of God through marriage (Revelation 19:6–9; 21:1–2). As followers of Jesus, our place in the family of God is guarded, secure, confident, and protected. Those who have bowed their knees and surrendered their hearts to Jesus Christ are part of His eternal family. We were created for relationship. We were created for family. We were created for community.

Questions for Reflection

Reality—What type of tree presently reflects your life? Redwood, sequoia, weeping willow, pine, or aspen? Is this working for you? Why, or why not? Which tree would you like to reflect your life?

Rewind and Review—Which of the five factors that impact community have significant traction in your life? In the life of your church?

Reflect on how Jesus experienced both the joys and wounds of community. How is His example applicable to your embracing His call to community in spite of the risks?

Reflect—What might happen if you move toward Jesus's call to genuine community? "I am afraid of _____. I might lose _____. I might be rejected or opposed by _____. I don't want to deal with the difficulty of _____."

Where is your church or ministry staff on the Team Scale? How confident are you in this assessment? Why is it there?

Where do you want your church staff to be on the Team Scale? Why? Is this a realistic goal? What adjustments must be made to get there? Is there enough buy-in from the staff to reach your goal? What will likely be sacrificed to get there? What *needs* to be sacrificed to get there?

Remember—Reflect on the fact that you have been grafted into the family of God through the shed blood of Jesus (Colossians 1:19–20), the miracle of adoption (Romans 8:15–17), and

marriage (Revelation 19:6–9; 21:1–2). What difference does this
make to you?

Respond—Where might you take a practical step of faith this week
toward genuine friendship and genuine community?

Chapter 4

Embracing Weakness in a Strength-Glorified Culture

I admit it; I have a tendency to think more of myself than I should. But God has memorable ways of dealing with that, especially when I step into ministry in third world settings.

Though I live in the United States, a big part of my heart lives with the pastors and people of Haiti and Trinidad. Simply traveling there hits my reset button. I return to the States with renewed perspectives on my walk with the Lord, my marriage, my family, and the work of pastoral ministry. That's why I'm so eager to take business leaders with me. Uber-confident professionals who find their self-worth in position, wealth, and power soon discover the acclaim they've earned in America adds up to a big fat nothing in the third world. I've seen men and women who lead multimillion-dollar companies with thousands of employees weep while ministering among the poor. I've witnessed arrogant, prideful, self-confident leaders reduced to mush at their first encounter with a child with the distended belly and orange hair indicative of malnutrition.

And sometimes it's my turn to learn.

I was leading a team in Haiti and a local pastor invited me to preach in his small church located in Marmalade, a beautiful mountain village located about two hours outside of Gonaïves, a city located in northern Haiti. The pastor informed me I would be the first white man to deliver the Sunday morning message to his congregation. He assured me he would spread the word (that I was white) and a larger-than-normal crowd could be expected (because I was white).

The night before the service I spent time preparing to preach the gospel to the congregation. I've filled pulpits for years in Haiti so this was nothing out of the ordinary. That evening I prayed the prayer I've prayed hundreds of times before. "Oh Lord, use my message to bring glory to Your name. Use my words to glorify the name of Jesus that many may come to a saving faith. May I faithfully preach the message of gospel grace so that many would see what Jesus accomplished in their place by giving His life at Calvary. Amen."

The next morning I finished my prep and continued to pray with the same heart and words. "Lord, use my message to bring glory to Your name!" I prayed on the two-hour bus ride as I watched the beautiful Haitian countryside out of my window. When we arrived at the church, I felt as if was "prayed up" and ready to go. Good thing. The pastor had not exaggerated his claims. We were immediately mobbed by children—a joy experienced by anyone who has spent time in the third world. The church was full, and there was an equal number of people trying to get in. This was a morning of standing room only. I felt a rush of adrenaline.

I settled in to my place on the platform in the open-air church. I was eager for what was about to happen. The worship portion of the service lasted over an hour. The musicians played instruments that looked as if they'd been through five hurricanes, probably because they had. But there was nothing damaged about the musicians who used them. They were full of talent and full of zeal. The congregation was passionate. Intense. And fully engaged. This was worship Haitian-style.

During the final worship song, I observed a group of about a dozen people unexpectedly walk through the side door of the church into the center aisle and slowly make their way toward the platform. They huddled together, many with their arms around each other. Some were in tears. I turned to my translator and asked what was happening. He went to the area in front of the platform where the pastor and several church leaders joined the group and began talking and praying with them. For some, tears turned to smiles. For others, tears began to roll. There were shouts of joy from the small group as the pastor prayed.

My translator returned to the platform, leaned toward me, and said, "These people came forward to give their lives to Jesus Christ. They have been running from God and this morning they felt compelled to end their rebellion and surrender their lives to Jesus."

I responded, "How is that possible? I have yet to preach!" Okay, I didn't say that out loud. But, honestly, the thought ran through my mind. Then it hit me! *The Spirit of God is thick in this place today! I'm going to be part of a revival!* I went into the pulpit supremely confident that something spectacular was about to happen.

I preached from 1 Samuel 17, the story of David and Goliath. I assured the people the application of the story is not "be like David." The point of the story is *not* "face your enemies and the Lord will be with you." The point of the story is that David fought as the legal representative of the people. David wasn't just fighting *for* Israel; he was fighting *as* Israel. In other words, whatever happened to David was imputed to the people of Israel. It's a story that points us to Jesus. God sent Jesus not as an example, but as a savior. Jesus's righteousness was imputed to His people as our legal representative and savior in the great cosmic battle.

I finished the message with sweat pouring down my face and expectations rising in my heart. I issued the invitation. I urged people to surrender their lives to Jesus Christ. I waited for them to fill the aisle and make their way to the platform.

No one moved. Zero. Zilch. Nada. Each person who trusted the Lord that day did so before I said a single word. The saving work of Jesus was accomplished in worship, not in my preaching. As I moved from the podium to my seat, the Lord impressed upon me that I had been praying the wrong prayer. When I say "impressed upon me," I mean He hit me over the head with a spiritual two-by-four. As I sat on the platform, I fully appreciated that God didn't need me.

Over the course of my lifetime, I have come to understand that God has multitudes of ways to humble His people. God is phenomenally creative in strategies that shift our eyes off ourselves to focus on Jesus. My loving heavenly Father gently reminds me that Jesus is the champion—and I am not. He reminds me that because He is strong, I can be weak. Because He absorbed death, I can live life. I need regular reminding. All too often I look to my strengths rather than embracing my weakness and allowing the power of Jesus Christ to work through me. All too often I fail to remember that God, who is unlimited in His power, His grace, and His compassion, delights in working in spite of human limitations. *All too often.* It is a phrase I use far too often.

Pastors have a special challenge in realizing we are not indispensable to the accomplishment of the agenda of the Lord. God can and will bring about His purposes by whatever means He chooses. When the Lord includes us in His plans, it is an incredible honor. But when I believe I am a critical component to the agenda of the Lord, I am forced into unsustainable, exhausting efforts to protect my public image.

Embracing Weakness

Weakness. Why is this something we avoid in the church? Why do we want people to focus on our front stage strengths while seldom calling attention to our back stage weaknesses? Why do we love to tell stories that highlight our assets rather than focus on our liabilities? You must understand that Jesus is the hero and, in His supreme kindness, He can and does use our weakness for His glory.

One of the major impediments to embracing the six relationships is our belief that we should never reveal our back stage weakness. To reveal our weakness could mean confronting fear and insecurities stuffed into the deep recesses of the darkest corners of our hearts. And yet, Paul the apostle gladly and openly embraced his weakness.

> To keep me from becoming conceited because of the surpassing greatness of the revelations, a thorn was given me in the flesh, a messenger of Satan to harass me, to keep me from being conceited. Three times I pleaded with the Lord about this, that it should leave me. But he said to me, "My grace is

> sufficient for you, for my power is made perfect in
> weakness." Therefore I will boast all the more gladly
> of my weaknesses, so that the power of Christ may
> rest upon me. For the sake of Christ, then, I am
> content with weaknesses, insults, hardships, perse-
> cutions, and calamities. For when I am weak, then
> I am strong. (2 Corinthians 12:7–10)

In other words, in order to keep Paul from becoming too full of himself, God humbled him through a severe struggle that wouldn't go away. This passage raises several questions.

While Paul identifies the thorn as a messenger of Satan, we must not forget that God allowed it. God is the redeeming agent behind the bitter experience. Satan does nothing to keep us from being conceited. His goal is to produce pride, not prevent it. That's how he commonly slays believers: with pride in what we have done, or despair over what we haven't done. But God is at work here too. While Satan is seeking to use Paul's thorn to destroy, the Lord Jesus is using the thorn to redeem.

Why was the thorn given? From our self-adulating, self-laudatory, and self-absorbed society's viewpoint, it seems as if the Lord is hold-ing Paul back from his full potential. If Paul wants to post a dozen selfies on his Instagram account, what's the harm in that? Few would argue that we are conditioned to tirelessly try to find ways to be thought highly of by others. We would never say it, but we secretly crave affirmation. If I could just get some people to notice me, clap for me, approve of me, then, and only then, will I be satisfied. But the truth is that satisfaction comes only when you forget yourself and are absorbed in the person of Jesus Christ. You will be fulfilled when you grow into a deeper, richer, and wider appreciation and love for His amazing grace.

What was Paul's thorn? This is one of the questions scholars have debated down through the centuries. Some of the more common suggested thorns are headaches, spiritual opposition, eyesight or speech problems, malaria, and agony at the rejection of the gospel. This is the only occurrence of the word "thorn" in the New Testament. In the Old Testament, the word appears twice, both times referring to the enemies of Israel. While scholars can't specifically identify Paul's thorn, I am well acquainted with my own. It's a thorn that has ultimately driven me into a place of embracing my weakness and learning utter dependency on the Lord Jesus. My thorn drove me to acknowledge—and accept—the need for a boss, a trainer, a coach, a counselor, a mentor, and a friend.

My Thorn in the Flesh

From the time I was a child, I dreaded, despised, and literally hated the first day of school. A new school year meant a new homeroom. A new homeroom meant a new teacher. And a new teacher was a whole new opportunity to humiliate and embarrass myself in front of my peers. Teachers would predictably go around the classroom and ask us to share our names and what we did over the summer. As other children effortlessly shared their stories, my breathing became labored. Panic swept through my stiffened body. When it came close to my turn to speak, I would often feign illness or a need to use the restroom, anything to get out of the room. Sometimes my escape plan was successful, but more often it led to increased humiliation. Why? Because I literally couldn't say my name. I couldn't say "Jimmy." I couldn't say my name because I was, and am to this day, a stutterer.

My parents were convinced my stutter was a childhood phenomenon that I would outgrow in time. When I hit five, they enrolled me in speech lessons, beginning to fear this was more than a childhood tic. Thus began fourteen years of speech therapy, which concluded only when I departed for college. If you've seen *The King's Speech*, then you've seen my life. This excellent movie portrayed the true story of King George VI of England (played by Colin Firth) and his ascension to the throne, hindered by his severe stutter. Geoffrey Rush plays Lionel Logue, the innovative speech therapist who helped the stuttering monarch overcome his inability to speak in public. I have been through every therapy portrayed in the movie. I have gone through entire therapy sessions lying on the floor. I've spoken over music wearing headphones. I've practiced diaphragmatic breathing. I've used pacing techniques with a metronome. One speech therapist convinced my parents that playing card games would slow my thinking, which in theory should slow my speech, which in turn would cure my stutter. In the following three years I played gin rummy, hearts, and poker with Dr. Nicholson twice a week. I became really great at cards—but not at speaking. It did nothing for my stutter.

Like most everyone struggling with a weakness, I remember turning my anger toward God. Even as a child I questioned, why me? Of all people, why did I have to be the one with a glaring weakness? Why did I have to be the one with a stutter? At times, my anger targeted my parents. Why would they name me Jimmy? A hard "J" is one of the greatest challenges to a stutterer. Why did we live on Courtleigh? A hard "C" was agony. Were my parents trying to humiliate me? Why didn't they name me Sean or Mike and live on Lincoln Street?

My stuttering dictated my plan for life. I needed a strategy to cope. I would find an occupation that didn't require me to interact with people. I would avoid telephone conversations; in fact, no speaking at all. I abandoned the idea of marriage. The thought of publicly making vows was debilitating. While I loved politics, I discarded the idea of running for office. Politicians are required to speak! I would live as a recluse far away from civilization.

But at the tender age of twelve, the Lord Jesus clearly and undeniably called me to be a pastor. The call to pastoral ministry followed a whirlwind year of life transformation. At the age of eleven, I surrendered my life to Jesus after talking with my older brother, Kenny, in his basement bedroom. The next year was filled with increasing joy as I was privileged to have mature believers pour into my life.

On the particular day of my call to vocational ministry, while I can't tell you the theme of the message, I can tell you the outcome was an indescribable, overwhelming sense that I hadn't surrendered everything to Jesus. And when I say "everything," I primarily mean my future plans. Since that day, I have come to understand that surrendering our lives to Jesus also means surrendering our agendas to Jesus. We don't come to the Lord in order for Him to rearrange our agendas. Rather, we come to Jesus to get a new agenda.

I remember slowly walking to the front of my church at the conclusion of a Sunday morning worship service at Central Christian Church in Wichita, Kansas. Reverend George Wood, a wonderfully kind and gifted pastor, met me at the altar. I wanted to tell him about my call, but I knew I couldn't risk being humiliated in front of the entire congregation. I wrote it out on a sheet of paper and handed my "call" to him. I wrote that the Lord had told me it was time to surrender everything to Him. I knew this meant that the Lord wanted me to be a pastor. I will never forget George praying over me—right then and there—asking the Lord to use me as a pastor to advance His kingdom.

Though most of the people around me celebrated my newfound call, I considered this the lowest point of my life. While many look back on their calls to ministry with fond memories, I saw my call to vocational pastoral ministry as a cruel trick being played by an unkind God. What kind of a loving God would call a stutterer to preach? Would God call a blind man to race automobiles? Would God call a deaf man to play the timpani in an orchestra? Was this some coldhearted cosmic joke?

We are told that Paul pleaded with the Lord three times to take away his thorn; I lost count when I hit a thousand. For years and years, even before I was a believer, I prayed daily asking the Lord to take away my weakness. Clearly, just as Christ said no to Paul's prayer, He said no to me. During my lifetime, I have come to understand that whenever God says no to our deepest pleadings, the no is always wrapped in the context of His compassionate goodness and love. The promise of Romans 8:28 is that God will use everything for our ultimate good and His ultimate glory. The Lord's answers to our prayers are never negative—except in the most superficial sense, because they are furthering God's plan for our good. Over time, I have come to see my thorn as something inherently evil that the Lord Jesus has unquestionably redeemed for my good and His glory.

When God Uses Weakness to Increase Our Dependency

Raising five children has allowed Sally and me to experience every stage of life—over and over again. But the pattern is the same. When a child is born, there is 100 percent dependency on the parents. Parents feed, bathe, and change the child, generally sustaining the child's life. Newborns are weak and helpless. If the parents were to leave a baby alone at home while they took a vacation, the child would not survive. As children grow and slowly mature (emphasis on slowly), surprising things take place. They begin to feed themselves, walk, and talk! Soon, children begin to dress themselves, take on household chores, and actually function as a productive family member! Later, they can stay home alone and may even take on responsibility for younger siblings. Some may begin to drive and hold down their first jobs. Some go on to college, while others enter the workplace. Eventually, they are no longer dependent on the parents. Life is a journey from 100 percent dependence to 100 percent independence.

Not so in our walk with God. While human development moves from utter dependence to complete independence, our spiritual journey is from unmitigated independence from God to 100 percent dependence on the Lord Jesus. We are to grow from self-strength to weakness. From power to vulnerability. And from control to surrender. We learn to embrace our limitations, allowing the goodness of the Lord to be magnified. When we embrace the pain of our thorn, it drives us away from self-reliance to greater dependency on Jesus. This is the theme of Paul's second letter to the Corinthians.

The Glory of Paul's Weakness

Paul tells his readers the hardships endured in Asia were burdens too heavy to bear.

> We do not want you to be unaware, brothers, of the affliction we experienced in Asia. For we were so utterly burdened beyond our strength that we despaired of life itself. Indeed, we felt that we had received the sentence of death. But that was to make us rely not on ourselves but on God who raises the dead. (2 Corinthians 1:8–9)

The picture Paul gives is that of being crushed by something exceedingly heavy—to a point where they feared for their lives. Why would God lay a life-threatening burden on Paul and his companions? Paul tells us that the hardships and intense pressure were given to expose their weakness and drive them to more fully rely on the Lord. Paul refers to the resurrection to highlight the strength of the Lord as juxtaposed to his own weakness. Paul and his companions needed a power far beyond themselves.

The key statement regarding weakness in Paul's second Corinthian letter is found in 4:7–11.

> But we have this treasure in jars of clay, to show that the surpassing power belongs to God and not to us. We are afflicted in every way, but not crushed; perplexed, but not driven to despair; persecuted,

but not forsaken; struck down, but not destroyed;
always carrying in the body the death of Jesus, so
that the life of Jesus may also be manifested in our
bodies. For we who live are always being given over
to death for Jesus' sake, so that the life of Jesus may
be manifested in our mortal flesh.

Once again, Paul stretches the limits of language to make clear
that the power of the gospel to see the glory of Christ is not human,
but wholly divine. Paul tells us we have the most powerful treasure
in the weakest delivery system: our frail human bodies. It is like pure
gold bars being carried about in a battered, filthy gym bag. Human
weakness is no impediment to the glory of God. In fact, just as the
brilliance of diamonds is always more striking when contrasted with
a black background, the worth of the gospel is more evident against
the backdrop of human frailty. God has entrusted the indestructible,
imperishable treasure of the gospel to weak, fragile jars of clay.

Here's the incredible thing about Paul's ministry. The longer he
walked with God, the less willing he was to depend on himself. It was
as if he signed a personal "declaration of dependence" and steadily
grew into a state of total dependence on the Lord Jesus. We know
this because Paul allows his readers numerous looks behind the curtain to see his struggles. In Galatians, likely Paul's first letter written
in approximately AD 50 or 51, Paul straightaway lays claim to the
title "apostle"—the highest office in the church.

Paul, an apostle—not from men nor through man,
but through Jesus Christ and God the Father, who

> raised him from the dead—and all the brothers
> who are with me.
>
> To the churches in Galatia ... (Galatians
> 1:1–2)

Yet six years later, Paul writes his first letter to the Corinthian church and says,

> For I am the least of the apostles, unworthy to be
> called an apostle, because I persecuted the church
> of God. (1 Corinthians 15:9)

In a period of six years, Paul hasn't progressed from "apostle" to "super apostle." Instead, he has gone from "apostle" to "least of the apostles." And in seven more years, approximately AD 61 or 62, Paul writes a letter to the church at Ephesus and says,

> Of this gospel I was made a minister according
> to the gift of God's grace, which was given me by
> the working of his power. To me, though I am the
> very least of all the saints, this grace was given, to
> preach to the Gentiles the unsearchable riches of
> Christ, and to bring to light for everyone what is
> the plan of the mystery hidden for ages in God
> who created all things. (Ephesians 3:7–9)

Now, Paul tells us that if you were to line up all believers in the world, he would be at the back of the line.

At this point you may be thinking that Paul is using hyperbole to make a point, but I don't believe this is exaggeration. I think Paul was coming into a deeper, fuller, and richer understanding of grace that allowed him to view the depth of his depravity with unparalleled honesty. As Paul weighed his sin with supreme clarity, he did believe he would be at the back of the line.

And finally, near the end of his life, in his first letter to Timothy, his son in the faith, Paul writes,

> I thank him who has given me strength, Christ Jesus our Lord, because he judged me faithful, appointing me to his service, though formerly I was a blasphemer, persecutor, and insolent opponent. But I received mercy because I had acted ignorantly in unbelief, and the grace of our Lord overflowed for me with the faith and love that are in Christ Jesus. The saying is trustworthy and deserving of full acceptance, that Christ Jesus came into the world to save sinners, of whom I am the foremost. But I received mercy for this reason, that in me, as the foremost, Jesus Christ might display his perfect patience as an example to those who were to believe in him for eternal life. To the King of the ages, immortal, invisible, the only God, be honor and glory forever and ever. Amen. (1 Timothy 1:12–17)

Over the course of his ministry, Paul went from apostle to the least of the apostles, to the least of all of God's people, to the worst sinner in the entire world. Shouldn't he be increasing in confidence and spiritual authority? Should we question Paul's spiritual maturity? Who in his right mind would knowingly seek spiritual direction and counsel from the worst sinner in the entire world? But Paul wasn't regressing. He was growing in his relationship with the Lord Jesus precisely because he matured from independence to *total* dependence on the Lord Jesus. By embracing his weakness, Paul announced his dependence. He stepped out of the illusion of strength and into the actual strength of a sinner who depended on God for his power. Paul came to understand his weakness could never trump the abundant supply of God's grace. In fact, the power of God led Paul to find glory in his weakness.

Paul tells us that the Lord responded to his pleading that the thorn would be removed with a simple truth, *"My grace is sufficient for you, for my power is made perfect in weakness."*

Confessing the Sin behind the Sin

Confession is good for the soul. We tell our congregations that all the time. Scripture instructs us to confess our sins to our heavenly Father (1 John 1:9) and to one another (James 5:16). The confession of sin pushes back against posing, pretending, and hiding (Proverbs 28:13). Yet in my conversations with pastors, I find I continually need to encourage them to confess their sins too. And then, to confess the sin behind the sin. Most have no idea what I'm talking about.

Recently, a pastor contacted PastorServe because he was looking for a safe, confidential, gospel-centered place to confess a particular sin (not at all uncommon). He disclosed that he had been struggling mightily with the debilitating sin of lust. "In fact," he told me, "just last night I was in a restaurant with my wife and I was overcome with lust for another woman at a nearby table." Through his tears, he confessed to me that he was overwhelmed with guilt, shame, and disappointment that he would commit such an atrocious sin in the very presence of his wife. He saw precious little hope for his sinful behavior.

I encouraged him to confess that particular sin of lust to the Lord. We prayed together and he sincerely cried out to Jesus, confessing the sin of lust, then asking the Lord's forgiveness. At the conclusion of the prayer, I asked him a simple question: "What is the sin behind the sin?" In other words, what was the sin that had caused him to lust?

After some thought, the pastor told me that he must have a shallow view of happiness, because he believed (albeit for a moment) that this stranger could genuinely make him happy. I encouraged him to confess this to the Lord. He again prayed, confessing his sinfully skewed perspective of happiness. When he finished his prayer, I again asked, "What is the sin behind that sin?" After lengthy reflection, he replied, "I guess … I thought that she could make me happy … because I don't believe that Jesus alone can make me happy." Okay, now we are getting closer to the root of the sin.

Following a time of confession, we returned to the question—"What sin lies behind not believing that Jesus can meet your needs?" His answer is commonly the root of most every sin: "Because I don't believe in the sufficiency of God's grace."

In conversations like these I am astonished how often pastors conclude that they struggle with a lack of belief in the sufficiency of Christ. And the same is true for myself.

Let's say I suffer from road rage. What's behind that? I have an obsession with being in control. What's behind that? I can't trust Jesus with control. What's behind that? I think I'm better at controlling the situation than God. What's the root of that? I don't believe that God's grace is sufficient to meet my every need.

Every confession deserves the process of backtracking. It's like a massive tree with a million leaves. Once you begin to confess the sin behind the sin, you backtrack your way from the leaves to smaller limbs, to larger branches, to the trunk, and ultimately to the root. And the root is almost always "not believing that Jesus Christ is able." We don't believe He is able to fill emptiness. We don't believe He can satisfy our deepest longings. We lust because we don't believe God is enough. Greed grips our hearts because we do not believe God is enough. We gossip because we don't believe that God is enough. We reject weakness, choosing instead to live in our isolationist kingdom of one where we are king and final authority because we don't believe that God is enough.

When God Uses Weakness to Strengthen Pastors

Paul not only acknowledges his weakness, he commits to *boasting* about it.

> Therefore I will boast all the more gladly of my
> weaknesses, so that the power of Christ may rest

upon me. For the sake of Christ, then, I am content with weaknesses, insults, hardships, persecutions, and calamities. For when I am weak, then I am strong. (2 Corinthians 12:9–10)

Paul saw human weakness as an opportunity to display the Lord's divine sovereign power. Don't be confused. Paul was not a theological masochist who glorified suffering. Rather, he came to embrace the fact that his thorn in the flesh was essential to acknowledging his constant weakness and Christ's constant strength. What he summarizes as weaknesses he details in four additional words: "insults, hardships, persecutions, and calamities." Often God's purpose is to make your weakness a showcase for Jesus's power. God's plan is not to eliminate our weaknesses (no matter how many times we plead with Him) but to cause us to rely solely on the Holy Spirit to endure. The deepest need you and I have in the midst of insults, hardships, persecutions, and calamities is not quick relief but the absolute confidence that what is happening to us is part of the greater purpose of God.

This is one of the most difficult concepts for pastors to grasp—and for good reason. Your congregation expects you to be strong. People want to follow strong leaders. If your back stage life doesn't match your onstage persona, they would prefer you keep that to yourself. Unfortunately, the expectations of a robust, tough, "never let 'em see you sweat" pastor is ludicrous—and why there is a mass exodus of pastors from the ministry in years two through four. Once congregational expectations set in, pastors realize their job descriptions don't allow them to embrace weakness and admit brokenness, and they conclude they don't have what it takes to lead. If you're a pastor, there are three potential paths to follow: One, walk away from the pastoral ministry. Two, become a professional pretender, never allowing anyone a glimpse behind the curtain at your back stage weakness. Or three, embrace the gospel of weakness and allow the strength of the Lord to shine through your powerlessness, your ineffectiveness, and your insecurities.

The Gospel of Weakness

The gospel is the story of an all-powerful, divine Father graciously sending His only Son to live a life that would be largely characterized by human weakness. Power in weakness is shorthand for the cross of Jesus Christ. The Father could have sent His Son in strength, glory, and judgment, but He could not have walked among those whom He came to redeem. Philippians 2 reminds us that Jesus emptied Himself (willingly laid aside strength), making Himself nothing (willingly embraced weakness). The only way to atone for the sins of mankind was for Jesus to hang on a cross, in weakness. While many saw the cross as the ultimate defeat of the divine, God triumphed through weakness and defeat, accomplishing our justification. In God's plan of redemption, there was weakness (the cross) before there was power (the resurrection). This powerful gift of divine reconciliation can be understood and received only in weakness. In order to have genuine faith, we admit that we can't make things right on our own. Salvation comes to those who genuinely admit how weak they really are.

G. K. Chesterton famously said that a paradox was a truth standing on its head calling out for attention. The greatest paradox is that God became man. From the cross comes resurrection. Out of death comes life. From repentance comes hope. Out of weakness comes strength. I would come to see this more clearly as I gradually came to see weakness as a close friend.

Questions for Reflection

Reality—What is an area of weakness in your life that causes you to reflect on the strength of Jesus Christ?

Rewind and Review—Dietrich Bonhoeffer wrote, "When we grow tired, God works." How have you seen this in your own life?

Jimmy pointed out that as Paul matured in Christ, his growth was reflected in language that some would take as spiritual regression. Why do you think Paul called himself the worst sinner? Was he using hyperbole to make a point?

Reflect—There are expectations, sometimes wildly unrealistic, in every church. What impractical expectations have been placed on you? How can you effectively address these expectations?

Jimmy said, "Your congregation expects you to be strong." What is one area of your life where you are pretending to be strong? What toll is this posturing taking on your life and ministry?

Review 2 Corinthians 12:9–10. How can you gladly boast in your weakness so that Christ's power may rest on you? What does it mean to be "content with weaknesses, insults, hardships, persecutions, and calamities"?

Remember—Jimmy said, "The only way to atone for the sins of mankind was for Jesus to hang on a cross, in weakness. While many saw the cross as the ultimate defeat of the divine, God triumphed through weakness and defeat, accomplishing our justification. In God's plan of redemption, there was weakness (the cross) before there was power (the resurrection)." How does this truth encourage you?

Respond—With whom do you feel safe enough to confess the sin behind the sin in your life? How often do you engage in back stage conversations of this nature?

In the midst of continually fulfilling your daily and weekly responsibilities, when was the last time you truly paused to reflect on the "gospel of weakness"—the story of an all-powerful, divine Father graciously sending His only Son to live a life that would be largely characterized by human weakness? What implications does the "gospel of weakness" have for your life and ministry?

Chapter 5

Paul's Thorn and Charlie's Angels

I should be making a whole lot more money! Why? Because I fit the supremely rich-guy demographic. I am a 6'3" white American male with an advanced graduate degree. Malcolm Gladwell, in his fascinating book *Blink*, tells us that in the United States, 14.5 percent of all men are 6'0" or taller. And yet, among CEOs of Fortune 500 companies, the percentage is 58. Even more striking, 3.9 percent of adult men are 6'2" or taller (that's me), and among Fortune 500 CEOs, an astonishing 30 percent are 6'2" or taller. Of the tens of millions of American men below 5'6", a grand total of ten have reached the level of a Fortune 500 CEO, which says that being short is as much, or more, of a handicap to corporate success as being a woman or African American.

Gladwell goes on to tell us that beautiful people earn 5 percent more an hour than their less attractive coworkers. The United States Census Bureau reports that white men with a college diploma earn 30 percent more than black men with equivalent college diplomas. White women who are college graduates make about 40 percent less than white men. Our culture has spoken. If you want to get ahead, really ahead, it helps to be a tall white American male.

The Babylonian-Mesopotamian culture, the civilization that gave us Abraham, Isaac, Jacob, and many other biblical leaders in the

Genesis stories, was dominated by a very particular leadership profile; in this case, the firstborn male. Women and second-born males were superfluous. Everyone knew it was wise to choose the strong over the weak, the wealthy over the poor, and the attractive over the plain. In short, you hit the genetic lottery if you were a good-looking, strong, wealthy firstborn male. Aren't you glad times have radically changed over the last four thousand years? (Yes, that was pure sarcasm.)

To be sure, weakness is a consistent theme throughout Scripture. God can and will use pain and weakness to bring us to a place of humility so we can hear His voice more clearly. In *The Problem of Pain*, C. S. Lewis writes, "We can ignore even pleasure. But pain insists upon being attended to. God whispers to us in our pleasures, speaks in our conscience, but shouts in our pains: it is his megaphone to rouse a deaf world."

Many believe the Bible is the story of strong leaders who were used by God to accomplish remarkable deeds, but the story of the Bible is more accurately described as God using weak, broken, flawed, sinful, messy people to accomplish His purposes. The back stage of leading figures in Genesis is likely the filthiest in all of Scripture, and God lifts the curtain to allow us to see what is really going on.

From the beginning, God makes it clear He will fulfill His kingdom agenda in a countercultural manner: He will use the weak, the second born, the women, and the children to do the work regularly reserved for firstborn males. Over and over in the Scriptures—*over and over*—when God chooses someone to do His work, He deliberately selects the unexpected one, the unlikely.

Throughout the story of Scripture, there is a scarlet thread that runs through the generations, the line through which God the Father carries the seed that ultimately leads to Jesus. When that scarlet thread intersects lives, it is almost always the younger, less attractive, weaker who are used of the Lord. When it came time to choose a member of the family to fulfill critical responsibility, God does not go the way of the world. He chooses the younger Abel, not firstborn Cain; the second-born Isaac, not the firstborn Ishmael. God selected weaker mama's boy Jacob and not the stronger outdoorsman Esau. Little Ephraim was chosen over Manasseh, and Perez was selected before Zerah. Judah, the fourth-born son of Jacob, was chosen to carry the scarlet thread, not firstborn Reuben or better-known Joseph. God chose tongue-tied Moses to deliver the people from Egyptian slavery, not his older brother Aaron. David was chosen over his older, larger, stronger brothers.

Gideon was literally the runt of Israel. He was chosen from the weakest tribe (Manasseh) and the weakest clan (extended family), and he himself was the weakling of the family (Judges 6:14–15). And yet, the Lord used Gideon to deliver all of Israel. Gideon started with an army of thirty-two thousand. Not a bad number if one is planning on rumbling with the Midianites; yet, God made it clear Gideon wasn't weak enough (Judges 7:2). The problem was this: if the Israelites fought and defeated the Midianites at full strength, they might take credit for the victory. You might even say that to keep the Israelites humble, God gave them a thorn in the flesh—Gideon! In the blink of an eye, God reduced the number of Israel's army to ten thousand, and then to three hundred, less than 1 percent of the original army! Now Israel was weak enough to give glory only to the Lord.

We could go on and on. God chose barren, old Sarah over a younger, more attractive Hagar. God chose ugly-duckling Leah (the mother of Judah) over beauty-queen Rachel. Nearly every judge is a broken mess, many bordering on embarrassing. Hey, kids, remember to be more like Samson? How can we explain Samson to our children? But God delights in using the weak and the despised and the forgotten of this world to accomplish His divine purposes! Paul tells us this very thing in 1 Corinthians 1:27–29.

> But God chose what is foolish in the world to shame the wise; God chose what is weak in the world to shame the strong; God chose what is low and despised in the world, even things that are not, to bring to nothing things that are, so that no human being might boast in the presence of God.

No one wants to be associated with the foolish, weak, lowly, and despised, but this is often where we find ourselves. We need to admit it. This is me! My personal 2 Corinthians 12 could easily read, "Because of the fact that I am a tall, educated white male, I am prone to a ridiculous amount of pride and arrogance. In order to keep me from thinking too much of myself, to keep me humble and on my knees, God graciously gave me a thorn in my flesh, a stutter, to keep my eyes off myself and on Jesus."

We need to realize that it is commonly through broken people that God does remarkable acts, which bring honor and glory to His name. God's economy opposes the economy of the world. You may be strong, smart, rich, good looking, and exceedingly gifted, but these are characteristics that may hinder you from doing the work of the kingdom. The antidote? Surrender everything. Yield all of your strengths, gifts, assets, and wisdom to the Lord Jesus. It's been said that

> God can achieve His purpose either through the absence of human power and resources or the abandonment of reliance upon them … All through history God has chosen and used *nobodies* because of their unusual dependence upon Him made possible by the unique display of His power and grace. He chose and used *some bodies* only when they renounced dependence upon their natural abilities and resources.[1]

What Was Paul's Thorn in the Flesh?

While I have never claimed unique spiritual insight into God's Word, there is a first time for everything! With absolute certainty, I know Paul's thorn in the flesh. What has been debated for centuries is now revealed! Please, stick with me through these next couple of (ahem) painful paragraphs; this ultimately ends at a good place.

From 1976 to 1981 one of the most popular television shows in American was *Charlie's Angels* (I warned you I was going to stoop low), produced by Aaron Spelling, one of television's early innovators. And while there are an abundance of personality profiles and assessments, I prefer to assess pastors by simply asking *who was their favorite angel*. The series ultimately included six: Kate Jackson (you are a rational, balanced realist), Farrah Fawcett-Majors (you have an active fantasy life), Jaclyn Smith (you are high maintenance and can likely never be pleased), Cheryl Ladd (you likely have a deep mother wound), Shelley Hack (you might want to see a counselor to address your insecurities), and Tanya Roberts (you likely watched *Sheena, Queen of the Jungle* on Netflix one too many times and you might want to see that counselor today).

Aaron Spelling knew women would watch *Charlie's Angels* because of the groundbreaking concept that women could be simultaneously beautiful, smart, empowered, and tough. He knew men would sneak a peek to view attractive women, but it would take a hook to get men to become a regular part of the audience. Spelling found his hook in Charlie Townsend, an eccentric millionaire who would speak to the angels only via speakerphone; Charlie was never seen. Only an occasional hand or leg would slip into America's living rooms. Spelling knew that as long as Charlie's face was never seen, every man could fantasize that Charlie looked—just like him! This was the genius of *Charlie's Angels*. Spelling understood a powerful, fundamental truth: that which is unknown is universal.

Now here's the big reveal. *God has graciously allowed Paul's thorn in the flesh to serve as the "Charlie" of Christian suffering.* What was Paul's thorn in the flesh? That's easy. His thorn was stuttering. And if you have poor eyesight, I believe Paul's thorn in the flesh was poor eyesight. And if you are deaf, I believe Paul's thorn in the flesh was auditory issues. If you suffer from debilitating migraine headaches, I believe Paul's thorn in the flesh was migraine headaches. If you struggle with depression, I believe Paul's thorn in the flesh was depression. If you are enduring fibromyalgia, I believe Paul's thorn in the flesh was fibromyalgia. I could go on and on. Thank God that

Paul never specifically named his thorn because I know many, *many* people who have found life-giving comfort and strength through the passages surrounding the unnamed thorn. In the United States alone, more than fifty-seven million people have a disability. Paul's unnamed thorn has been a great comfort to many of the more than *one billion* around the world suffering from a disability. God used Paul's thorn in the flesh to focus his attention on Jesus Christ. It's my ongoing prayer that God would use my thorn in the flesh to keep me in a place of dependence, humility, and trust with an unyielding desire to bring glory to His name.

To be sure, my stuttering has improved over the years. If you hear me speak once, you may not notice. If you hear me speak multiple times, you will detect a slight stutter. If you spend any amount of time with me, you will hear a consistent stutter. Those closest to me have experienced days when I struggle to utter a single sentence. Is it at times embarrassing? Of course. Have I experienced humiliation? Too many times to count. Do I avoid situations in which I sense that my speech will be a problem? Definitely. And yet I have been asked if I would trade my stutter for perfected elocution if that meant I witnessed a lesser level of God's influence. Not on your life.

The Gospel of Weakness

Why does the church around the world continue to grow among the poorest, weakest, most vulnerable nations? Why is the gospel message bringing visible, transformational revival to nearly every part of the world—except North America and western Europe? Is it because we associate abundance with independence and strength? Yet this is how the gospel functions—it saves people who admit they are weak and in need of a savior. Power in weakness is shorthand for the cross of Jesus Christ. Like Paul pleading to the Father on three occasions to take away his thorn, so, too, in the Garden of Gethsemane, three times Jesus pleaded with His Father to take the cup away. In both cases, God the Father said no.

Acknowledging our need for the six relationships will be derailed *if we fail to acknowledge weakness*. If we believe we are strong, independent, self-reliant leaders, we will be profoundly threatened by any one relationship, let alone six. If we are determined to live an incongruent front stage–back stage life, allowing no one to look into the reality of our brokenness, we build an isolationist prison from which some never escape.

The church seeks leaders who are strong enough to lead the local body. I get that. But I believe the more pertinent question may be, is this leader weak enough to lead this body? I have found that those who believe they have no need for the six relationships are living protected lives characterized by isolation, fear, doubt, and shame. You see, the struggle is to believe that God will use you and that *He does not wait until you achieve perfection* to do it. In your weakness He can and will use you to lead.

How Grace Changes Our Perspective

Earlier in the chapter, I mentioned that Ephraim was chosen over Manasseh. While this story may be unfamiliar to many, it may be the supreme portrait of man's limited perspective and God's beautiful sovereignty. In Genesis 48:8–20, Jacob (now known as Israel) has been reunited with Joseph. Jacob is nearing the end of his life and Joseph knows that it is time to bring his two boys, Ephraim and Manasseh, to his father to be blessed.

The blessing of the sons, particularly the firstborn, was a significant cultural event. Commonly held in public, the ceremony was an opportunity for the father to pronounce a blessing over his boys for all to hear. While some today would see this as an antiquated practice, blessing carried rich significance for the parent and the child. Jacob's life pursuit had been to obtain blessing, and when he deceived his own father (Genesis 27), he learned that genuine words of blessing spoken over a deceptive life mean little to nothing. It remains true today that real words of blessing and affirmation spoken over someone living a life characterized by posing and pretending leave one feeling deceptive, phony, and empty.

While all blessings carried power, not all were created equal. The primary blessing was always given with the right hand—the hand of control, authority, and power—while secondary blessings came from the left hand. So, naturally, Joseph took Manasseh, the firstborn son, and brought him to Jacob's right hand. As the firstborn male, he would receive the lion's share of family authority, power, and inheritance. But Israel did something extraordinary: he crossed his hands, placing his right hand on the younger Ephraim and his left hand on the head of Manasseh. And pandemonium erupted!

Joseph was exasperated, disturbed, and just plain furious! He removed his father's hands, interrupting the blessing. This was an intensely sacred ceremony; you simply didn't interrupt. It would be similar to interrupting a pastor in the middle of pronouncing a bride and groom husband and wife. I can hear Joseph saying, "Whoa, whoa … Dad! Hang on just a second. Let's uncross those hands"— and off to the side, "you old blind fool. Wrong son" (nervous chuckle as Joseph grabs his father's hands and places them on the intended subjects).

Now, maybe Joseph thought it was an honest mistake. Maybe he thought his father's poor eyesight was the problem. But Israel understood that just as the Lord had placed his older brother, Esau, behind him, so, too, Manasseh would be placed behind the younger Ephraim.

Why? Why was Jacob placed ahead of Esau? And why did he bless Ephraim with the right hand? Israel crossed his hands and blessed Ephraim *because the Lord led him to cross his hands*. God delights to use the weak, the underdog, the second best to do His work. God can even use a child to do a work an adult might never be able to accomplish. And that is the lesson I learned in 2001 in Trinidad.

How Grace Changed My Perspective

I believe the Lord Jesus is the hope of the young, the excluded, the weak, the marginalized, the unimportant, the broken, and the failures. Sometimes, it takes one of my own family members to drive home that truth.

By the time I was twenty-five years old, I was well on my way to visiting every country in the world. While I was being discipled by Paul Borthwick at Grace Chapel in Lexington, Massachusetts, the

Lord hit me with a profound truth: My plan to visit as many countries as possible was purely selfish. It was all about me. The mission
became less about sharing the gospel and more about unique stamps
in my passport. The Lord impressed on me that rather than go an
inch deep in one hundred countries, it would be more strategic to
go a mile deep in only a few. Trinidad was one of those countries the
Lord impressed on my heart.

In 2001, I was asked to lead a church-planting training conference for pastors and leaders in Trinidad who would be starting a
church in Campoo—a region well known for its fervent Muslims
and devout Hindus. Because I had previously planted a church and
frequently trained church planters, and because this would be my
thirty-fifth trip to Trinidad, the challenge felt like it was very much
in my sweet spot.

The formal name of the English-speaking former British colony
is Trinidad and Tobago—T&T for short. Most people know T&T
for its incredible beaches, delectable food (shark and bake at Maracas
Beach is my favorite), the steelpan (invented in Trinidad), the annual
carnival, and the Soca Warriors—the national football (soccer) team.
While some continue to describe Trinidad as third world, it is on the
edge of the first world. It has a thriving economy, robust tourism,
and relative government stability. All of this makes T&T an ideal
first-time-out-of-the-country mission trip destination, and Sally and
I decided that this would be a great trip for our daughter Megan,
who was eleven at the time.

On day one of the trip, Megan and I arrived in Campoo where I
would begin the training at a community center, which was located
across the street from a Hindu bar and a few random shops. Now,

you have to understand that my five children have been obligated to hear their dad preach on countless occasions. My kids know my stories as well as I know them myself. Megan was thrilled to come with her dad to Trinidad. She was not thrilled at the prospect of sitting through a couple of days of church-planting seminars. So, like any protective parent, I encouraged my eleven-year-old to wander the streets of a hostile community to see if she could meet a new friend. (Okay, that's a stretch, but thank God her mother wasn't aware of what was happening.)

Megan had seen a little girl who looked to be about her age on a balcony above a Hindu bar. I watched as Megan walked across the street and asked the little girl if she wanted to play. During breaks in the conference, I walked outside and I could see Megan and her new friend on the balcony. At the end of the day, on the way back to the mission compound, Megan recounted her day. She had learned the Trinidadian girl's name was Keisha. Keisha was Hindu and her father owned the bar. Megan and Keisha hadn't exactly become BFFs, but they had enjoyed the time together. The next day Megan once again spent the day with her new friend as I taught.

The new church's grand opening was only a month away. For the grand opening service, the plan was to show *The Jesus Film* in the community center. They hoped the showing of a movie would attract the curious, allowing Christians to get to know some of the residents of Campoo. While trust in Jesus was high, expectations were quite low, as everyone understood the challenge. The training completed, Megan and I headed for home.

My schedule had me back in Trinidad only five weeks after I had completed the church-planter training. I was met at the airport by a group of enthusiastic leaders who informed me that the new church in Campoo was thriving—defying logic and expectation. In my arrogance (are you catching a theme?) I remember thinking, *Well, of course the church plant is going well. Wasn't I just here five weeks ago?*

And then the real story began to spill out. On the night of the grand opening, the church leaders had arrived to get everything set up, only to find that the community center had been padlocked. Apparently, news of a Christian church had spread and several Muslims and Hindus had petitioned the community leaders; as a result, the Christian church was denied any further access to the Campoo community center. No community center meant no access to power, which meant no showing of *The Jesus Film*. The grand opening was not going to happen. As they packed their supplies to leave, the owner of the Hindu bar approached the group and inquired what was happening. They explained the situation and assured the man that they would regroup; they firmly believed the Lord had led them to plant a Christian church in Campoo. The man said, "Don't cancel church tonight. I will close half of my bar and you can show the film tonight in my building." And so, astonished and thankful, the team prepared for the grand opening service of a Christian church in a Hindu bar! When the service began, many of the regular bar patrons (all Hindu men) were curious and decided to stay. After *The Jesus Film* was shown, the lead pastor of the church-planting team, himself a former Hindu, shared his testimony.

What happened that night sounds like a story straight from one of the Gospels or the early church. There was genuine transformation, as several of the Hindus gave their lives to Jesus Christ. They acknowledged that Jesus was the only God. While many Hindus will readily express their desire to follow Jesus, in reality they are adding Him to the more than eight million gods they already worship. When you are worshipping eight million gods, what's one more? And yet, these Hindus declared Jesus to be the one true God. A revival started that night that spread to other parts of Campoo. .

As the night came to a close, the pastor sat down with the bar owner to ask one bewildering question: *Why would a Hindu host a Christian church in his bar?* His answer still gives me chills and usually brings me to tears, no matter how many times I tell the story. He said, "For many months I watched your team come to the community center preparing to begin this new church. I watched as you met people from this neighborhood. I didn't believe that what you were doing was a good thing. However, five weeks ago, when a little girl from your group walked across the street and spent two days playing with my daughter, something in my heart changed and I knew that what you were doing was right. Then, I resolved to help you in any way I could."

Now, review with me: Who is the pastor? Me! Who has been to Trinidad dozens and dozens of times? Me! Who trains church planters and pastors around the world? Me! And who did God use to launch a revival in a Hindu and Muslim community? An eleven-year-old girl. In that moment, *God, like Israel, crossed His hands*. He took His right hand of power and authority and placed it on the head of an eleven-year-old and took His weaker left hand and placed it on the head of an experienced pastor.

God made it very clear: *I will not share My glory with another. If you believe you are indispensable to My plan, I'll gladly use a child to do My work. I can and will use whoever, whatever, whenever I choose. I delight in working in and through those whom the world categorizes as weak, excluded, marginalized, and incapable.*

Whenever God calls a broken vessel to lead the treasure of a local church, He crosses His hands. And until we pastors acknowledge that the only hope we have is the gospel of Jesus Christ, there will continue to be an increasing chasm between our front stage and back stage lives. We will continue to live incongruent lives, which lead to hypocritical, fear-based, inauthentic ministries.

The Implications of an Incongruent Life

Allow me to wade into dangerously awkward waters. While this may surprise a naive few, it needs to be acknowledged that a number of female congregants have schoolgirl crushes on their male pastors. All right, I said it; now let's wade into the troubled waters. Why do women harbor these feelings? The answer is actually quite simple. Women tend to project a sliver of their pastor's life onto a broad scale, which leads to nonsensical conclusions. And before you call me sexist, trust me, men do the same thing with women in different contexts.

Let me explain. Let's say that there is a particular woman who attends a local church once a week. Other than Sunday morning worship service, there is little to no contact with the pastor. During that lone hour of limited pastoral interaction, the pastor is clearly the in-charge shepherd leader. He is handsome, well dressed, well spoken, and has a great sense of humor. The pastor seldom, if ever, talks about his weaknesses, his brokenness, or his personal sin. Instead, he shares stories revealing his athletic giftedness as well as his servant spirit. In nearly every message he speaks well of his beautiful wife and his gifted children. To top off the illusion, he commonly sheds a tear as he reads a John Milton or C. S. Lewis poem to close his message. The pastor is a striking picture of giftedness, strength, control, leadership, athletic prowess, vulnerability, humor, and honest emotion. In other words, he is the human embodiment of many women's dreams. Women want to be with him; men just want to be him. (Lest you think this is a hypothetical story, those exact words were used to describe this pastor.) If he is like this for one hour, the woman concludes, he is most certainly like this the other 167 hours of the week.

As one who has worked with thousands of pastors, I know that no pastor can maintain this facade for 168 hours per week. Though he would never disclose his brokenness, I know that the pastor is fragmented and weak. He has a temper, is generally a slob, and does not have the respect of his staff. Sadly, he is commonly disrespectful of his spouse and he secretly abhors poetry. And to top it off, he has pitiful taste in clothes. This pastor lives a front stage–back stage life. He is adored on the front stage by those with limited contact and loathed on the back stage by those with extensive contact. This pastor rejects the six relationships for fear of exposure. In short, he does not believe the gospel. He does not believe that God can and does use the least vessel to do the greatest work. The congregation's picture of the pastor only lifts him higher and higher so that when the fall comes (and the facade *will* come crashing down), many will be disillusioned. The Lord Jesus never intended for us to live dual lives—but this is the direction our culture, particularly Western culture, has taken us. There is a widening gap between the public and private. How can this be addressed?

Questions for Reflection

Reality—Why is it that so many cultures favor "good-looking, strong, wealthy firstborn" men?

Rewind and Review—What explanations can you offer for God's use of lesser-qualified people throughout the Bible's storyline?

When you read "God can achieve His purpose either through the absence of human power and resources or through the absence of reliance upon them," why do you think that is so?

Reflect—Can you identify a "thorn in the flesh" that God has used, is using, or maybe desires to use to make you "strong in your weakness"?

How can weakness be so necessary when so much of this book is about the importance of six relationships to help you thrive in ministry?

Facing the incongruence of the front stage and back stage of your ministry and life can be a doorway to admitting personal weakness. How do the examples from Scripture and this chapter encourage you to learn and practice reliance on God for life and ministry?

Do you agree God does not just call us to love and serve the weak but to become weak? How will this impact your life?

First Corinthians 1:27–29 reads, "But God chose what is foolish in the world to shame the wise; God chose what is weak in the world to shame the strong; God chose what is low and despised in the world, even things that are not, to bring to nothing things that are, so that no human being might boast in the presence of God." How does this passage specifically apply to you?

Remember—Jimmy reflected on Genesis 48 when telling the story about his daughter in Trinidad. There was another time when God crossed His hands—when Jesus took our curse in order that we might receive the blessing of the firstborn son. How can this truth bring refreshment to your heart today?

Respond—How can the gospel help you realize that your personal strength, success, gifts, and experiences are not the ultimate source of success in ministry? What difference can that make this week?

Chapter 6

Leave Me Alone!

"Please respect my privacy," the young pastor begged the woman. "Just because I'm a pastor at the church you attend, this doesn't give you the right to pry into every corner of my life."

It was a hard thing to say, but the young pastor just couldn't take it anymore. Soon after arriving at the church, the older woman had approached him inquiring into his sports teams, his favorite restaurants, even his preferred coffee. He initially assumed she was being friendly, just making conversation. However, over the past months the questions had become much more invasive. She wanted to know how the pastor and his wife spent their evenings, what movies they attended, and which television programs they enjoyed watching. As an election drew near, she insisted on knowing which candidates he favored. Each week had brought more personal questions that seemed to cross an unspoken boundary. Now, she undeniably crossed the line when, following a Sunday morning worship service, she approached the pastor and said, "Good morning, Pastor. I was driving by your house this week and I noticed that you had three trash bags on the curb for trash pickup. I'm just wondering, what are you and your wife doing to fill three trash bags?" I trust you would agree that when members of our church begin picking through our trash (literally), something needs to be done. And yet, what are appropriate boundaries? How do you determine when someone has gone too far?

As much as you might want to meet your favorite group following a concert, not everyone is allowed back stage to hang out with the band. There is a general understanding that the front stage audience is allowed back stage only via personal invitation. Likewise, not everyone in the church is going to be allowed into the inner sanctum of the pastor. Most pastors invite a carefully selected group to know them back stage as well as front stage. When uninvited people in the church try to force their way back stage, into the private life of a pastor, we rightly resist. I remember a talkative member of my congregation coming to me with an intense desire to confess his most secret sins. After nearly an hour of pouring out the darkness of his heart, he said to me, "Whew! That was emotionally therapeutic to share my deepest, darkest sins. Okay, Pastor, now it's your turn. What are your worst sins?"

Pastors understand that serving a church naturally means surrendering a portion of their privacy. Yet the desire to maintain personal boundaries can go to the extreme, driving pastors deeper and deeper into the dreaded black hole of isolation. When, out of fear, paranoia, or embarrassment, we allow no one back stage to enter into our real brokenness, we walk a path that passes through the hall of isolation and ends at the pit of destruction. How have we taken healthy boundaries and turned them into justification for sequestered living?

The Value of Privacy

Because of my love for the poor and my involvement in the third world, I am regularly invited to speak at mission conferences. One of my favorite messages revolves around the topic "three things that make the average American rich." People usually respond by nodding their heads in agreement. But I'm *not* referring to being spiritually rich, emotionally rich, or relationally rich, but *rich* rich. I'm taking about being financially, materially wealthy. *Rich* is a relative term. If someone makes $50,000 in Southern California, he may feel like he is barely scraping by. If someone makes $50,000 in Liberia, he has reached the top of the wealth pyramid. For someone to be classified as rich, it means that he possesses significantly more than his neighbor. Working with that definition, I conclude that there are three things that make the average American rich: choice, opportunity, and privacy.

Many in the world today live life void of basic choice. More than a billion people wake each day and put on the same thing, eat the same food (commonly rice and beans), and engage in the same daily activities as they did the day before. These people will encounter only a handful of choices every day. Conversely, those living in Western culture are presented with hundreds of thousands of choices each day. Think about it. In America, we wake up and decide what we will drink to get our batteries charged for the day. We choose a quiet spot in the house or apartment to spend time reading and praying. We decide which shirt, pants, and shoes we will wear—choosing from an embarrassing number of options. We decide what to have for breakfast. Personally, I can make scrambled eggs, have a quick bowl of cereal, or make a protein smoothie. If you stop off at a coffee shop on the way to a morning meeting, you face hundreds of choices. You may decide where you will have lunch and then choose from an extensive menu. If you swing by the grocery store, there will be close to a hundred thousand choices. For example, there are more than fifty different toothpastes alone in the average grocery store. Fifty! If you have an excess of choices in your average day, you are rich.

Second, if you have opportunity, you are rich. Let me briefly explain. Presently, who is the best golfer in the world? I'm guessing that a number of names immediately run through your mind. Whoever you select, I would argue the likelihood is very high that person is *not* the best golfer in the world. I would contend that they are the best golfer in the world *of those who have been privileged to have the opportunity to learn how to play golf.* While close to thirty million people play golf in the United States, less than 1 percent of the world has ever had the opportunity to play golf. More than 50 percent of the golf courses in the world are in the United States. And within the United States, the majority of golfers are middle- and upper-class white, the majority living in the suburbs. The odds are staggeringly high that the athlete with the greatest golf potential is a part of the 99 percent who never learned how to play golf. So, while I can respect a well-played golf shot, I have immensely more athletic respect for the winner of the Olympic 100-meter dash.

Are all Olympic gold medals created equal? Absolutely not! Winning the gold medal in the 100-yard dash and winning the gold medal in the equestrian dressage are vastly different. While I have no doubt that it is a thrill to win a gold medal in yachting, I also know that the yachting community constitutes less than a fraction of a fraction of the world's population. That is why the 100-yard dash in the Olympics and the World Cup in soccer are the two most important sporting events in the world—simply because they are perhaps the only two equal-opportunity competitions in the entire world of sports. What about the 200-meter dash? Not every country has a track on which to practice turns. Swimming? Far from it! The majority of the world has never had the opportunity to swim in a pool. If you have the opportunity to play sports, to get an education, to find a job, you are rich.

Third, and most pertinent to our discussion, if you have privacy, you are rich. I remember taking a tour with my family of Plimoth Plantation (yes, that's how it is spelled) in Plymouth, Massachusetts. Plimoth is a seventeenth-century living history museum where "inhabitants" of the plantation take on the personalities of historic pilgrim figures, seldom, if ever, breaking character. In one particularly small home, a woman explained that she and her husband were blessed to have eight children. As I looked around the tiny home, I inquired about "alone time with her husband" and how they made that happen in a one-room house surrounded by eight children. The "pilgrim wife" asked me what I meant by "alone time with her husband" (she loved seeing me break out in a sweat). "You know," I sheepishly replied, "alone time, to be intimate with your spouse." Her response could be painted across the centuries and the majority of countries around the world. "I *am* intimate with my husband," she said, "but there is no such thing as *alone time*."

If I need to be alone, I have multiple options readily available. I can rise before the family wakes up and spend time alone (with my dog) in the living room. Or I can find a quiet place by going downstairs into my office. I can take a walk in a nearby park, or I can get into my car and drive to a remote spot and walk around a secluded lake. Honestly, I'm embarrassed at the abundance of opportunities available to me to be alone.

The majority of the world does not share the luxury of privacy. The first time I take someone to Haiti, they usually comment on the number of people who are walking the streets, day or night. The reason why the streets are always crowded in Haiti (the same reason the streets are crowded in any third world country) is that there are more people than beds, which means that the typical family will sleep in shifts. And because Haiti has more than 75 percent unemployment, when it is not your turn to sleep, and because there is nowhere to go in your one-room Haitian home, and because there is no job to go to, you walk the streets—because there is no other option! The majority of the world does not have the luxury of privacy. Even using the restroom becomes a public event in many places in the world (as I personally learned serving with YWAM in Cambodian refugee camps in the 1980s). While we may fight for privacy, it is important to understand that we are fighting for a luxury that is largely unknown outside of Western culture. The idea of privacy and the adjacent concept of separating our private lives from our public lives is a recent Western phenomenon.

Separating Our Private Lives from Our Public Lives

Up until the 1960s, there appeared to be only a slight separation between the public and private sectors. In the early history of the United States (like Plimoth Plantation), those we knew in the public arena, we likewise knew in the private arena. People were primarily known and valued by their private lives and not by their work. Everyone personally knew the blacksmith, the farmer, the owner of the local general store, the banker, and the local pastor in both the public sector and the private sector. There was no sign on the local general store that read, "What happens in the textile section stays in the textile section."

Despite the fact that this will age me, I will tell you that as a child growing up in Wichita, Kansas, milk was delivered to our home twice a week by Mr. Bonus, the milkman. Our family knew Mr. Bonus. We went to school with his three children. He lived a couple of streets over, and I was often in his home. Our TV repairman was Mr. Hull. The Hulls were friends of our family. My older brother, Kenny, and Steve Hull were the best of friends. Our family bought gas at the nearby Hudson station where our fuel was regularly pumped by Will, whose aunt owned the gas station and was one of my parents' best friends. My dentist, Dr. Pistotnick, was regularly at our home. Our cars were repaired by Pat, our animals were cared for by Mr. Farmer (yes, he lived on a farm and that was his real name), and our trash was hauled away by One-Eyed Johnny (that's a story for another time). Nearly every person who came into our home was a personal friend. We didn't primarily identify our friends by their occupation but simply by the fact that they were our friends.

Quick, what is the name of the person who works on your car? Who fixed your furnace the last time it broke? What's the name of the guy who works the counter at the gas station where you regularly fill up? Do you know the name of your plumber? Your electrician? What's the name of the waitress at the restaurant you frequent? I'm not asking if you know anything about their personal life. I'm simply asking if you know their name. Sadly, most do not. When I have asked people if they know the name of their auto mechanic, the common response is, "Who cares what his name is! I just want to know if he can fix my car." In another time, those we did business with in public we also knew in private. They were our neighbors. But do you know who lives in the apartment next to yours? Who lives directly above you? If you live in a neighborhood, who lives next door or across the street? In another time, there was a thin line separating public and private. The curtain between the front stage and the back stage was sheer if not invisible. Now we have moved from connected community to detached isolationism. What happened to our culture?

When the president of the United States was impeached for breach of trust with the American public for having a sexual relationship with a young White House intern and, shortly after the impeachment, was reelected to a second term as president, things radically changed. Because the American public reasoned that what took place in private life had little to no impact on his public leadership, the pivotal wedge was driven deeper into the gap, forever separating the public and private sectors.

Interestingly, the public-private gap is largely nonexistent in most third world countries. I have found that where economic opportunity is at a minimum, there is a minimal gap between the public and private sectors. Where economic opportunity abounds, the gap widens. Therefore, it is not surprising that when questionable private character is exposed in governmental leaders in France,

England, Russia, and other first world countries, it is done so with little to no public consequence.

Symptoms of an Increasingly Privatized Culture

Our fascination with an increasingly privatized lifestyle is reflected in multiple sectors of first world culture. Take, for example, the trends in architecture over the past fifty years. The style of buildings speaks volumes about our history, our values, our systems, our cultural direction, and … our theology. Our pull to living privatized lives is most clearly reflected in the average American suburban home. What has architecturally taken place in suburbia is a tragic representation of what has happened in the lives of the American people. Going further, the trends in the American home mirror what has happened to clergy in the United States and why ministry leadership is in an isolation crisis.

Unquestionably, the average American suburban home has undergone enormous transformations in the past fifty years. These significant shifts revolve around the front yard, the front porch, the front door, and most important, the relationship between the dining room and the master bedroom. Each change is symptomatic of the direction of our culture and the ultimate, tragic destination of comprehensive privatization. Even if you reside in an apartment in an urban community, you have been impacted by the transformation of the typical American home.

Growing up in the 1960s, I spent my childhood in the front yard. Neighborhood kickball games with dozens of neighbors were a nightly event. We rode our bikes (without helmets), walked to school (without parents), and stayed out playing until after dark (without worry). In the summer, my mother could be found in the front yard every night watering a designated portion of the lawn. We hosted neighborhood basketball games in our driveway and neighborhood ice cream socials in our front yard.

I clearly remember in 1967 when my parents tackled the most radical architectural transformation ever seen in our neighborhood. They constructed a back deck surrounded by a six-foot privacy fence. This was unusual because: (1) No one I knew had a back deck. (2) Why would anyone want to spend more time in the back yard? And (3) what were we doing in the back yard that demanded privacy? For years, the front porch had been our evening refugee. The front porch gave us access to our neighborhood and our community. Now, our back deck would become a place to escape from the world.

It wasn't until the '80s that I saw my first garage door opener. Growing up in a modest neighborhood, the concept of a garage door opener was as foreign as paying for water or spending four dollars for a cup of coffee. I was befuddled by the idea of installing a machine to raise and lower your garage door. What need did we have to close our garage? In fact, we commonly left our garage door open all night. And yet, the garage door opener suddenly allowed families to raise the drawbridge, cross the moat, and enter into their castle with zero contact from neighbors. The garage door opener was a significant leap down the path of privatization. Gated communities were a natural progression.

Sadly, where I presently live, there is little community. Neighborhood games in the front yard have been replaced by video games in the entertainment room. The watering of the yard is taken care of in the middle of the night by a sprinkler system. Nowadays, the back yard is the preferred play area. Why? It's "safer." We can keep an eye on the kids (from the back deck). Everyone has a garage door opener, and to leave a garage open overnight would likely lead a watchful neighbor to call 911. The shift from the front yard–front porch to the back yard–back deck was a shift from community to isolation. From friendship to loneliness. From public to private. It was only natural for the interior of the home to follow the flow toward personal segregation.

Over the centuries, homes have evolved from a place of shelter to a place of community to a place of personal retreat. Biblical commands to practice hospitality (Hebrews 13:2; 1 Peter 4:9; Matthew 25:34–46) are fulfilled via an annual Thanksgiving trip to drop off a turkey in a "bad neighborhood." In an earlier time, it was not unusual to have friends drop by the house—unannounced—to spend an evening with my family. We called this entertaining company. Have things changed? In our present culture, an unexpected knock on the front door after 8:00 p.m. is reason to unlock the gun cabinet and call 911.

It was only natural for the interior layout of the typical American home to follow the privatization path. The most significant architectural transformation in the average first world suburban home in the past one hundred years is the relationship between the dining room and the master bedroom. For hundreds of years in United States, the largest room in the typical house was the dining room. It was the place of community, connection, laughter, games, homework, and meals with extended family. The dining room was where the family gathered for family meetings and commonly family worship. It was the focal point of the home.

Somewhere in the 1980s a significant cultural shift occurred when architects began designing homes with a new central focus. Homes were constructed around a room that by square footage alone commonly dwarfed the other rooms in the home. The family room? The living room? No and no. The center of the home became the master bedroom. It is a fascinating exercise to track the historic size of the average dining room versus the size of the average master bedroom.

For many Americans in the eighteenth and nineteenth centuries, homes were primarily functional. The majority of Americans, especially those who lived in regions vulnerable to cold winters, slept in one room. Or if they were immensely blessed, they had two bedrooms—one for the parents, and one for the children. As one would guess, the "master" bedroom traditionally was the personal quarters of a home's owners. It had nothing to do with size. The word fell out of vogue when slavery was abolished.

In 1970, the average American home was fourteen hundred square feet. Bedrooms in the home were all approximately the same size. No bathroom was directly connected to any one bedroom. Now, the average American home is twenty-seven hundred square feet, nearly doubling in the last forty years. Interestingly, four factors significantly influenced this transformation: the availability of land, the introduction of central heating, the advent of the forty-hour workweek, and the reintroduction of the master bedroom.

Urban sprawl led to planned neighborhoods and homes being constructed on large tracts of land. Central heating and the low energy costs of the 1980s (following the energy crisis of the 1970s) allowed the home to be heated for a reasonable cost, which removed the final barrier to supersizing our homes. And the introduction of the forty-hour workweek meant the home was more than a place to sleep in between work shifts. The home could now be viewed as a refuge where a family could relax in the evenings and play on the weekends. The master bedroom was the final piece of the increasingly large home. Suddenly, a master bedroom, complete with an enormous "private" bathroom and walk-in his-and-her closets, became a standard part of any new home construction. Master bedrooms were regularly built with a fireplace, a separate sitting room, an entertainment center, and in some cases even a separate entrance. No contact with the neighbors? Heck, you don't even need to have contact with your own family! Today, many master bedrooms are self-contained homes within a home.

While the square footage of the master bedroom was exponentially swelling, the square footage of the dining room radically decreased. Whereas the dining room was typically the largest room in any home, it is now one of the smaller rooms in a new home. The dining room has become a room that is seldom, if ever, used, as most meals are consumed at the kitchen table. In fact, many homes are now constructed with no dining room. Why waste square footage on a room that will seldom be used? The square footage shift from the dining room to master bedroom is a shift from generosity and hospitality to distance and isolation, from community to retreat, and from public to private. At the end of a long workweek, we can enter our gated community (keeping the unwanted away), raise our garage door, step into our fortress (avoiding any contact with troublesome neighbors), and retreat into our master bedroom (even avoiding our own families). And it is this cultural movement that significantly contributes to widening the gap between the public front stage and the private back stage.

If you don't possess the resources to dictate the style of home or apartment in which you live, you can still make a commitment to practice hospitality (see Romans 12:13). Host a meal for people with whom you have casual, daily contact. Go to a local college and inquire about hosting a meal for international students, the majority of whom will never step foot into a private home.

Do you live in a single-family home? Spend some time in your front yard. Do you live in an apartment complex? Spend time in community areas. Greet neighbors who are walking their dogs. Make homemade ice cream and invite the neighbors. Throw a couple of additional burgers on the grill and invite the neighbor who does everything in his or her power to avoid contact with anyone. Serve your community!

Appropriate Boundaries

Unquestionably, we all want and merit some measure of privacy. No one wants to explain to their congregation what's in their trash. Pastors and their families need to work to create boundaries that allow for family time away from the crush of unrealistic expectations. I am heartbroken at the number of pastors I meet with who tell me that they have never had the opportunity to take a family vacation— apart from work. In other words, the only way a vacation happens is when the pastor speaks at a retreat, conference, or family camp and brings his family along. Time with the family is nearly impossible in this setting, as nearly everyone wants a little piece of the speaker.

The number one inquiry we receive at PastorServe revolves around privacy and family boundaries. The dilemma commonly sounds something like this: "I feel as if I have no boundaries in my role as a pastor. While I understand my family can't live in isolation, I am struggling to balance my commitment to say yes to the ministry and my commitment to say yes to my family. I am finding it difficult, if not impossible, to spend an appropriate, healthy amount of time with my family without feeling incredibly guilty, like I am cheating the church."

We have a standard response to this concern (and for some of you, this will change your life): *While we appreciate the tension and the reason behind the question, you are thinking of the issue in the wrong paradigm. All of life is ministry, and your family is your primary ministry.* Read that last sentence again. When a pastor leaves the church office to spend time at his daughter's soccer game, he is not leaving the ministry to spend time with his family. He is leaving his secondary ministry to spend time in his primary ministry.

Please don't misunderstand me. A need for pastoral privacy unquestionably exists. Every pastor needs to know when it's time to take a timeout from the front stage. No one is arguing the need to create boundaries. The problem materializes when the pursuit for privacy evolves into a deeply dysfunctional discontinuity between the front stage persona and back stage behavior, between what the congregation thinks and what the family knows. When a pastor fears back stage exposure, the front stage will lack authenticity, humility, brokenness, honesty, and above all, gospel grace. There is a cognitive dissonance as we pose, pretend, harbor secrets, and live ethically uncomfortable, tension-filled, conflicted lives.

Repairing the Cultural Clash

The cultural gap between life's front stage and back stage is widening. Society encourages us to lead intensely private lives and instructs us to allow no one to intrude into our back stage. We have moved from being a people defined by the front porch and the dining room to being a new society known for its back decks and master bedrooms. We have evolved from being known in our undivided life to being identified primarily by our occupation. We have traveled from wholeness and authenticity into a culture with a beautiful front stage and an inaccessible back stage. But Jesus came to bring freedom from a conflicted, inauthentic, fictitious life. Jesus lived His life to free us from the shackles of privatized inauthenticity.

Questions for Reflection

Reality—Has anyone ever dug through your trash? Has someone gone too far when inquiring about your personal life? How have you handled the meddling?

Rewind and Review—Do you classify yourself as rich? Do you agree with Jimmy's definition of what it means to be rich? How can this new definition change your perspective on your present situation?

Share examples of the growing separation between private and public. What trends have you observed during your lifetime that would have contributed to the separation of private and public life? Are there steps you can take in your own life to reverse any of them?

What theological statements are being made by the homes or apartments in your community?

Reflect—In your church or ministry, are you trending toward authenticity and relational health or toward isolation and loneliness? Personally, are you trending toward relational health and authenticity or toward individualism and isolation?

Have you ever given anyone a "back stage pass" to your life? If so, to whom? If not, what are the barriers preventing you from giving someone that kind of access?

Remember—Philippians 2:5–11 reminds us that Jesus left the perfect fellowship of His home and entered into our broken world. How does that truth bring comfort to your soul?

Respond—Review the biblical commands to practice hospitality (Hebrews 13:2; 1 Peter 4:9; Matthew 25:34–46). How can you apply these commands?

What can you do to increase or enhance community in your neighborhood?

Do you know the name of your auto mechanic, the attendant at the gas station, or the waiter or waitress at your favorite restaurant? How can learning names—and stories—of those with whom you have regular contact be used ultimately by the Lord Jesus to advance the kingdom of God?

Section 2

Thrive

The Six Relationships Every Pastor Needs

The following six chapters are the heart and soul of a healthy pastoral ecosystem: three professional relationships and three personal relationships. This is the foundation.

And yet, I write with trepidation knowing that the next six chapters could potentially cause damage by contributing to an increase in one's Maturity Gap Index. The three professional relationships (boss, trainer, and coach) will largely contribute to the front stage of a leader's ministry while the three personal relationships (counselor, mentor, and friend) will primarily impact the back stage of a leader. If you take the first three chapters of this section to heart, committing to fulfilling these relationships in your life while ignoring the concluding three chapters, then this book has only increased your maturity gap. If you are reading this book on a sinking ship and you only have time for three chapters, start with counselor, mentor, and friend.

Working with thousands of pastors over several decades has taught me that the number one barrier to the six relationships is the sin of pride. Those who most commonly resist the six relationships are those who arrogantly believe they can go it alone. I pray that you will read the following six chapters with an open mind and softened heart, knowing the Lord has created us to live in community, needing one another.

Six relationships do not necessarily equate to six people filling the six roles. A coach could also serve in the roles of mentor, trainer, and friend. A mentor might additionally wear the hats of coach, trainer, counselor, and friend. A boss can serve as a trainer. But—and this is key—a boss can't concurrently wear the hat of coach or counselor. Even the simultaneous role of mentor and coach can create unique challenges. At PastorServe, we encourage a minimum of three people (four is ideal) to fill the six relationships. You might have a boss who also serves as a trainer; you might have a mentor who is also a counselor, and your coach may in reality be a close friend. If you're a high achiever, go for six different people to get the absolute most from the relationship network.

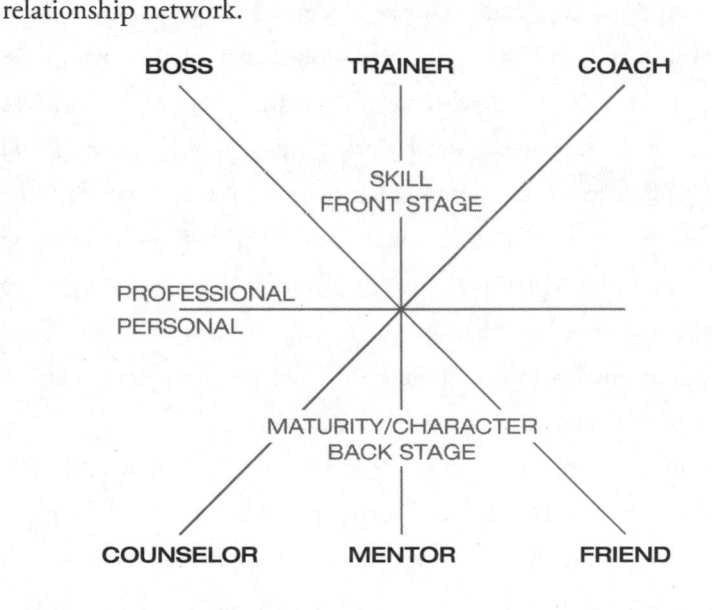

Chapter 7

Everyone Needs a Boss

In 1982, my Maturity Gap Index was ginormous. While I was beginning to see how the Lord could use my gifting to advance His kingdom-of-God agenda, I was also swimming in extreme doses of immaturity and character deficiency. I was serving as a youth intern at the historic College Church in Wheaton, Illinois, as I closed out my senior year of college. Only two weeks into my one-year internship, the youth pastor was relieved of his position. I was to "serve in the position of interim youth pastor" because it was made clear to me that I was not an official College Church pastor. While I would be *fulfilling* the job description of youth pastor, I wasn't the youth pastor.

I remember Senior Pastor Kent Hughes calling me into his office and explaining the situation and the need for me to immediately step into the primary role of youth leadership. Kent sympathetically expressed his understanding that this put me in a difficult position as I was going to be a full-time student and a nearly full-time church employee. Kent pulled a calculator from his desk, punched in several numbers, and announced, "And we can pay you twelve thousand a year."

"I'll take it!" I shouted, remembering that it was indeed a privilege to serve as an intern at College Church. In fact, why shouldn't I pay the church for the opportunity to learn in such an intellectually and spiritually stimulating environment? The other two interns (one of whom was my older brother, Kenny) were making a whopping hundred dollars a month, so I suddenly felt as though I had hit the lottery. Later that night I called my fiancée, Sally, who was teaching in Kansas, and told her our financial ship had come in!

I will forever be grateful for my time at College Church, as it was an ideal first church-staff position. I was immensely privileged to serve on an incredible team of godly men and women who passionately loved Jesus. Kent Hughes served as senior pastor. Kent's wife, Barbara, was an incredible teacher and herself a gifted leader. Larry Fullerton served as senior associate, Jerry Root was the college pastor, Paul Stough served in pastoral care, and Olena Mae Welsh directed the special needs ministry. Together, these six leaders have impacted hundreds of thousands, if not millions, of leaders around the world. Each one of them uniquely shaped my life. I am the man I am today largely because of my two years at College Church. While I was officially an intern, I was treated with all the privileges and responsibilities of any College Church pastor. I was given the opportunity to preach at College Church (with many of my Wheaton professors in the audience). College Church allowed me to regularly connect with spiritual giants such as John Stott, J. I. Packer, Ralph Winter, James Boice, R. C. Sproul, and a host of other godly leaders. Some of the best stories of my life, which could fill several volumes, took place in those two years. Like the time I overslept on J. I. Packer. But I digress … While I appreciated each of the pastoral staff, Kent Hughes was my boss, my mentor, and in many ways my hero. I looked up to Kent with deep admiration, grateful for his impact on my life and the opportunity to rub shoulders with him every day.

September 13, 1982, the day that would radically change my life, began like any other Monday. I had been on staff at the church for fewer than three weeks, balancing my nonpastoral youth pastor position at College Church, maintaining my status as a full-time student at Wheaton College, and preparing for my upcoming wedding. I was living in Jerry Root's attic with two gifted friends who were also pursuing pastoral ministry. In my spare time I enjoyed—oh wait, there was no spare time. Pastor Hughes (everyone else on staff called him Kent; I called him Pastor Hughes at the time) caught me in the morning and asked if I would be free for lunch later that day. I assured him that whatever I had could be canceled if it meant an opportunity to spend time with my pastor.

Kent and I walked to a nearby restaurant. I sat in a booth across from him, literally squirming with excitement, as I was already looking forward to calling Sally and telling her about the lunch. I complimented Kent on his message the day before, assuring him that it had made an impact on my life. After ordering, Kent jumped right in to the purpose for the meeting. Apparently we weren't going to just hang out as guys and talk about the Cubs. Kent began by affirming my gifts. He let me know that, although we were only weeks into my leadership of the youth ministry, he had heard glowing reports. He mentioned that he had stood in the hall as I taught the high school group the week before and he was impressed with my gift for combining serious teaching with lighthearted humor. He talked about how parents were thrilled that I had agreed to accept the interim position. He affirmed my contributions in staff meeting. In short, this was shaping up to be the greatest meeting of my life. How could it get any better? My hero, mentor, pastor, and sudden admirer saying nicer things than I could imagine! Somebody pinch me!

And then Kent looked me squarely in my eyes and said the following words, which I can remember as if it took place five minutes ago. Kent said, "However, I want you to know that you have a Messiah complex. Listen, I am extremely grateful for your ministry and I believe that you are an exceptionally gifted young man. Everything I am going to say is said in an entirely constructive spirit. I am going to highlight some troubling areas of your life, which you need to address because I have genuine affection and admiration for you."

I began to sink into the booth, praying it would somehow swallow me and allow me to disappear forever. It was at that point that Kent started down a list of seven additional areas of my life that needed immediate attention. The areas included: (1) I appeared, and indeed was, manipulative; (2) I came across as overly aggressive; (3) I was not a good listener; (4) I tended to alienate adults; (5) I was working too hard to gain a following among the youth; (6) I needed to be careful when discussing my salary; and (7) I should not forget that I was not the youth pastor—I was only doing the job of a youth pastor.

Finally, Kent said, "Now, Jimmy, I know this has been hard to hear, so I have typed everything I just said to you in a letter" (which he slid across the table as he continued to talk). "I want you to take this home, pray about what I have said, and ask the Lord to do a great work in your life." I sat in stunned silence. The food arrived, but I don't remember touching my cheeseburger and fries.

You might be wondering how I can remember with such precise detail a conversation that took place in 1982. Because as I write this chapter, I hold in my hand the letter that Kent slid across the table to me that day. I have read and reread that letter hundreds, if not more than a thousand, times. The letter is one of my life treasures. If the house were on fire (and everyone was safely outside), I'd grab my Bible, my laptop, photo albums, a bucket with the kids' art projects over the years, my father-in-law's original paintings, my autographed Kansas University basketballs, my Green Bay Packer memorabilia, and the letter from Kent (and maybe the chair that was used by Chaplain Evan Welsh at Wheaton College). Okay, let's pray my house doesn't burn because I would never make it out alive! I have shared this story in conferences around the world, and at the conclusion of the story, I produce the letter and read it. There are always those who are flabbergasted that I have kept the letter all these years. The reason is simple. On that day, my boss loved me enough to call me out. He saw that I needed to improve, and he cared enough to be honest. That day, September 13, 1982, my Maturity Gap Index was significantly reduced. On that day, someone confronted the glaring immaturity of a brash, arrogant twenty-one-year-old. That day was … life changing. It was life changing because I had a boss who was in a position of authority enabling him to call me out.

Biblical Church Government

Throughout the history of the church we have seen three basic forms of church government: episcopal, congregational, and presbyterian. In the episcopal and presbyterian forms of church government, biblical authority (a boss) is a nonissue, as the structure ensures that pastors and priests operate under authority. The congregational form of government is not so clear cut.

If you are serving in a staff-led independent church, without the oversight of a supervising board, be careful. That's the nicest way I can say it. If that appeared spineless, allow me to say it in a different tone: If you don't have a boss, you are tiptoeing through a minefield. You have placed yourself in a lone-ranger position that has contributed to leading many pastors down the road of ministry demise.

If you are leading a church from a position of being the primary leader as the head of staff with no board to whom you are accountable, you are operating outside the bounds of Scripture. There is no church in the New Testament functioning with only one elder (or one pastor, one bishop, or one overseer). Each church is to have a plurality of elders (Acts 14:23; 20:17; Philippians 1:1), not a one-person rule. Throughout the New Testament, church leadership continually points to one central theme: plurality. The church is to be led by a plurality of godly leaders. By submitting pastors to elders (or deacons) who love the Lord Jesus, the church creates a healthy checks-and-balances of leadership direction, pastoral care, and financial accountability.

Unquestionably, the number one reason why pastors struggle with anyone in the role of boss is pride. I have heard the argument over and over again: "Why should I place myself under the authority of someone who has no graduate-level ministry training? Why subject myself to a group of people who may or may not be walking with the Lord Jesus?" The answer? Because the Bible instructs pastors to place themselves under the authority of godly leadership. It's pretty straightforward. Everyone needs a boss.

The Barrier of Pride

Why the struggle with pride? There are a number of lists of the "deadly sins." One is found in Proverbs 6:16–19. The sins include haughty eyes (pride), a lying tongue, hands that shed innocent blood, a heart that devises wicked plans, feet that make haste to run to evil (always looking for trouble), a false witness who breathes out lies, and one who sows discord among brothers.

The gospel of Mark contains the only list of vices in the Gospels. Jesus is teaching the crowds when He says,

> For from within, out of the heart of man, come evil thoughts, sexual immorality, theft, murder, adultery, coveting, wickedness, deceit, sensuality, envy, slander, pride, foolishness. All these evil things come from within, and they defile a person. (Mark 7:21–23)

The classic historical list of deadly sins is attributed to the fourth-century Egyptian monk Evagrius Ponticus, who expanded the traditional list to include eight deadly sins. His sins included gluttony, fornication, greed, pride, envy, anger, boasting, and acedia (while some define acedia as sloth or even listlessness, I define acedia as a life driven by persistent question—what's in it for me?).

In the sixth century, Pope Gregory the Great once again revised the list, returning to the original number of seven sins. His list included pride, envy, anger, sloth, greed, gluttony, and lust. The official Catholic list adds vanity to the original seven.

Why the trip down "seven deadly sins lane"? Because it is noteworthy that pride is the only sin appearing on every list. It is significant that Solomon, Mark, early church fathers, and Pope Gregory each identified pride as one of the deadly sins, if not *the* debilitating sin. In my work with community business leaders, I invite them to list the seven sins they struggle with the most. Incredibly, in all the years I have conducted this informal survey, pride and lust have appeared, without a single exception, on every list. Unquestionably, pride is a debilitating sin.

Biblical synonyms for pride include conceit (Jeremiah 48:29; Romans 11:20), superiority (1 Peter 5:5), insolence (Romans 1:30), arrogance (Proverbs 8:13; Isaiah 2:11; Isaiah 2:17; Isaiah 9:9), boasting (1 Corinthians 1:31), contempt (Psalm 31:18), wrongdoing (Job 33:17), and self-centeredness (1 Corinthians 13:4–7). Self-centeredness and self-love are totally antithetical to the teachings of Scripture.

Practically, pride can be defined as taking credit for what God is doing, being self-congratulatory in my accomplishments, as well as having a lack of humility, an insatiable desire for man's approval, and thinking I don't need the Lord.

Pride led to Uzziah's downfall (2 Chronicles 26:16). Pride hardened the heart of Nebuchadnezzar (Daniel 5:20). Proverbs 16:18 tells us that pride goes before destruction. We know that the prideful do not seek God (Psalm 10:4). Pride also brings conflict (Proverbs 13:10), deception (Obadiah 1:3), and a false sense of self-confidence (Psalm 10:4).

Everything about pride is self-centered. Pride is self-seeking, self-reliant, self-absorbed, self-interested, self-exalting, and selfish! Pride seeks to justify oneself, admire oneself, promote oneself, and approve of oneself. Pride convinces us we are self-sufficient (I don't need you), self-confident (I know I don't need you), and self-assured (I feel good about knowing that I don't need you).

How does pastoral pride happen? Through a lack of humility. Leaders who resist anyone in a role of authority are not humble before the Lord. They are convinced no one can lead at the level in which they lead. Because we should desire to lead in all humility (James 4:6; 1 Peter 5:5) and because placing ourselves beneath authority can play a key role in our learning to lead with humility, it only makes sense to place yourself in a role in which you can clearly identify your boss. In the majority of denominations, networks, and many independent churches, this is a nonissue. The role of a leadership team—a governing board, elders, deacons—allows you to have a boss.

Thank God for your boss. Commit to pray regularly for your boss.

Pastoral Care—Apart from Your Boss

As we walk through the importance of the six relationships for the thriving pastor, here is the one section in which I will digress from the norm. Here is my argument, which I will attempt to support: *It is both unrealistic and unwise for a boss to serve in a pastoral position to fellow pastors.* Stated another way, *if you are wearing a boss hat, and you want to pastor brothers and sisters under your ecclesiastical authority, the odds are low that those beneath will ever come to you. While there are certainly exceptions, the majority of pastors, feeling the absence of safety, will hesitate to be vulnerable to anyone who possesses the authority to terminate them.*

A Baptist regional director once informed me that while he appreciated the ministry of PastorServe and was thankful for the work we did with other denominations around the country, there was no need for us in his denomination. He explained the elaborate system for pastoral care that provided care for two hundred churches and more than four hundred pastors serving in his particular district. When I gently informed him that PastorServe was presently working with more than thirty Baptist churches in his district, he became defensive.

"That's not possible," he said. "Our pastors know if they have a problem, they are to call me. I'm their boss."

"And that is exactly why they *don't* call you," I replied. "They don't call precisely because you are their boss."

The same story has been repeated over and over again. One well-known denomination reluctantly brought in PastorServe to be a part of their annual assembly of pastors. I say "reluctantly" because while we were invited by the regional host, others around the nation were extremely unhappy that an outside ministry was being brought in when a system for pastoral care was already in place. In fact, there were multiple layers of pastoral care available to every pastor within this denomination. If a pastor felt unsafe with his appointed agent of pastoral care, he could move to another level—up the pastoral-care chain. It was predicted by some that PastorServe would not meet with a single pastor. Others believed our presence was a waste of time and money.

In reality, we ministered to more than eighty pastors (slightly more than 11 percent of all attendees), the majority of whom were in crisis. We know from well-documented statistics this represents only the tip of the iceberg. Some sessions included wives and children. To no one on the PastorServe team's surprise, the situations addressed were varied: moral failure, betrayal, unexpected firing, ongoing conflict with leadership, burnout, church splits, severe injury and illness, sense of isolation and abandonment, exhaustion from cleaning up the mess of someone else's moral failure, lost sense of call, deep discouragement, marriage and family tensions, seemingly no way to finish well. The ministry settings were as diverse as the denomination, churches from fifty to thousands; wealthy communities and poor communities; urban, rural, and suburban; civilian and military; Anglo, Hispanic, African American, Asian; seasoned veterans and new to ministry. In nearly every conversation, there was an undercurrent of testing the waters, asking, "Are you safe?" There was one striking commonality between nearly every pastor. Each one said, "I would never go to our denomination for pastoral care. One, they wouldn't know what to do; and two, they aren't safe."

Pastoral Care in the Church

The same applies to churches. While there are some exceptions in which grace is a predominant theme, the majority of churches that provide internal pastoral care are failing. I know this because PastorServe receives more than twenty thousand requests for assistance from pastors each year, many mentioning they have no place to go for safe, confidential, objective care. And some of the stories are nothing short of heartbreaking.

A church contacted PastorServe in regard to Steve, a pastor who had served for more than twenty years in a large West Coast suburban Evangelical church. Steve was struggling with the lure of pornography. He had been "caught" when the church ran routine checks and was now facing discipline and potential termination. The board of elders asked me to conduct an assessment and make a recommendation. Before making the trip, I learned Steve was well loved by the congregation.

I flew to Los Angeles and met with Steve, several members of the church staff, and eventually the elder board. Steve shared his love for the church. He also discussed his difficult marriage and confessed he had sought false intimacy through online pornography. Steve matter-of-factly shared some disturbing statistics, which were verified by other pastors at the church: he regularly worked sixty-plus hours each week and had taken an average of two weeks' vacation for the past twenty years. Steve had never had a sabbatical, an extended vacation, or even a study leave. In short, Steve was exhausted. He needed a break that would allow him to address his sin, pour into his marriage, pursue counseling to explore other deep and internal issues, recharge his batteries, and gain some much-needed perspective.

When I met with the elder board that evening, I commended them for leading a church that was known for its commitment to world missions and the poor. After a lengthy discussion about Steve's sin, I recommended he be given a three-month sabbatical. I laid forth a plan for the sabbatical that included everything from intensive coaching and counseling, a week for him and his wife at SonScape Retreats, the leading Christian marriage retreat center in the world, and some much-needed rest, including an extended vacation with his family. I explained that I did not believe Steve's sin warranted firing. He had not acted out and, aside from his pornography addiction (which was serious), there were no inappropriate relationships with women.

His elders were exasperated and deeply offended by my recommendation. One said, "You are asking us to give Steve a three-month break from the church, and you are recommending that we pay him while he is away? And you want us to pay for counseling and coaching for Steve during this time away? And we are paying PastorServe to give us this advice!" The tone of voice was sharply accusatory, making me feel like I was under attack.

And the bad news was only just beginning. The board informed me that while they had asked me to come to make a recommendation, they had earlier in the day decided to fire Steve, providing him a six-week severance package. One of the elders turned to me and said, "Well, what would you do if you were an elder in this church?"

I took several deep breaths and prayed to the Lord for careful words before responding. "That's hard to say, as I'm not an elder in this church," I began. "But I can tell you what I would do if I were a member of this church. I would immediately resign my membership and run far away from you and your ungracious leadership. If this is how you treat one of your own, someone who has given his life to this congregation, how are you going to treat me when my sin is revealed?"

You can likely imagine the outcome of the night. Steve was fired and that was that. The church hired a new pastor and moved on. I don't think it was the right outcome, but I am happy to report that Steve loves Jesus, received coaching and counseling, is a shepherd to many, and is engaged (though not employed) in a wonderful church. Our paths crossed just last week.

Similar stories continually come across my desk. And every time a story like this is revealed, it drives pastors deeper into the back stage of isolation. It convinces them that there really is no place to go where they can safely process their wounds, their doubts, and their sin.

While every pastor needs a boss, every pastor also needs a safe place to confess his or her sin. You may be convinced that your church is doing an effective job of providing internal pastoral care, but I strongly encourage you to allow your church staff to provide confidential input regarding the present level of pastoral care. Most boards and lead pastors overestimate the level and availability of care presently provided.

If you simultaneously wear the hats of boss and pastoral shepherd, I implore you to provide an alternative avenue of care. I am not advocating for PastorServe; I am advocating for the care of every pastor. There are a number of wonderful ministries serving pastors around the world. At a minimum, connect with a local trusted pastor (not from your denomination or tribe) and ask the pastor if he or she would be open to talking with your staff members if they felt like they needed an outside, objective, nonauthoritative pastoral voice. Offer to do the same for his or her church.

Questions for Reflection

Reality—Under what form of government do you presently serve? Does your form of government require you to serve under a boss? If yes, who serves in the role of your boss? What are the strengths and weaknesses of your form of church government?

What are the present blessings and struggles with your boss? Who are you presently serving in the role of boss?

Rewind and Review—What do Luke 18:9–14; Galatians 6:3–4; Romans 12:3; 2 Corinthians 5:12; and James 4:6 tell us about pride? How does each passage speak truth into your present situation?

Pride was the first sin as we see in the downfall of Satan in Ezekiel 28 and Isaiah 14. What was the root of Satan's pride? Do you ever see evidence of this same root in your heart?

Reflect—Pride and false humility have a great deal in common— essentially being opposite sides of the same coin. How is false humility most commonly demonstrated in your life?

Jimmy listed a number of biblical synonyms for pride, including conceit, superiority, insolence, arrogance, boasting, and self-centeredness. Which description of pride most commonly describes you? Why are you susceptible to this particular form of pride?

How has pride made your life difficult? What might lead you to a humbler heart?

Remember—Philippians 2:6–8 reminds us that Jesus Christ humbled Himself by becoming obedient to death on a cross. How can Jesus's humble submission to the will of God the Father grant you hope as you seek to live the life of a servant?

Respond—If you don't serve beneath anyone in a position of authority, what can you do to invite authority into your life? If you do have a boss, how can you serve with increased humility?

Chapter 8

Continuing Education Isn't Just for Teachers

"Sorry. That will never happen. I don't have the time and the church doesn't have the money!"

Exasperated and clearly frustrated, Roy had just finished telling me about a mammoth problem in his church. Two church staff members were engaged in an intense personal conflict that had broken through the boundaries of confidentiality and created division within the staff, which was now being felt by some within the congregation. What had initially started as a private conflict was now a public battle. As the staff gradually caved in to the pressure to choose sides, the disagreement spiraled into insults, gossip, even slander. The staff ministry team suddenly went from joyfully serving alongside one another as close friends to cold, barely speaking working relationships.

As the pastor and I spoke about a plan to address the conflict, I asked if he had received any training in conflict resolution. I could instantly feel his defenses rise. No, he had never had any training in the arena of conflict resolution, though he knew it was important. He vaguely remembered one course he had taken in seminary that had one class lecture dedicated to conflict resolution. Now he could see that he was woefully incapable of effectively addressing the growing staff division. Someday, he said, he would like to be trained in conflict resolution, but today wasn't that day! When I gently mentioned an upcoming two-day conference that was dedicated to peacemaking, his response let me know I had crossed an invisible boundary. In a raised voice, he told me, "Sorry. That will never happen. I don't have the time and the church doesn't have the money!"

The same story could be repeated over and over again. A pastor confesses that he would like to have been trained in leadership development, evangelism, missions, discipleship, and a host of other areas of pastoral competency, but there was never the time nor the money. Year after year, when the church budget is finalized, and the final cuts are made, continuing education is commonly one of the first things to go.

Yet continuing education, or pastoral competency training, is fundamental to the ongoing life of the church, the soul of the pastor, and the health of the pastoral staff. Without a commitment to a trainer, one of the key relationships is missing, which weakens the entire pastoral ecosystem.

Of the six relationships, trainer is the one relationship that can be short term. While there needs to be a long-term commitment to training, there may be a short-term relationship with a particular trainer. The boss relationship may last months or decades. Coaching relationships generally last a minimum of one year. Mentors can be with us throughout our lives, counselors can be with us for a season, and friends, we pray, are with us through all seasons. The person in the role of trainer can change several times in one day. The emphasis is not on a relationship with a specific trainer, but rather a commitment specifically to ongoing training. This is mandatory in literally hundreds of occupations—why not pastoral ministry?

Mandatory Continuing Education

In many businesses around the world, funding for continuing education is never off the budget. Why? Simply because in many top-tier occupations, continuing education is necessary and nonnegotiable. An increasing number of occupations in America require continuing education. Many professionals in your congregation are continually seeking out the finest continuing education opportunities. Are there doctors, nurses, pharmacists, dentists, and occupational therapists in your church who serve in the medical field? They will lose their licenses to practice if they do not obtain the proper number of continuing education credits. Lawyers in your church? Without the proper amount of CLE (continuing legal education) credits, they won't practice law for long. The list goes on and on. Accountants, financial professionals, engineers, and architects all need to meet regular continuing education requirements. Insurance agents, real estate agents, and even sports agents must meet educational standards if they want to continue to call themselves agents.

You may be an experienced sports agent with a number of clients in Major League Baseball and the National Basketball Association, but if you want to work in the National Football League, the NFL Players Association requires a healthy amount of specialized continuing education. If you are involved in any governmental work involving nuclear, electrical, or space, there is a staggering amount of annual training. The fields of computer repair and automotive repair require annual recertification through continuing education seminars. Although requirements vary from state to state, teachers are required to participate in continuing education courses or conferences in order to maintain their licenses and sharpen their instructional skills. In many professions, failure to complete ongoing education can result in license suspension or revocation, penalties, and increased training requirements.

Do you work for the Department of Energy? It's going to take you eighty hours of continuing education every two years to continue in your job. The Department of Defense? It's going to take a whole lot of study to stay current. Most branches of the military use a tuition assistance program that pays 100 percent of the cost to help employees meet the requirements.

If your profession requires a license or certification, you are going to need continuing education. Do you work in the field of human resources? You will need to attend continuing education classes to stay current with employment laws, salary trends, and other employment-related issues.

And why wouldn't you want to see a physician actively participating in continuing education? If I have a significant health crisis, I want my doctor to treat me with the newest medical procedures. No one wants to hear their doctor say, "We know there is an improved procedure for this particular surgery, but no one in our practice has been trained in it. So we are just going to need you to bite on this piece of wood while I remove the bullet."

The Gap in Pastoral Continuing Education

Knowing the way pastors think, it's not hard to surmise the argument you may be forming in your head: *This is an apples-to-oranges argument. You have listed occupations where the field is continually changing. As a pastor, I am privileged to work in a field that never changes. The eternal Word of God is not in flux.*

It *is* an apples-to-oranges argument. I agree. But it's based on fundamentally flawed logic. Nearly every professional occupational field trains aspirants in *every* competency necessary to provide a *baseline minimal standard* of professionalism to his or her profession and clients. This cannot be said for pastors and ministry leadership. PastorServe has dealt with thousands of pastors who reported they were never adequately trained to confront the challenges facing them in pastoral ministry. In 1998, the Francis A. Schaeffer Institute of Church Leadership Development, based out of Covenant Theological Seminary in St. Louis, continued pastoral research that had been initiated earlier in 1989 by the Fuller Institute. As a part of their research, 1,050 pastors were surveyed from two pastors conferences held in Orange County and Pasadena, California. Seven hundred ninety (790 or 75 percent) of the pastors surveyed felt they were unqualified and/or poorly trained by their seminaries to lead and manage the church or to counsel others. This left them disheartened in their ability to pastor.

While pastors appreciate courses in preaching, Christian education, and church history, when they arrive at their first church, it's like being handed the keys to a small business, for which they are unprepared. Immediately, they are asked to create a budget, read a financial spreadsheet, make personnel decisions, begin a class in leadership development, mediate a church conflict, and help the church understand the purpose of suffering as a longtime member has just passed away. Resign? Many pastors turn and run!

If you are seeking an apples-to-apples argument, let's draw a parallel to medical school. Suppose a doctor did the majority of his training and learned how to take a blood sample but wasn't required to take several related science courses—specifically those involving blood. Or a doctor attends medical school and never learns how to diagnose basic medical issues. The doctor is trained in the history of medical advances and the art of ancient medical scripts, though. Is that a problem? You bet it is! And yet some of the most fundamental baseline competencies are not taught in the world's finest Bible colleges and seminaries. And this lack of training leaves pastors feeling overwhelmed, underprepared, and inadequate to face the challenges that lie before them. It is a travesty that we expect pastors to serve in challenging areas of ministry in which they have minimal training.

I lay the problem of an absence of baseline pastoral competency primarily at the feet of our Bible colleges and seminaries. Pastors and ministry leaders need continuing education because the basics of their occupational challenges were not taught in their educational institutions. I have personally had conversations with seminary presidents who readily agree with this assessment; but adding seminary courses to the core curriculum means eliminating others. And precious few departments and professors are prepared to place their specialized fields of study on the chopping block. I applaud alternative forms of pastoral education that address real-life pastoral ministry, often requiring students to serve in local church settings throughout their educational training. For an excellent example, see World Impact's TUMI Training (www.tumi.org).

Baseline Leadership Competencies

PastorServe took three years to personally interview hundreds of pastors in order to discover baseline pastoral competencies. After initially arriving at a list containing close to one hundred competencies, we began the process of identifying those competencies that are critical to pastoral ministry. The list was cut to fifty. Some items were combined, which cut the list to thirty. Finally, after much prayer, discussion, arguing, and more prayer, we arrived at the PastorServe 24 Leadership Competencies.

Vertical Foundations
- Kingdom Prayer and Fasting (Awareness of Spiritual Warfare)
- Worship—Understanding of Christ-Centered Worship
- Doctrinal Soundness
- Understanding of Suffering/Personal Limitations/ Embracing the Cross

Horizontal Foundations
- Personal Life of Pastor—Personal Health, Vibrant Marriage/Family (Vacation)
- Personal Integrity and Accountability (Moral Purity, Personal Financial Health)
- Intimate Friendships (Not Isolated)
- Likability/Sense of Humor

Building the Body of Believers

- Gospel-Driven Mission, Vision, Philosophy of Ministry/Faith Driven
- Kingdom of God Attitude (Networking/Gathering/Collaboration)
- Evangelism (Personal Evangelism Skill/Passion)
- Gospel-Centered Communication (Preaching, Teaching, Written Communication)

Leading the Body of Believers

- Leadership—Personal/Christ-Centered Leadership (Decision Making, Problem Solving, Motivation, Leading through Change)
- Life Planning and Management (Calling, Time Management, Stress Management)
- Ministry Management, Systems, and Infrastructure (Mobilizing and Delegating/Working with Teams/Communication)
- Leadership Development (Raising Up the Next Generation of Leaders)

Serving the Body of Believers

- Nurture and Cell-Group Understanding (Biblical Gospel Community)
- Discipleship/Assimilation (Desire to Develop Devoted Followers of Christ)
- Servant/Shepherd Understanding (Counseling, Empathy, Listening Skills)

- Conflict Management/Peacemaking

Extending the Body of Believers
- Theology of Missions/Awareness of Issues Confronting Global Church
- Church Growth, Church Planting, Reproduction, Multiplication
- Passion for Local Ministries of Mercy and Justice (Understands Racial/Social Issues Confronting Church)
- Generosity/Stewardship—Biblical Understanding

We have received pushback in several of the areas of competency, none more than likability and sense of humor. But here's the unabashed truth: If people don't like you, you are not going to thrive in your pastoral position. Likability is essential to effective ministry. And there are little things you can do to make yourself more likable. I doubt you had a course on that in seminary!

As we have talked through the competencies with pastors, we have come to understand that there are a number of topics rarely, if at all, addressed in the majority of Bible colleges and seminaries.

Take a couple of minutes right now to rank yourself in each of the twenty-four competency areas by personal proficiency. In the margin, grade yourself on a scale from 1 to 5.

1. High Competency—Mastered Competency
   "I'm killing it in this area."

2. Exceeds Competency

"I have a healthy skill set in this competency."

3. Baseline Competency

"I can get by."

4. Low Competency—Below Baseline Proficiency

"I know enough to know what I don't know."

5. No Competency

"I openly admit I am clueless in this competency."

If this were a commercial for a miracle drug, at this point there would be a soft voice speaking a hundred miles per hour giving you all the side effects of the drug. I love it when the announcer says, "May cause dizziness, nausea, dry mouth, constipation, fainting upon standing, and unusual changes in behavior, thoughts of suicide, compulsive gambling, insomnia, sleep driving, nightmares, and stroke." That really makes me want to run out and pick up that drug!

Okay, here's my caution before taking the competency assessment: This self-evaluation will be most useful when you prayerfully combine it with feedback from others. Ask other leaders, friends, your spouse, coworkers on committees, and so on for their feedback as well. Give them the competencies, and have them check off items that fit you. Most of all, look at yourself through God's eyes, and work with the results.

If there is one competency you should work to develop in the next year, what would it be? Where do you most need to mature in wisdom? What changes would bring the greatest glory to God and greatest blessing to His people? Confess your sins and failings to God, remembering that Christ is your faithful high priest and shepherd—the Pastor of pastors (Hebrews 4:16)! Prayerfully set goals. Ask people to pray for you and hold you accountable. Are there Bible passages or books you should study? Are there plans you should make? Do you need advice from wise Christians about how to go about changing? Make plans to include study in your daily routine. Believe the gospel.

The Pros and Cons of Committing to Training

I encourage churches to commit to continuing education for their pastoral staff. Often, a board of elders, deacons, or leadership team will make the commitment. I encourage the church to write the commitment into the church bylaws. Make this a nonnegotiable line item in the annual budget. There are several pros and a few cons when making this commitment.

First, it mandates education for your pastoral staff. You are making a statement that you believe continuing education is vital to the health of the church pastoral staff. Second, it demonstrates professionalism. Third, it will improve pastoral health, and that directly benefits members of the congregation. Additionally, new skills can be learned that will have a direct impact on the church body. Fourth, continuing education encourages networking. By attending conferences and educational seminars, I network with other pastors who are a part of the professional clergy community. Through their expertise and experience, I am shaped and molded to be a better pastor.

In the cons list, there is a cost that means something else will need to be cut from the church budget. Making this a nonnegotiable can make one feel selfish for making pastoral needs a top priority. Budgeting for the entire staff to attend a conference in another city can be expensive. Another con (although I would rather call this a natural consequence) is time. A commitment to continuing education will certainly pull pastors away from the church.

Eight Practical Steps toward Continuing Education and Competency Training

This is where the rubber meets the road. When developing a plan for training and continuing education, do not throw a pastors conference into the annual budget and calendar and call it good. Take intentional steps to ensure the training plan is comprehensive, varied, and well thought through to achieve spiritual encouragement, intellectual stimulus, emotional connection, and physical health for the pastoral staff.

As part of your training plan, develop your church's specific pastoral ecosystem. What does it mean to have a healthy, growing, and competent pastoral team? What is the goal of the training? Unique to your church, what are the factors that represent pastoral health? Allow your staff to give significant input. Define the destination before beginning the journey. Here are eight steps to make the commitment a productive one.

1. Commit to get out of town a minimum of once every two years with your pastoral team for a general pastoral conference. There are a number of excellent pastors conferences around the world.

2. Commit to get out of town a minimum of once every two years with your pastoral team for a *specialized* pastoral conference. This is one of the major gaps in continuing education. Don't always attend a general-topic pastoral conference. At least once every couple of years, attend a conference that deals directly with one of the PastorServe 24 Leadership Competencies. Is your team weak in the pulpit? Attend a workshop hosted by the Charles Simeon Trust. Are you struggling in the area of conflict management? Attend the annual Peacemaker Conference. Is your church struggling in the area of stewardship? Attend the annual GenerousChurch conference. The list of excellent workshops and conferences is extensive —and you can review them and others on the PastorServe website.

3. When attending a conference away from your home base, use the time in another city to visit healthy churches. Going into another church environment is one of the best ways to receive training. Are you able to schedule a weekend in the city hosting the conference? If so, it is not difficult to visit three to four churches in one weekend. Once you have decided which churches to visit, contact each lead pastor to arrange for a ninety-minute meeting following worship service. Ideally, take the pastor and spouse out for lunch after church (or dinner after an evening service). Take a card thanking the pastor and include a $100 gift card to a nice restaurant. A number of pastors will be hesitant to meet because they are busy, just like you, so share your intentions. Explain that you are coming to learn. Ask for a copy of their bylaws and organizational structure before the visit. Send each pastor a list of questions a minimum of one week before the visit:

- What are the nuances of this church?
- What is your leadership structure? How do you interact with the staff?
- What are your top three best practices that contribute to the health of this church?
- What are the kingdom movements that are important to you?
- Tell us about your vision, direction, calling.
- What is the relationship between elders (assuming you have elders) and staff?
- What does your preaching team look like? How often are you personally filling the pulpit? Do you have a staff teaching team?
- What does leadership development look like in your church?
- What role does prayer play in the life of your church?
- Are you an affiliated church (denomination, network)? How has your affiliation helped your congregation?
- Will you please pray for my church and my needs? (List your needs.)
- Do *not* ask, "What do you think we should we do?"

4. Bring in an outside speaker for an annual multiday retreat to train your staff. Go far enough away that no one will be tempted to spend the night in their own residence. There is value in spending extended time together. Personally, this is my sweet spot. I find tremendous joy in teaching and training pastoral teams in a retreat setting.

5. Bring in an outside speaker for an annual one-day staff training. Ask a local pastor or friend who is an expert in a specific pastoral competency to train your team.

6. Always be reading a book together as a staff. Alternate between classics and contemporary works. Occasionally read a biography together as a staff. Check the PastorServe website for a list of suggested titles.

7. Develop self-directed learning contracts. At the outset of every year, each staff member commits to pursue a specific pastoral competency by developing a self-directed learning contract, which is a collaboratively written agreement between a staff member and a supervisor that clearly defines what is to be learned or achieved, how it will be learned or achieved, and how that learning will be evaluated.

There are many different ways to design a learning contract, incorporating as many or as few elements as desired. Despite this flexibility, there is a general format that the majority of self-directed learning contracts follow:

- Identify the competency to be mastered.
- Specify the methods and strategies that will be used to master the competency.
- Specify resources to be used in order to master the competency.
- Specify the type of evidence that will be used to demonstrate competency mastery.

For example, a pastoral staff member expresses a desire to become a better preacher. He then meets with his supervisor to discuss his desire and his learning plan. The supervisor retains the right to adjust, expand, and redirect the learning plan. The staff member may say, "I need to become a better preacher." The supervisor may respond by saying, "Actually, you are a great preacher. Your problem is that you need to develop more depth in your preaching." In that case, the plan may include training in theology as well as communication skills.

8. Develop a plan for the staff to systematically study the PastorServe 24 Leadership Competencies. Tackle one area of competency each month, and complete the study in two years, or address eight competencies each year (taking off the summer months and December).

Questions for Reflection

Reality—If time and money were no barrier, what training would you most like to receive? Why?

What priority is continuing education given in your church? Does each staff member have an allotted amount for continuing education?

How are you presently pursuing continuing education? What conferences have been the most helpful to you?

Have you ever read a book together as a staff? What books have been helpful to tackle together as a team?

On a scale of 1 to 10, how eager are you to learn right now? Explain your answer.

Rewind and Review—Jimmy listed several institutions that require continuing education for their members. Why is it that churches often downgrade the need for continuing education for their pastors?

What training did you receive before you entered full-time ministry? In what ways were you well prepared for your current ministry? In what areas was there inadequate preparation or training?

Reflect—Do you think churches should require continuing education for their pastors? Why or why not?

What are some of the best general conferences you've attended? Which specialized conferences have been helpful? What made the conference so good? Specifically, who has been a helpful trainer to you? What key truths have you gleaned from this trainer?

Jimmy asked you to rank yourself on a scale of 1 to 5 in the 24 Leadership Competencies. Share your results. Is there a general area in which you are stronger than others? Is there a general area in which you are weak? What could you do to strengthen your weaker areas?

Remember—Ultimately, we learn from the greatest teacher, Jesus Christ. In the Gospels, Jesus is called Teacher, Good Teacher, Rabbi, a teacher come from God, and a man who told you the truth He heard from God. Why do you think the Gospels place such an emphasis on Jesus as a teacher? How can you daily sit at the feet of Jesus and learn from Him?

Respond—What steps do you need to take to get your church to provide financial resources for continuing education for the pastoral staff? What are the pros and cons of mandatory continuing education being added to your church bylaws?

Have you attended another church with the specific purpose of learning? If not, what prevented this? Insecurity? Time? Exhaustion? Financial resources?

Chapter 9

Hey, Coach! Put Me In!

When Sally and I began the process of planting a church in Kansas City in 1992, a new phenomenon was sweeping through the church-planting community. I was assigned a church-planting coach. While I had grown up around athletic coaches, a ministry coach was a new idea, and I readily embraced it.

I was coached by Corb Heimburger, who, in addition to being a first-rate coach, became a dear friend and mentor. Corb lived in St. Louis while I was planting in Kansas City. In addition to our regular phone conversations, once a month Corb and I would meet halfway at a restaurant in Columbia near the campus of the University of Missouri (which was always challenging for a Kansas Jayhawk fan like me). As I look back on my years of church planting, I can't fathom planting and leading a church apart from the regular interaction with Corb. He wasn't there to tell me what to do. He was consistently there to process with me, ask me hard questions, and push me in skill development.

I frequently speak with pastors who assure me that they have a coach. When I ask about the nature of their meetings, I often hear some version of the following: "My coach and I try to meet a minimum of once a month. When we get together, my coach asks me about the church and how things are going. We usually have a great conversation lasting around an hour. I always walk away with a number of great ideas—and a boost of encouragement." I love the fact that the pastor receives regular encouragement, but this is *not* a coaching relationship. What I have just described is a friend.

Coaching is a process, not a position or a title. It's using one's desire, knowledge, and skills to help others succeed through regular interaction. I don't disagree that in selected contexts effective coaching can be as brief as giving another person a few words of encouragement. The underlying assumption of coaching is that we can all help one another. We *are* coaching when we say anything to anyone to help improve their performance. Without question, the ultimate goal is to help others reach new levels of personal commitment and performance. However, in the context of consistent pastoral coaching, we will use the following definition:

> Successful coaching is regular conversations (as opposed to a monologue) that follow a systematic process centered on a defined set of skills that can be learned and developed, which leads to improved and eventually superior performance.

Coaching is not an exact science. There are blurred lines of role delineation that allow, and at times demand, the coach to wear a number of different hats. While a coach is different from a consultant, a coach can give advice and provide solutions. A coach is different from a counselor, although exploring how performance roadblocks are tied to someone's past can be a part of coaching. A coach can and will teach during coaching sessions, although the coach is not defined as a trainer.

Generally speaking, a coach does not need to be an expert in the client's field. In fact, extreme expertise can be a hindrance, as some individuals may not have the ability to coach when a particular skill came so naturally to them. For example, some of the best players in professional sports have gone on to become some of the worst coaches. Superior athletic coaches are generally those who were known as students of the game rather than stars of the game. In coaching, the client is the expert. It's not the job of the coach to have all the answers; it is the job of the coach to ask the questions that lead the client to find his own answers.

Difficult to Reach Your Potential Apart from a Coach

How many top-level athletes who participate in individual sports (tennis, golf, skiing, to name a few) or semi-individual sports (track and field, gymnastics, swimming, and so on) can you name who do not have a coach? My guess is that maybe one or two come to mind, and only if you are an ardent sports fan. All the top swimmers in the world engage individual coaches, as do tennis stars, runners, and gymnasts. The top golf pros? Of course. Tiger Woods made headlines when he hired a new coach (for the fourth time).

Quick, without consulting Google, what do the names Jack Grout, Glen Mills, Harry "Hoppy" Hopman, and Bob Bowman have in common? All four are widely recognized as some of the greatest coaches in sports history. Jack Grout served as a coach to golf legend Jack Nicklaus throughout his career. Glen Mills coached a rather speedy young Jamaican named Usain Bolt. Australian Harry

Hopman is regarded by most as the greatest tennis coach in history, having coached more than a dozen Grand Slam champions, including Ken Rosewall, Rod Laver, and John McEnroe. Finally, Bob Bowman coached swimming phenom Michael Phelps to a record number of Olympic gold medals.

It's interesting to note that elite individual athletes commonly employ a coach, a sports psychologist, a manager, and an athletic trainer. And to top it off, many travel with an entourage (I'm guessing their mentor meets them at the athletic venue). When individual athletes are asked why they shell out big dollars to employ a coach, the question is viewed as irrational and ridiculous.

So I am perplexed when pastors resist coaching. Many continue to view the need for coaching as a sure sign of weakness. Funny, most top-tier athletes and Fortune 500 executives view the lack of a coach as a sure sign of stupidity. The greatest team-sport athletes readily acknowledge their need for coaches. Soccer legend Cristiano Ronaldo repeatedly points to coach Carlo Ancelotti as the key to his personal success as well as the accomplishments of his team Real Madrid, for example. John Buchanan is widely regarded as the best coach in cricket history (for those who scoff, cricket is widely regarded as the second most popular sport in the world). And Buchanan's players (regarded as the best) regularly attribute their successes to their coach.

One of my favorite coaching stories comes from legendary North Carolina basketball coach Dean Smith. Following the 1982–83 season, in which North Carolina won the national championship on a Michael Jordan shot, Smith wrote two letters to Michael during the summer. Rather than mention the national championship shot, Coach Smith (a former Kansas Jayhawk player) instead addressed the parts of his game Michael needed to work on over the summer. Coach Smith wrote, "Shoot the ball the same way each time, the same arc.... In pick-up games, try to be a point guard, working on your dribbling and starting the ball low.... Don't always reach for the ball but contain your man." In conclusion, Smith wrote, "Michael, if you do improve on these items we mentioned, you will be a much better basketball player." How great is that? And do you know what Michael Jordan did? Everything his coach advised him to do! And things turned out okay for Michael.

Coaching at the Highest Levels

In his excellent August 13, 2012, post, "Why Every CEO Needs a Coach," on the *Psychology Today* blog, Ray Williams makes the case for why CEOs of leading businesses need an executive coach. Williams makes the point that the proof is in the pudding. In the past two decades, 30 percent of Fortune 500 CEOs have lasted less than three years. Top executive failure rates are as high as 75 percent and rarely less than 30 percent. Chief executives now are lasting 7.6 years on a global average, down from 9.5 years just twenty years ago. According to the *Harvard Business Review*, two out of five new CEOs fail in their first eighteen months on the job. To be sure, leading has never been more difficult.

Williams also notes,

> Top executives who feel that they can handle it all by themselves are more likely to burn out, make poor decisions or make no decisions—potentially resulting

in significant loss of opportunities, human resources
and financial resources. The job of CEO is unique
from several perspectives: No one else needs to hear
the truth more, and gets it less from employees; no
one else is the focus of criticism when things go wrong;
no one else is the final decision maker on difficult
and often lose-lose decisions; and finally, no one else
enjoys the almost hero-celebrity status and rewards.[1]

In the top businesses around the world, coaching is in no way
associated with inferior performance. According to the *Denver Post*,
nine out of ten executives believe coaching is well worth their time
and dollars. John Russell, former CEO of Harley-Davidson Europe
and the Shakespeare Trust, has often been quoted saying, "I never
cease to be amazed at the power of the coaching process to draw out
the skills or talent that was previously hidden within an individual,
and which invariably finds a way to solve a problem previously
thought unsolvable."[2]

Coaching cannot and should not fill a motivational gap. While
coaching can encourage commitment—people will do superior work
because there is a personal commitment to doing so—if someone is
unmotivated, coaching will not "fix them." Coaching is not for the
faint of heart. For those who value straightforward, clear-cut feedback, coaching will be a welcome friend.

It is vital that coaching occur in the proper context. It is difficult
to coach a leader who has no voice in the function or direction of his
or her work. People become committed to strive for superior work to
the degree that they:

- operate well under a clearly defined vision, mission, and values
- have clarity of expectations and a definition of success
- have sway and authority over what they do
- believe that their fears, insecurities, failures, and emotions have been acknowledged and understood
- possess the necessary competencies to perform the assigned job
- are loved, appreciated, and thanked for their performance

Over the decades, I have been privileged to coach dozens and dozens of pastors. Unquestionably, some of most difficult coaching assignments involved pastors who were: (1) not the lead pastor; (2) serving as lead pastor under a board who, failing to understand their shepherding and governance role, micromanaged the pastoral staff; and (3) serving as lead pastor despite not possessing the pastoral competencies necessary to effectively lead a church. When a pastor possesses no authority to implement change, coaching can begin to feel like an endless cycle of unfulfilled expectations.

Behaviors That Cause Leaders to Fail

David Dotlich and Peter C. Cairo, in their book *Why CEOs Fail: The 11 Behaviors That Can Derail Your Climb to the Top—and How to*

Manage Them, hit the nail squarely on the head when they laid out the reasons why so many leaders fail. Crippling behaviors they identify, which I have personally witnessed crossing over into pastoral leadership, include:

> Arrogance—you think you're right, and everyone else is wrong
>
> Melodrama—you need to be the center of attention
>
> Excessive Caution—you're afraid to make decisions
>
> Habitual Distrust—you focus on the negatives
>
> Aloofness—you're disengaged and disconnected
>
> Eccentricity—you try to be different just for the sake of it
>
> Passive Resistance—what you say is not what you really believe
>
> Perfectionism—you get the little things right and the big things wrong
>
> Eagerness to Please—you try to win the popularity contest

The authors insightfully stress that each of the behaviors is a dark side of an important strength. For example, the charismatic leader can cross the line into melodrama. Similarly, in a church, vision-driven decisiveness and self-confidence can morph into arrogance.

Look over the list. Do any of these behaviors ring an inner bell? If you are brave (or foolishly overconfident), ask your coworkers and spouse to look over the list. One central impediment to leadership is a failure to address blind spots (see chapter 12, on friendship, for a full discussion of blind spots). Coaches can and should speak into unattended blinded areas in the life of a leader, whereas a staff, board, and even family often will not.

Over years of consulting, PastorServe has done hundreds of church health assessments. I am no longer surprised when there is a wide gap between what the leader believes and what the staff knows. Sadly, there is a general lack of self-awareness that plagues a high percentage of leaders. In acute cases, though the pastor may regularly invite opinions, he or she has in reality created a culture in which openness and honesty are not viable options for anyone on the team who wants to have a job next Monday morning. I have spoken with lead pastors who assured me that they led an incredibly healthy church and, therefore, had no need for a staff assessment or, for that matter, a personal coach; only to be contacted the next day by church staff members who were in the bowels of discouragement as they felt as though an assessment was their one thread of hope for honesty and open dialogue. No one needs to hear the truth more than overconfident lead pastors, and no one will hear the truth less than overconfident lead pastors. I maintain that while pastoral associates and assistants can benefit from coaching, every lead pastor needs a coach.

Dispelling a Coaching Myth

Allow me to state the obvious. Jack Nicklaus is a better golfer than Jack Grout. Michael Jordan was a better basketball player than Dean Smith. Usain Bolt can outrun Glen Mills, and I would put money on Michael Phelps in a swim-off with Bob Bowman. The role of coach in no way conveys superior personal proficiency. In fact, in the world of sports, I struggle to think of more than a handful of professional coaches who, at any time in their athletic careers, exceeded the athletic ability of the current best player on his or her team. It's the same in the boardroom.

Translated into the church, large church pastors do not need to be coached by larger church pastors. The mind-set that says "I don't want to be coached by someone who has never pastored a church as large as mine" is shortsighted, foolish, and downright arrogant. Being an experienced pastor never qualified anyone to be a pastoral coach. In fact, experience can work against the coach when coaching.

What is true in the world of sports coaching is true in the world of pastoral coaching. The pastors of large churches generally (there are exceptions) make the worst coaches. Look at any list of the worst coaches in professional basketball history. The names Isiah Thomas, George "The Iceman" Gervin, Elgin Baylor, and Willis Reed appear on every list. And they were NBA stars! NBA success does not always equate to quality NBA coaching.

So, too, in the church world; the best coaches often pastored small churches, often from "the second chair" (in fact, the best coach on the PastorServe team never served as a lead pastor). Many of these small church pastors are incredibly insightful, competent, bold, and caring. Successful pastors who become coaches must learn to sufficiently withhold their personal expertise in order to coach well. The tendency of the coach is to become a teller ("When I pastored my church, we did it this way, and therefore, so should you"). An effective pastoral coach will learn to leverage personal and pastoral experience to benefit the pastor in the coaching relationship. Good coaches will not use their coaching platforms to "clone" their own experiences.

PastorServe began coaching pastors in 1999, and we were one of the first national ministries to train and certify pastoral coaches. Presently, PastorServe coaches pastors both young and old, leading churches from fifty congregants to several thousand. We coach pastors from a wide variety of denominations and theological backgrounds. And nearly every pastor we coach, despite the wide-ranging backgrounds, faces the same handful of challenges.

Models for Coaching from the Scriptures

The superior model for coaching is found in the Bible. Some of the primary character qualities of coaches are found in the following passages.

- Philippians 2:3–4 emphasizes humility and a genuine concern for others. "Do nothing from selfish ambition or conceit, but in humility count others more significant than yourselves. Let each of you look not only to his own interests, but also to the interests of others."
- Hebrews 10:24–25 underscores the need to be loving, thoughtful, considerate, and encouraging. "And let us consider how to stir up one another to love and good works, not neglecting to meet together, as is the habit of some, but encouraging one another, and all the more as you see the Day drawing near."

- Psalm 18:35 highlights the need for humility and gentleness coupled with a concern for others. "You have given me the shield of your salvation, and your right hand supported me, and your gentleness made me great."
- James 1:19–20 speaks of humility, a concern for others, the need to listen before you speak, and self-control. "Know this, my beloved brothers: let every person be quick to hear, slow to speak, slow to anger; for the anger of man does not produce the righteousness of God."
- Proverbs 18:13 again emphasizes the need to practice active listening. "If one gives an answer before he hears, it is his folly and shame."

Perhaps the best model for a coach is the Holy Spirit. Scripture tells us that the Holy Spirit is a comforter and advocate (John 14:26), empowers believers (Jude 1:20), illuminates the hearts of believers (Ephesians 1:17–18), and convicts believers (John 16:8). The Holy Spirit instructs (John 14:26), lifts up Jesus (Luke 4:1), and gives good gifts (Galatians 5:22–23). We need to consistently ask the Lord to allow the Holy Spirit to be mirrored in our lives.

Six Key Qualities to Look for in a Coach

Now that I've made the case for coaching, allow me to highlight qualities to look for when selecting a coach. There is a coaching skill set that can be readily recognized: six key qualities you want to seek out in your coach.

First and foremost, you need to like your coach. Coaching is all about relationships. There comes a time to challenge in coaching. How will you respond when confronted by your coach? If the relationship is not grounded, it simply will not work. Do you think that because you are a highly respected person the coach has no right to call you out? Coaching will involve conversations about deficits in performance. There will come a time in the coaching relationship to address:

- clarification of performance expectations
- identification of shortfalls
- identification of weak core competencies
- mutually agreed-upon strategies to improve
- commitment to continuous improvement

Are you going to be okay when confronted?

Second, effective coaching always begins with a healthy, realistic self-evaluation. An effective coach is constantly learning and growing in self-awareness. Successful coaches turn the mirror on themselves, gaining a clear perception of their own agendas and biases so as not to project unhealthy expectations on the pastor they coach. In short, who is your coach's coach? What is he doing to regularly improve as a coach?

Coaches do not work out their own problems through the ones they are coaching. I was coaching a bright young pastor in Michigan who was facing some difficult challenges in his church, the majority of which were centered on one obstinate, stubborn member of his board of elders. One evening I was invited to spend time with the elders, training them in ways they could effectively lead and shepherd the congregation. I hadn't been teaching for ten minutes before it became woefully obvious who was the problem elder. Suddenly, I felt a wave of anger toward this arrogant, pigheaded buffoon who had no business serving on a board of spiritual leaders. I called for a break, took a deep breath, and said a prayer, and the Lord brought me instantaneous insight (which doesn't happen every day). Years earlier, I had suffered through a season with a difficult board member in a church who made my life very difficult, but it was ridiculous to think that attacking the Michigan church elder was somehow going to apply a healing balm to my wound from years earlier, which obviously remained open. Just as many people have a father wound, so, too, many pastors have an elder wound. The Holy Spirit showed me that the issue wasn't so much this elder who sat before me; the problem was my heart, which clearly hadn't effectively processed the pain of earlier conflicts. The bottom line: coaches do not process personal issues through current coaching situations.

Third, effective coaches embrace the vision and mission of the pastor. Everyone brings a personal agenda into any given situation. The pressing question becomes whether the coach's agenda is in line with the pastor's agenda. We hope that everyone is mutually seeking the Lord's agenda, but the coach must honestly ask himself if he is bringing a personal agenda to the coaching relationship.

I have coached pastors in churches in which I fundamentally disagreed with their overall direction. They have a differing (though orthodox) theology, a different view of church growth (they want to grow a church of twenty thousand), a different perspective on training leaders within their congregation (they believe that because elders only govern, they really don't need to be trained), and a differing view on the role of small groups in the church. While a coach can offer suggestions, it is not the role of the coach to seek to change the vision of the church. If a coach subtly works to ever so slightly modify the goals to fulfill a personal agenda, the coach is in reality working against the pastor. This lack of integrity should excuse the coach from the position.

Coaches should understand the boundaries of the coaching role. The coach is not there to tell, direct, make judgments, impose agendas, or force people to change against their will. Telling people what to do—rather than creating mutual discovery—will lead to unhealthy dependency. Telling is associated with a parent-child relationship. Coaching is associated with a peer-peer relationship. Telling is demeaning. Coaching is encouraging. Telling says "I think you should." Coaching says "Let's think about." Telling always expounds on what worked for you. Coaching always explores what could work in this situation. Additionally, beware of coaches who neglect to take responsibility for improving the performances of the pastors they are coaching.

Fourth, effective coaches are skilled in the area of active listening. Can they go through an entire conversation only asking questions and avoiding making statements? When looking for active listeners, I search for a coach who can acknowledge me in the conversation. This can be as subtle as an occasional, "Hmm … I see. Okay, yes, I understand." "So that is the heart of the problem? Yes, I follow that." These small words make a big statement. They tell me the coach is tracking with me in the conversation.

I look for a coach who understands the difference between a closed probe and an open probe. A closed probe is a question that encourages a yes, no, or specific response such as "How much money is left in the budget?" or "Have you discussed this with your worship leader?" An open probe encourages elaboration. "Tell me how you are doing with this project." "How are you feeling about your leadership team today?" If you are trying to gather information, use an open probe. If you need to focus on one specific issue, a closed probe can be helpful.

Here's a free tip that has little to do with coaching and everything to do with life and marriage. Men tend to use three times more closed probes than open probes. When several closed probes are strung together (as men love to do), it appears as if the man is in complete control of the conversation. This leads to a monologue as opposed to dialogue. To encourage wives to share more intimately with their husbands, use more open probes!

Reflecting is a vital part of any conversation. The best example of reflection is any waiter, any waitress, or any drive-through worker always repeating the order. Reflecting briefly restates what another has just said. Why is this so difficult? Because listening is a learned skill. It doesn't come naturally. To reflect, we must listen. Reflecting forces listening and builds listening skills.

I want a coach who can walk the fine line between listening and self-disclosure. This is where so many coaching relationships jump the rails and crash. This is a dangerous but necessary component of active listening. Self-disclosure is an opportunity to very briefly share a bit of your own story for the express purpose of advancing the conversation. It is not license to launch into a lengthy telling mode.

Self-disclosure is a simple, relevant statement that communicates that the coach can empathize with the pastor. "Can I share a brief thought? I experienced a similar staff challenge ten years ago. My heart goes out to you, as I know personally this is painful." That brief statement can make a big difference.

Finally, an effective listener will always summarize at the conclusion of a conversation. A brief summarization is a safeguard to avoid potentially tragic misunderstandings. What were the main points you covered? What are the next steps? I have learned an immense amount about summarization from watching my friend Justin. I know of no one more skilled in summarization. Every conversation ends with a review of what we just covered, next steps, and deadlines. Justin is the living, breathing embodiment of SMART Goals (specific, measurable, attainable, realistic/relevant, timely/time bound).

Fifth, and near the top of importance, effective coaches are skilled in the area of asking questions. Any coach who attempts to serve a pastor without asking a myriad of questions is likely not doing an effective job. By asking key questions, probing into areas of competency, and taking the pastor beyond perceived limitations of their own knowledge, the coach effectively pushes the pastor into new realms of skill sets, insight, and performance. Successful coaches are disciplined and follow a clearly defined process using specific communication skills. They do not say whatever comes to mind. Coaches focus on developing a process rather than striving to control the content of the coaching conversation.

Coaches listen without evaluating or putting the other person on the defensive. They avoid questions that start with why or how, as these can raise a person's defenses. I look for coaches who begin questions with what, when, or who. For example:

- What are the reasons you …
- What was the process you went through to …
- What steps did you take to …
- When did you make the decision to …

Some of the most effective coaches can go for several hours without making a single statement—the entire conversation is directed through questions. I believe that any effective coaching session is going to cover four areas first set forth by Sir John Whitmore in his coaching classic, *Coaching for Performance: GROWing Human Potential and Purpose—The Principles and Practice of Coaching and Leadership*. Whitmore uses GROW as his coaching guide.

> **G**—What is the **GOAL** of our time together? The primary temptation in coaching is to move to respond to or solve a problem before a reality check.
> **R**—What is the **REALITY** of the present situation? This is like finding the map in the mall that tells us "You Are Here." If we really want to get to point B, we need to be realistic about point A.
> **O**—What are the available **OPTIONS** and **OPPORTUNITIES**? This always takes time, as there is always another option.
> **W**—What **WILL** you do? **WHERE** do we go from here? What SMART Goals will you set as a result

of this coaching conversation? Often, the root issue of a problem will surface just when a coaching conversation is concluding.

Knowing that random conversations guided by a random agenda produce random results, PastorServe uses seven simple questions prior to every coaching appointment. Three days before the coaching appointment, it is the responsibility of the pastor to email answers to the following seven questions, spending no more than fifteen minutes on the exercise. I am not looking for a lengthy essay. I am looking for brief statements that will safeguard that the coaching appointment will be guided, specific, and valuable. The following questions *must* be submitted prior to the coaching appointment. Failure to submit questions results in a rescheduling of the coaching appointment.

1. How can I be praying for you in preparation for our next appointment?

2. Tell me what you are presently celebrating in Jesus Christ.

3. It is vital that I understand your expectations for our meeting. Tell me what would be the single most helpful thing for you to take away from our time together.

4. What progress have you made on action items or SMART Goals from previous conversations?

5. Tell me about one ministry challenge you are presently facing.

6. Tell me about one personal challenge you are presently facing.

7. Provide an update on how you are doing emotionally, physically, and spiritually by giving me an update on how your three gauges read.

Emotional Energy

E_____1/4_____1/2_____3/4_____F

Physical Energy

E_____1/4_____1/2_____3/4_____F

Spiritual Life

E_____1/4_____1/2_____3/4_____F

Sixth and finally, an effective pastoral coach will assist in coaching the pastor through change. Coaching involves inviting people to change; yet it must be done without putting the person on the defensive. When people become defensive, they become resistant to options for change. We face several options when confronted with change: (1) we can be swept along by change; (2) we can learn how to work with change; or (3) we can make change happen (change agents).

Part of encouraging change is learning to be concrete in coaching conversations. When a pastor discloses that his staff has remarked that they feel demeaned in staff meetings, it's not helpful for a coach to respond, "You know, you really need to learn to be a team player on your staff." It's much more helpful when the coach provides concrete

suggestions: "Let's talk about how you could be immediately respon-
sive to requests from the staff. Additionally, let's talk about never
making others on your staff look foolish or incompetent in front of
their peers. Knowing you want to make these changes, what are some
ways that you think this could be communicated to your staff?"

In his book *Next Generation Leader*, Andy Stanley has these words
to offer about coaching: "You will never maximize your potential in
any area without coaching. It is impossible. You may be good. You
may even be better than everyone else. But without outside input
you will never be as good as you could be."

Every pastor needs outside input. And every pastor needs a
boss, a trainer, and a coach. These three professional roles are vital
if a pastor is wholeheartedly committed to improving his or her
skill level and pastoral competencies. We now turn to the more sen-
sitive areas of personal relationships: the relationships of counselor,
mentor, and friend.

Questions for Reflection

Reality—Are you presently being coached? Who serves in the role of
your coach? For whom are you presently serving in the role of coach?

Have you ever experienced being coached as it's described in
this chapter? If so, how did coaching benefit you personally and/or
vocationally?

Rewind and Review—How has this chapter helped bring some
clarity to your preconceived ideas about what leadership coaching
is and isn't?

Look over the list provided by Dotlich and Cairo. Do any of these behaviors describe your standard methods of operation? How are they revealed in your life?

Reflect—Do you agree or disagree with the following statement: "No one needs to hear the truth more than overconfident lead pastors, and no one will hear the truth less than overconfident lead pastors"? Why, or why not?

Let's assume it's true that many pastors do resist being coached. What do you believe are some of the reasons for this resistance? Would you be opposed to being coached during this season of your life? Why, or why not?

Coaching helps leaders move forward in areas of their lives where they feel stuck, plateaued, discouraged, or disillusioned. Reflect on your personal and professional life for a few moments. Where do you feel stuck, plateaued, discouraged, or disillusioned?

Imagine you are sitting with your coach right now. He asks the question, "What is the single most helpful thing for you to take away from our time together today?" What do you need to process together right now? How do you respond?

Being brutally honest, what do your life gauges read right now?

Remember—Psalm 18:35 reminds us, "You have given me the shield of your salvation, and your right hand supported me, and your gentleness made me great." While the passage encourages the need for humility and gentleness coupled with a concern for others, it reminds us first and foremost of the Lord's concern for us. How does this truth encourage your heart today?

Respond—What steps do you need to take to secure a coach? If you do invite a coach into your life in the near future, what qualities would you want to see in this individual before hiring him or her? Why?

Chapter 10

Counselor: Scrubbing the Wound

Joel called me from Washington state. He mentioned he would be passing through Kansas City and would like to meet in person. As we compared calendars, we realized the only time we could connect would be at midnight at a local coffee shop, which was closed, but they had a nice outside seating area.

We sat down and Joel began. "I wanted to meet so I could confess something to you." I assured him that I was a sinner who was in need of grace, just like him. Our conversation would remain confidential (he has granted me permission to share this story). He continued. "I know you hear a lot of confessions, but I don't want you to use my confession as an example when talking with other pastors." I assured him that he would not become the example story. But he said, "Let me be clear. Not only do I not want you to reference my story; I don't even want you to vaguely refer to my story by changing my name. I don't want my story to ever be mentioned again, and if I ever hear you say anything vaguely similar to what I am about to share with you, I'll know you violated confidentiality and broke your promise to me."

I honestly began to think he might be about to confess murder or some monstrous crime. At that point in my career, I had heard it *all*. My heart began to race. Again, I assured him that if the confession was not criminal or did not involve hurting another person, particularly a minor, his confession was 100 percent confidential. After a lengthy pause, with tears filling his eyes and his voice cracking, he slowly and painfully said, "I am struggling with Internet pornography, and I don't know what to do."

As detailed in chapter 1, Satan has a limited toolbox. His primary tool is to tell believers lies, which we often believe. One of Satan's primary lies is that we are the *only one* who has a back stage that doesn't match the front stage. We are the only person living a dual existence.

Thank God I didn't laugh. It took only a couple of seconds to realize this was no joke, that Satan had convinced Joel he was the only pastor in the world (his words) struggling with pornography— and he saw no way out. The call to me was his final lunge toward freedom. I gently assured Joel that if he ever heard that I was speaking about this particular sin, it was not a reference to him; I was referring to one of the other dozen pastors who had reached out to PastorServe earlier *that week* with the same challenges. He sat in stunned silence. He thought I was patronizing him. I assured him that while the sting of sin can be a good thing to drive us toward genuine repentance, I was not patronizing him. Other pastors were struggling with this same sin. Sin loves isolation, and Joel had been cut off from any community.

"You are not alone." Powerful words. One reason why so many resist counseling is we convince ourselves our sinful issues are unique. "No other person, certainly no pastor, is struggling with this particular sin the way I struggle with this sin." We see counseling as the line that should never be crossed, lest our dysfunction be revealed. The risk is simply too high. And so we live and minister with the unceasing, condemning voice in the back of our heads, "If my church only knew …"

Psalms of lament point us to the only One who can free us from captivity of back stage inauthenticity.

> When the righteous cry for help, the LORD hears
> and delivers them out of all their troubles.
> The LORD is near to the brokenhearted
> and saves the crushed in spirit.
>
> Many are the afflictions of the righteous,
> but the LORD delivers him out of them all.
> (Psalm 34:17–19)
>
> He heals the brokenhearted
> and binds up their wounds. (Psalm 147:3)

Only Jesus saves the crushed. Only Jesus frees us from captivity. Only Jesus allows us to honestly confront our deepest sin. Only Jesus grants us the freedom to confront our doubts. Only Jesus heals the brokenhearted. Only Jesus gives us the courage to open the back stage door and allow others to see our mess. Only Jesus speaks eternal words of gospel truth to our thirsty hearts.

Opening the Wound

I believe the majority of pastors, in one way or another, are wounded. I have heard more stories than I could ever recount about father

wounds, mother wounds, friendship wounds, family wounds, elder
wounds, congregation wounds, failure wounds, and the list goes on
and on. I believe it is wise to address these wounds with a professional gospel-centric counselor. Gospel-centric counselors believe
that the Lordship of Jesus and the grace of God have an impact on
every story on every page contained in every chapter in our life book.

Some who push back on counseling say that it is unwise to reopen
deep wounds. "If the Lord didn't reveal His purpose to you in the
midst of the pain, what makes you think He will reveal the purpose
now?" I heard one well-known church leader say that God wants all
believers to be spiritual emus, one of the only animals who, along with
the kangaroo, are unable to walk backward. "God never wants us to
be moving backwards, but only forwards," she said to an audience of
thousands of young, impressionable pastors. I wanted to throw up.

Counseling carries many parallels to the medical procedure
to heal a burn wound, which is one of the most painful because it
is one of the slowest healing. When a person's skin is burned, the
layers beneath the skin are burned too. Healing begins when you
meticulously scrub the dead skin until you reach a layer of living
skin—resulting in a great deal of pain to the patient. However, this
is necessary to enable the burn wound to heal from the inside out.
A burn left unscrubbed can heal quickly on the surface, but despite
the outward appearance of healing, the wound is infected on the
inside. This leads to gangrene, amputation, and in the more serious
cases, death. Many wounds in the church (and marriage, relationships, and several additional areas) are not sufficiently opened and
scrubbed. After a time, while they may outwardly appear to have
healed, there may be a deep, internal infection. Time does not heal

all wounds. Therefore, untreated, infected wounds must be opened and scrubbed to prevent lasting damage. One role of counseling is to reopen unhealed wounds and scrub them over and over again in order to bring real internal healing.

That said, there are wounds that may never heal, although an examination of them makes them bearable. Perhaps the most powerful story in J. R. R. Tolkien's classic Lord of the Rings series, which has been a comfort to countless pastors, concerns the wounds we suffer in the service of the Lord. In the first book of the trilogy, while at an inn, Frodo slips on the Ring, instantly becoming invisible. This immediately draws the Ringwraiths (the Black Riders) to him. When the Black Riders attack the inn, the hobbits are forced to trust Strider, a friend of Gandalf's, to escape. Strider takes them through the wilderness toward Rivendell, an elf haven. The Black Riders catch them halfway at Weathertop, a ruined fort, and stab Frodo with a magic Morgul blade, causing him to drift between life and death. His companions rush him to Rivendell where Lord Elrond has the power to save him.

As Frodo recovers, Gandalf and Elrond discuss the seriousness of the wound. Gandalf says, "He has a wound that will never heal. He will carry it the rest of his life. It is a burden he should not have to bear."

Fast-forward to the conclusion of the story in book 3. After the Ring has been destroyed and all appears to be right with the world, the hobbits head for home. They are desperately excited to return to the Shire. On the journey, Frodo suddenly expresses pain.

> "Are you in pain, Frodo?" said Gandalf quietly as he
> rode by Frodo's side.

"Well, yes I am," said Frodo. "It is my shoulder. The wound aches, and the memory of darkness is heavy on me. It was a year ago today."

"Alas! There are some wounds that cannot be wholly cured," said Gandalf.

"I fear it may be so with mine," said Frodo. "There is no real going back. Though I may come to the Shire, it will not seem the same; for I shall not be the same. I am wounded with knife, sting, and tooth, and a long burden. Where shall I find rest?"

Gandalf did not answer....

[Once back at the Shire,] one evening Sam came into the study and found his master looking very strange. He was very pale and his eyes seemed to see things far away.

"What's the matter, Mr. Frodo?" said Sam.

"I am wounded," he answered, "wounded; it will never really heal."[1]

It is later revealed that Frodo has bouts of sickness, from time to time, resulting from the wound and what he suffered on his quest. We later learn that time with his friends in the Shire will not heal the wound. Frodo can only be ultimately healed by traveling to the Undying Lands.

Tolkien is making a powerful point. There are some wounds that are so deep, they are never meant to heal in this lifetime. Over the years, many pastors ask me when the wound will finally heal. But there are some wounds (divorce, betrayal, false accusation, broken relationships) that are so deep, they will only finally heal when we see Jesus face to face. Our wounds remind us that there is another land where all wounds will heal, all tears will be dried, and all pain will be swallowed by the King of Kings and Lord of Lords.

Lamenting before the Lord

I am immensely grateful to the Lord for giving us the book of Psalms. The psalms settle my spirit and remind me I'm really not that abnormal. Have you ever had the experience of having the most bizarre, atypical thought, but then someone near you voices the exact same thought? You breathe a sigh of relief because maybe you're not as strange as you believed. The psalms do that for me, particularly the psalms of sorrow, doubt, pain, and heartbreak—the psalms of lament.

The theme of every psalm is YHWH pointing to Jesus Christ. Every psalm looks ahead to the truth of Jesus and the hope of the gospel. While I appreciate every genre of the psalms—royal, salvation history, thanksgiving, enthronement, praise, trust, wisdom, and even imprecatory—the psalms of lament tackle the themes of hurt and disappointment, things we often don't talk about in context of Christianity. Words such as "O LORD, how many are my foes! Many are rising against me" (Psalm 3:1); "Give ear to my words, O LORD; consider my groaning" (Psalm 5:1); and "O LORD, rebuke me not in your anger … Your arrows have sunk into me, and your hand has come down on me" (Psalm 38:1–2). This is raw, gut-wrenching, unfiltered, unprotected, unguarded, exposed emotion.

The psalms are so realistic. They push back with *every* word, *every* prayer, and *every* cry against Western, shallow, watered-down, prosperity-gospel theology. In many corners of Christianity, there is no place for the raw emotional vomiting so often expressed in the psalms, and as a result, an unfounded, unsupported, unjustified myth cripples a portion of the Christian church—that depression is a sign of weakness and should be judged as a failure that disqualifies believers from vocational Christian service. Simply put, because we have victory in Jesus, Christians should not experience mental health issues. The truth? Christians can and do struggle with hopelessness, burnout, and depression. Christians suffer breakdowns and severe anxiety attacks. Followers of Jesus can, and many do, experience mental health issues. But because of the stigma associated with depression, some Christians deal with it superficially: "Come on. Toughen up and confess your sin. Just pray more, get over it; just look forward. You just need more faith; God is able."

The Depths of Depression

If you suffer from depression and you feel overwhelmed and you are convinced you can't go on, you are in good company. Moses asked God to blot him out of the book of life (Exodus 32:32–33); Abraham gave us a vivid description of the sensation of terror when he said a "dreadful and great darkness fell upon him" (Genesis 15:12); Jacob wept for days, refusing comfort (Genesis 37:35); Isaiah cried, "Woe is me! For I am lost" (Isaiah 6:5); and Jeremiah wished he had never been born (Jeremiah 20:14–17). In fact, Jeremiah reached the point of calling God "a deceitful brook … waters that fail" (Jeremiah 15:18) and even accused God of deceiving and overpowering him (Jeremiah 20:7). The prophet Elijah came to a broom tree, sat down under it, and prayed that he might die: "It is enough; now, O LORD, take away my life" (1 Kings 19:4). Jonah said that for him, death was better than life (Jonah 4:3); and David and his people wept until there was no strength left to weep (1 Samuel 30:3–4). David continued, "I am utterly bowed down and prostrate; all the day I go about mourning.... I groan because of the tumult of my heart" (Psalm 38:6, 8). We could on and on with examples from the Scriptures of those who were discouraged, depressed, and unable to see the hope that lay before them. Remember, God could have shielded us from this depth of naked honesty. He could have withheld this information. And yet, the Lord allowed them to express their lament in the Holy Scriptures.

We could create a similar although much longer list from history. Well-known leaders such as William Cowper, the great hymn writer; Charles Haddon Spurgeon, who was known as the prince of preachers; President Abraham Lincoln; Mother Teresa; Martin Luther King; and many others had well-documented bouts with depression. Mother Teresa wrote, "I am told God loves me—and yet the reality of darkness and coldness and emptiness is so great that nothing touches my soul.... I want God with all the powers of my soul—and yet between us—there is terrible separation." On another occasion she wrote, "I feel just that terrible pain of loss—of God not wanting me—of God not being God—of God not really existing."[2]

Don't believe health-and-wealth liars, prosperity-gospel deceivers, gospel-of-success frauds, or television-evangelist charlatans who spout blatant untruths such as "If you are walking with Jesus, your bills will be paid, your marriage will be flawless, your children will be healthy, and you will not suffer from depression." This "I experience no pain because I'm happy in Jesus" mind-set results in suppressing agony, fear, and doubt, which leads to debilitating stress, damaging ulcers, and crippling guilt. Understand me: I am not encouraging a pity party. I am not throwing the pursuit of happiness to the wind. I am encouraging you to be real with God and with one another. I do know that lament is a deep ache in our hearts to remind us of our need for Jesus. Every sorrow and tear reminds me this world is not my destination; rather, I am journeying to a greater land where the sting and pain of *all* tears, *all* sorrows, and *all* heartache have been absorbed and absolved in Jesus Christ my Lord, Savior, Redeemer, Justifier, Adopter, and King.

If you are one of the many believers struggling with depression and/or mental health challenges, am I encouraging you to accept this as your lot in life? That's a difficult question. I don't believe God wants us to spend our lives in the emotional valley of depression. I believe God does want us to fully function as children of the King. I also believe there are unique lessons that can only be learned in the deep, darkened valleys of life. Ask Jesus to reveal Himself to you in fresh ways. Ask that you not be allowed to miss the lessons He is teaching you. *O Lord, while I long to come out of the valley of depression, do not allow me to step foot on emotionally level ground before understanding the teaching You are graciously presenting to me.*

It is well documented that the great hymn writer William Cowper struggled with depression and suicidal thoughts throughout his life. Cowper was best friends with John Newton, the theologian and pastor who wrote the hymn "Amazing Grace."

Cowper tried to take his life on multiple occasions. And yet, this man, who struggled so deeply with depression, penned some of the most powerful hymns we have ever known.

> God moves in a mysterious way
> His wonders to perform;
> He plants His footsteps in the sea,
> And rides upon the storm.
> —"God Moves in a Mysterious Way"

Newton was there throughout Cowper's life, loving him, counseling him, pastoring him, even giving up his vacation to stay with him. Of Newton, Cowper said, "A sincerer or more affectionate friend no man ever had."

In the midst of fighting demons, Cowper wrote what has become one of my favorite hymns, "There Is a Fountain Filled with Blood." Through depression, through the darkness, these words of truth and light poured forth. It is a great reminder that, through it all, God is there.

> There is a fountain filled with blood drawn from
> Emmanuel's veins;
> And sinners plunged beneath that flood lose all
> their guilty stains.

The Importance of Story

One of the most powerful counseling tools is allowing people a forum in which they can openly share their stories. What is important to them personally? What are the values that drive their actions? To draw out someone's story, first encourage him to tell his story in great detail, then learn to listen to the story (and tell your own story) progressively. Stories can be progressively shared as trust is established.

After someone has told his story, I often ask, "What represents your journey, your pain, your hurt, and God's salvation? Is there a particular song that speaks deeply to your heart?" When we have come through dark tunnels, we need to find a symbol to represent our pain and subsequent redemption. I encourage people who have a story involving both trauma and redemption to find a symbol to represent their journey, purchase it (or make it), and place it in a prominent place in their living quarters. It may be the words to a song or a poem they have framed. It may be a painting or a sculpture. In our home, there is a crystal cross on a shelf. While most would never notice the cross, to Sally and me, that cross is a powerful symbol of God's redemption during a particularly difficult time in our ministry together. Seeing the cross reminds us of the Lord's provision, kindness, mercy, and grace.

Pastors Need Pastoring, and Counselors Need Counseling

Like you, I have endured some difficult years of life. And like you, as I process the events of my life, one reality has continued to churn in the deep recesses of my heart—I need counseling!

Really. I need someone skilled in counseling to assist me in processing the events of my life, to help me make sense of the darkness I feel descending on me. The death of my parents, the death of family members, and the death of relationships have driven me to a place where I know I need outside assistance to understand my ever-fluctuating emotions. After the passing of my father, I engaged in a "counseling intensive" with my therapist, an exceptionally skilled believer, who helped me make sense of the deep pain I was experiencing. It was emotionally exhausting, yet incredibly helpful.

There are times when I need a safe place to go to process bewilderment, disappointment, and hurt. While I do a great deal of pastoral counseling, there are many occasions when *I* need a counselor. I need a friend and encourager who provides a safe place to share my feelings, unburden my heart, and process the events of my life. I need an outside voice to speak into my life providing encouragement, focus, guidance, and perspective. I need a safe place to go where I am allowed to share my story without criticism or condemnation. My counselor's office is that protected sanctuary where I can honestly release my doubts, questions, and confusion. Every counselor needs a counselor.

I'm certainly not advocating for pastors to enter into weekly or even monthly counseling appointments for the remainder of their lives (although for some that's not a bad idea). I am advocating for (1) pastors to acknowledge the value of gospel-centered counseling; (2) pastors to acknowledge the personal need for a counseling relationship; and (3) pastors to muster the courage to enter into a counseling relationship. While a coaching relationship is centered on regular interaction, the counseling relationship is an "as needed" relationship.

Doctors need medical care. Lawyers need legal advice. Counselors need counseling. Pastors need pastoring.

A favorite slogan of the legal profession is that a lawyer who defends himself in court has a fool for a client. In much the same way, a pastor who attempts to go it alone, refusing counseling, coaching, mentoring, and pastoring, is an isolated, drifting individual. This was never God's plan for His children.

Perspective

Sometimes in life, we need a little perspective. There are days when we desperately need to see life from a different vantage point. In the midst of these deep, dark fractures of life, we cry out to God for help, relief, and illumination. In the darkest night, I am *not* crying out to God to reveal a bright radiance that will miraculously reveal an opening near the top of the wall that triggers the immediate release from captivity. No, I am crying out to God, asking for a faint light to shine on the next step. Sometimes, the next step is everything. Sometimes, I get things so twisted, so wrong and ridiculously out of perspective that I lose sight of the next step. Sometimes—okay, all the time—I need a little perspective.

If you have read this far, you know I am a passionate Kansas basketball fan. This means I have occasionally celebrated and occasionally felt devastated by an untimely loss. It also means that as a Kansas basketball fan, I have times when I desperately need perspective. Lest you think I have lost my mind by using a game to illustrate the need for perspective, read on.

In the 2010 NCAA tournament, the Kansas University basketball team suffered a devastating loss to Northern Iowa. Kansas, who had been picked by many basketball experts to win the NCAA championship, crumbled in their loss to an athletically inferior team. For Northern Iowa, it was the greatest victory in school history. That said, does it make me less of a Kansas basketball fan that I wasn't devastated by KU's loss to Northern Iowa?

Don't get me wrong; I was bummed. I was frustrated, discouraged, and in a basketball state of shock (if such a thing exists). The loss to Northern Iowa was without question the most disheartening loss in the history of Kansas basketball, surpassing even the 1997 Arizona debacle in Birmingham, for which I was present. My schedule from November through March includes watching most of the Jayhawks' games. I am privileged to attend a number of games each year in Allen Fieldhouse, the greatest home court in college basketball. I regularly take out-of-town guests to Kansas games. Our pregame rituals include stopping at the nearby cemetery to pay our respects at the grave of Dr. James Naismith, the inventor of the game of basketball and the first coach of the Jayhawks, and the museum contained within Allen Fieldhouse. Many would say that I bleed crimson and blue.

Following the loss to Northern Iowa, I experienced emotions ranging from anger to disbelief. How could a team stocked with multiple stars and future NBA millionaires led by one of the best coaches in basketball collapse when playing before a friendly crowd? But on that Saturday in March 2010, I wouldn't say that I was devastated. After all, Kansas basketball is not life and death.

Perspective.

Don't misunderstand my sentiments. I am not playing the sour-grapes card. It's just that on that Saturday I was afforded a little perspective by which to judge the Kansas loss.

Perspective is a funny thing. We think we are having a bad day when we spill our first cup of coffee on our pants, until we learn that a coworker was released with little to no severance. Stopped for speeding on the way to the office, we convince ourselves that our day could not go worse, until we catch wind that Jill in accounting was diagnosed with stage-three breast cancer. Perspective allows us to measure what is truly important in life.

I have been regularly traveling to Haiti since the late '90s, making an average of three to four trips a year. I have worked with orphans, the elderly, pastors, business leaders—Haitians from every walk of life. I have had the privilege of supporting projects to build schools, orphanages, affordable housing, and medical clinics.

I received a massive dose of perspective on Tuesday, January 12, 2010, as I disembarked from a flight that had just landed in Kansas City. As I stood in the aisle of the plane waiting to deplane, head for my car, and be home in time for a late supper, my phone began to blow up with messages regarding an earthquake in Haiti. I quickly learned that a catastrophic magnitude 7.3 earthquake had struck with an epicenter near Léogâne, a city where I had been on multiple occasions. The next two weeks were spent coordinating the transportation of both people and supplies to assist in the aftermath of the tragedy. While I longed to fly to Haiti to be with my friends, I knew that I was playing a strategic role in the coordination of relief efforts.

I received a second dose of much-needed perspective on January 30 as the Kansas basketball team prepared to play Kansas State. I was eagerly anticipating the start of the game when I received an email from a Haitian pastor informing me that four hundred pastors who were distributing food throughout Haiti, in the aftermath of the earthquake, were literally starving. They were so concerned with feeding the masses that they were neglecting to feed themselves. The email, which arrived just moments before the game's tip-off, literally begged me for assistance. Suddenly, KU beating K-State wasn't my number one priority.

Perspective.

As committed as I am to watching Kansas basketball, I missed the loss to Northern Iowa. In fact, I didn't watch a second of the game.

Like you, I am a pastor, which means that there are times when people call and you go no matter what is presently holding your attention. Knowing this, I have a number of friends who love to call me during Kansas games to ask for help with a flat tire, assistance with their marriage, or any number of a thousand crises that demand my immediate attention. "Pastor, my car broke down and I'm stranded on the side of the road. It's dark, I'm scared, and I can't find anyone to give me a ride home. Can you pick me up?" My pastoral response? "Sure, find a ditch to hide in and I'll see you in about three hours."

On March 20, 2010, while Kansas was losing to Northern Iowa, I wasn't watching the game because I was leading a funeral service. As a pastor, I have presided over countless funerals. But that Saturday was the first time in my many years of pastoral ministry to lead a funeral for more than one person. A mass funeral brings tragedies to mind like an entire family losing their lives in a car accident or a husband and wife perishing in a plane crash. I never dreamed that my first mass funeral would be for eleven people. Standing atop rubble that was once the walls of a church, beneath blue tarps blowing in the breeze, I was leading a funeral service in Haiti for eleven people who had lost their lives in the January 12 earthquake. Nine of the eleven bodies had yet to be recovered. But it was time to bring this incredibly painful chapter to a close. My dear Haitian friend Pastor Moise Vaval asked me to conduct the funeral service. He had conducted funeral upon funeral for the previous two months. Moise and his lovely wife Francoise lost their oldest son in the earthquake when his school collapsed. Moise simply could not do another funeral. The emotions were rubbed raw, and he needed support.

The emotions of that day are indescribable and unforgettable. It was a poignant, grief-filled experience that will be forever etched on my heart and mind. The loss of life was overwhelmingly devastating to families, loved ones of the eleven, and to me.

Perspective. Life and death in Haiti.

Renise was a thirteen-year-old Haitian child whose life was literally saved by the earthquake. In 2008, at the tender age of eleven, Renise was sold into slavery, a legal and common practice in Haiti. As a child slave, known as a "restavek," Renise served her family from sunup to sundown. She was, in her words, "treated like a donkey." She slept on the floor while the family slept on beds. She was dehumanized as an insignificant child slave.

When Renise was twelve years old, she went to gather water, one of her daily rituals. There is no running water in the vast majority of Haitian homes. Most Haitians walk to the closest well (sometimes miles), fill a five-gallon bucket, and return home with water for cooking, cleaning, and bathing. Many Haitians have no access to clean water, which leads them to nearby streams to fill their buckets with contaminated water.

On this particular day, while Renise was walking to gather water, she was raped. She became pregnant, a fact she was able to hide from her "owners" until she was five months pregnant. When her family learned that she was expecting a child, they threw her out into the street, telling her that they could not live with the shame of a pregnant slave.

Now thirteen years old, pregnant, and on the streets of Port-au-Prince, Haiti, Renise was alone and starving, with no money, no family, and no hope. The date was January 9, 2010. For three days she lived with nothing, preparing for the inevitable —to die alone. Then, on January 12, the 7.3-magnitude earthquake struck Haiti. Astonishingly, because of the large number of aid workers who poured into the country, Renise was found walking the streets, pregnant and starving. She was taken to a local shelter where she was fed. Ultimately, she found her way to an orphan village run by the Kansas City–based Global Orphan Project.

On that Saturday, as Kansas was losing to Northern Iowa, Renise underwent a C-section and delivered a healthy five-pound eight-ounce baby girl. On the same day, at the same moment as the mass funeral, a new life entered the world.

March 20, 2010. Eleven people who tragically died remembered; a new life for a newborn baby girl and a new beginning for a thirteen-year-old former slave. Oh, and a Kansas loss to Northern Iowa. Earthquakes are devastating. KU losses are hard.

Perspective. Counseling provides me perspective.

I returned to Kansas City on Monday morning and encountered a number of Jayhawk fans who informed me they were "literally devastated by the loss." Devastated? Hmm. I gently reminded them that Saturday in the NCAA tournament was a game. Saturday in Haiti was literally life and death.

Disturb Us, Lord

Writing about the need to takes risks in life, which inevitably leads to anguish, C. S. Lewis reminds us in *The Four Loves*:

> To love at all is to be vulnerable. Love anything, and your heart will certainly be wrung and possibly be broken. If you want to make sure of keeping it intact, you must give it to no one, not even an animal. Wrap it carefully round with hobbies and little luxuries; avoid all entanglements; lock it up safe in the casket or coffin of your selfishness. But in that casket—safe, dark, motionless, airless—it will change. It will not be broken; it will become unbreakable, impenetrable, irredeemable. To love is to be vulnerable.[3]

No pun intended, but the Sir Francis Drake poem "Disturb Us" honestly disturbs me. Written in 1577, the poem reminds me that angst, pain, and heartache are natural results of following close after the Lord Jesus. There will be times that I choose not to play it safe and the result is wider seas, storms, and losing the sight of land. If you have no need for a counselor, maybe you have spent your life hugging the shoreline, failing to venture into deep waters where certain heartache awaits.

Disturb us, Lord, when
We are too well pleased with ourselves,
When our dreams have come true
Because we have dreamed too little,
When we arrived safely
Because we sailed too close to the shore.

Disturb us, Lord, when
With the abundance of things we possess
We have lost our thirst
For the waters of life;
Having fallen in love with life,
We have ceased to dream of eternity
And in our efforts to build a new earth,
We have allowed our vision
Of the new Heaven to dim.

Disturb us, Lord, to dare more boldly,
To venture on wider seas
Where storms will show your mastery;
Where losing sight of land,
We shall find the stars.

We ask You to push back
The horizons of our hopes;
And to push into the future
In strength, courage, hope, and love.

Questions for Reflection

Reality—Who presently serves in the role of your counselor? How often do you connect with your counselor?

What are your burn wounds, your "Morgul-blade wounds," and your "don't go there" places that have only healed superficially? Why have you lied to yourself about not needing help to scrub these wounds?

Rewind and Review—How is it helpful to know there are more psalms of lament than psalms of praise? What does that tell you about real life, God, others, and yourself?

Why is there such a gap between the raw emotional vomiting in the Psalms and our unhealthy, superficial handling of negative emotion? Why are these expressions so frequently on the lips of leaders in the Bible?

Reflect—Story is one of the most powerful tools the Lord has given. Take time to share your story with someone this week. Take the initiative to ask someone his story. Practice the listening tools discussed in the coaching chapter as you listen.

What are the laments in your life that cry out for a counselor? Where do you need perspective? Where do you need insight beyond your own? Where do you need someone in this storm alongside you? Where do you need help with wounds that haven't truly healed? Where do you need help to walk in gospel risk instead of self-saving behind a religious veneer?

Remember—What wounds have you suffered in life that you believe are so deep they were never meant to heal in this lifetime? How does the hope of heaven bring you comfort?

Psalm 147:3 says, "He heals the brokenhearted and binds up their wounds." How does this passage encourage you today? Jimmy said that only Jesus saves the crushed, only Jesus allows us to honestly confront our deepest sin, and only Jesus grants us the freedom to confront our doubts. If you believe these statements, how do they bring cheer to your heart?

Respond—What steps do you need to take to find a gospel-oriented, wise, safe, professional counselor?

Chapter 11

Mentor: The View from Above at the Labyrinth of Life

After the demise of a particularly well-known American church and the downfall of its equally well-known pastor, scholar and theologian Scot McKnight, the widely recognized authority on the New Testament, early Christianity, and the historical Jesus, made an insightful comment to *Leadership* magazine when reflecting on lessons to be learned from the pastor's failure. McKnight said, "Every young pastor needs to have a mentor relationship with a pastor who has been pastoring for at least twenty-five years in a church that is not a megachurch."

Personally, I know this to be true because I need mentors—a stable of mentors.

In case you have forgotten (I haven't), the unforgettable words from Pastor Kent Hughes at our lunch on September 13, 1982, were "I want you to know that you have a Messiah complex." I still have a tendency to take on a Messiah complex. I need to be continually reminded that I am not the rescuer, I am not the savior, and I am not the repairer of broken lives (I'm pretty sure that's Jesus). I still need to wake up every day and repeat the powerful words of John the Baptist: "I am not the Christ" (John 1:20). And when I forget this truth, I need a mentor to remind me.

I traveled to Grass Valley, California, to meet with Glenn, a wise leader who had been recommended to me by a trusted friend. I felt like I was going into my rescuer mode and I believed he would have a much-needed word of wisdom. His words to me that day proved to be life changing.

After hearing of my struggle to slow down and take the necessary time to pour into my marriage and family, Glenn took me to John chapter 5. He then led me through a discussion of the importance of seeking and following the leading of the Holy Spirit. And although the Holy Spirit is not mentioned in this passage, the Holy Spirit is all over it. John 5:3–9 presents Jesus coming to the pools at Bethesda, an infirmary to thousands of desperate, needy people looking for a miracle. John tells us:

> In these lay a multitude of invalids—blind, lame, and paralyzed. One man was there who had been an invalid for thirty-eight years. When Jesus saw him lying there and knew that he had already been there a long time, he said to him, "Do you want to be healed?" The sick man answered him, "Sir, I have no one to put me into the pool when the water is stirred up, and while I am going another steps down before me." Jesus said to him, "Get up, take up your bed, and walk." And at once the man was healed, and he took up his bed and walked.

From what we understand from John's account, Jesus went to Bethesda, where there were a multitude of extreme needs. We can only speculate as to the size of the crowd that "multitude" describes, but it was likely several thousand. This was not someone suffering in a private room at a nearby hospital. This was open, exposed, unprotected, painful human suffering. John tells us that Jesus entered into this sea of human need and proceeded to heal one person. One person. The obvious question is, why not heal more? Jesus had the divine power to heal everybody—but He chose to heal only one. No doubt on the way to the one man, Jesus stepped over and around a litany of disabled suffering people. And while it is speculation, I think it's a fair guess that there were thousands begging Him for His healing touch on His way out. They had just seen the Lord Jesus heal. Surely they should be the next in line for a divine touch from the Great Physician.

Here's the compelling question that gave me pause (and continues to cause me to stop and reflect). Later that day, did Jesus feel guilt and remorse for healing only the one man? Did Jesus slap His forehead and say, "What was I thinking! I just remembered! I'm God. I could have healed everyone. Why didn't I hang out for at least another ten minutes and heal a couple of additional people? Wow, I really regret my actions!"? Did Jesus ever think, say, or imply anything close to that? Of course not! Jesus's actions were not driven by opportunity or need. His actions were not dictated by the expectations of others. Jesus was guided solely by the prompting of the Holy Spirit. While we may struggle with regret, Jesus did not.

That hit me hard. All too often, I feel the need to work just a little harder to serve a few more pastors. Why? Okay, maybe it's a Messiah complex. Maybe it's an unquenchable longing to be indispensable to others. I need to be needed. I want to be wanted. I desire to be ... you get it. Perhaps it's me looking to find my affirmation in the words of others rather than the promise of Jesus. Think of it this way: If Jesus was content doing His Father's will and then calling it a day, and I cannot call it a day as I feel the compulsion to make that one last phone call, I have a problem! The Son of God could walk away from a need that He could obviously meet, and I cannot! Who in the heck do I think I am? Really!

Needs and opportunities confront pastors every day. And pastors are called to follow the leading of the Holy Spirit every day. Faced with an overwhelming to-do list, countless phone calls to be returned, long lines of people seeking a meeting with us, pastors need to look to the Holy Spirit to determine which appointment, which call, which task should take priority. This would mean that they would be following the leading of the Holy Spirit rather than allowing their schedule to be dictated by church members.

Pastors are so driven by the expectations of others that they go to the hospital instead of their child's Little League game. Because of expectations, pastors attend another church board meeting rather than going to the local bar to meet with the man struggling with his marriage. Even though they may be living a life controlled by the Lord, when pastors cease to fulfill the expectations of the church, they commonly get fired. Jesus was not driven by opportunity or need. Jesus was wholly directed by the prompting of the Holy Spirit. What would the church look like if pastors committed their daily schedule in prayer, asking for the schedule to be determined by the leading of the Holy Spirit—not by the expectations of their congregation? Knowing the Holy Spirit was my daily guide, what would it look like for a prayer life of discipline to become a prayer life of desperation? What would it look like to have a moment-by-moment connection that allows me to ask the Holy Spirit what I should do—and then do it?

Glenn hit me with all of that during our conversation in Grass Valley. And I needed everything he said.

Profile of a Mentor

A mentor is a teacher, a trainer, a sage, and a friend all rolled into one vital relationship. The word *mentor* originated in Homer's *Odyssey*, inspired by the character Mentor. The goddess Athena takes on the appearance of Mentor in order to guide young Telemachus through life's many challenges. So, too, a mentor is one who guides a person through life's many challenges. Mentoring is most often a lifetime relationship when two friends' lives intersect and become entangled over a long period of time. However, mentoring can also be a short-term, task-driven relationship. Or both. I believe every pastor needs multiple mentors—lifetime mentors who walk with him or her through life, and a team of short-term mentors committed to specific tasks.

I think it is wise for every pastor to have a preaching mentor (if you have no idea what a preaching mentor looks like, I encourage you to contact the Charles Simeon Trust). During a particularly hard season in your relationship with your spouse, you might have a marriage mentor. In processing a painful disagreement, you could use a conflict mentor. If you want to join the board of directors of a business, you may be asked to be mentored for one year by an outgoing board member. During the process of writing this book, I've had some people take on the role of literary mentors. Ideally, a pastor will have a number of mentors speaking into his or her life.

While it is important to select a capable, qualified mentor, the key to mentoring is actually the humility of the one being mentored. There are no fewer than a dozen words used to describe the recipient of the mentoring. You may be a mentee (not to be confused with manatee), an apprentice, an intern, or all three. You may be described as a trainee, a learner, a student, a pupil, or an understudy. You may be a follower, a disciple, or a protégé (if you are male) or protégée (if you are female). Each implies humility, a willingness to be directed, and the heart of a learner.

A mentor has the time to pour a portion of his or her life into another. The mentor is a mature follower of Jesus who is seeking to follow the Lord in every aspect of life. The mentor should be wise, gentle, caring, direct, and winsome. Any good mentor knows that the best relationships are peer to peer, each learning from the other. A mentor does not hide his failures or weaknesses. First Thessalonians 2:8 reads,

> So, being affectionately desirous of you, we were ready to share with you not only the gospel of God but also our own selves, because you had become very dear to us.

As the passage tells us, a key aspect of mentoring is the mentor and protégé both allowing the other into the back stage of his or her life. If mentoring is a series of presenting front stage perceptions while hiding back stage reality, the relationship will be essentially fruitless. A mentor will use his or her strengths, emotions, wisdom, resources, intellect, and life experience to help a protégé reach maximum potential as a follower of Jesus. By bringing real-life experience into the relationship, mentors help protégés avoid costly mistakes. Mentoring does not take place in a formal classroom but rather in the classrooms of everyday life such as the kitchen, the church office, the athletic field, and the local pub.

Whereas a coach has regular, consistent contact with his student, a mentor serves in more of an on-call capacity. Personally, I can go for long stretches without contacting certain mentors, but when I confront a challenge, an opportunity, a decision, or a crisis, I'm on the phone. One key word that describes a mentor is *availability*.

I encourage you to pray, investigate, and look for the best mentor who could effectively speak into your life. Aim high, and yet discuss expectations. If there is a leader you would like to learn from, ask him. I have had the incredible privilege to be mentored by some great Christian leaders. Some were short-term mentoring relationships while others have continued for my adult life. For the most part, they agreed to mentor me simply because I asked. I will forever be grateful for the impact long-term mentors George Wood, Dick Gorham, Kent Hughes, Jerry Root, Paul Borthwick, Corb Heimburger, Roger Sandberg, and many others have had on my life.

My Greatest Mentor

I chose to attend Wheaton College for a number of reasons. One, my brother had attended Wheaton and I fell in love with the college when I was in junior high. Two, my best friend, Bruce, was going to attend Wheaton, and we were determined to stick together. And, three, Wheaton was the home of the man I considered to be the greatest teacher in the world, Dr. Merrill C. Tenney, professor of New Testament.

Dr. Tenney was seventy-five years old when I arrived on the Wheaton campus in the fall of 1979. After I moved into the freshman dorm, I made my way to Dr. Tenney's office to ask about taking his graduate-level class on the Pastoral Epistles. During that initial meeting, I informed him that he was one of the primary reasons I had decided to attend Wheaton, and therefore, I asked if he would disciple me during my Wheaton years. To each of my questions, Dr. Tenney said … no!

"Mr. Dodd," he said (he would forever call me Mr. Dodd), "I am teaching a graduate-level class. This course is for upper-level seniors and grad-school students, not for freshmen who have yet to take courses as basic as New Testament introduction. Second, I need to spend my time with my students, not freshmen who will not be in any of the classes I teach. Good day, Mr. Dodd."

I left dejected but far from defeated.

While this story makes me look brash, arrogant, bullheaded, and bombastic, I'll tell it exactly how it happened. The first Monday of Dr. Tenney's Pastoral Epistles class (a Monday, Wednesday, Friday class), I sat on the front row. Though I was not enrolled in the class, I entered with the grad students and did everything in my power to look the part. It probably helped that I was 6'3" with a deep voice. With utter disgust, Dr. Tenney noticed me as he walked in the door. He ignored me throughout the class. I feverishly took notes, nodded at everything he said, and didn't make a sound. A mentee knows when to listen—and I knew that this was not my time to talk. After class, I approached him and again asked him to please admit me to the class. He was a bit agitated. He firmly told me to leave and not to come back. Again, dejected but not defeated!

On Wednesday, I was back on the front row, taking notes like a stenographer and nodding like a bobblehead. Again, after class, he *asked* me not to return. He had previously *told* me; so I sensed he was softening.

Friday morning, front row. At this point I knew he would either call campus security or agree to my request. Every teacher loves a student eager and willing to do anything to learn. And every mentor loves a protégé who has an open heart, ready to learn. Dr. Tenney could see that I was eager, willing, passionate, and dead serious about learning all I could from this master teacher. After class, he asked me to stay back so he could speak with me.

"Mr. Dodd, I have never in all my life seen anyone as persistent as you. While I may regret this, I'll allow you to take my class. And yes, we can begin to meet every week. But know this … you had better not fail this class!"

I didn't fail the class. Over my years at Wheaton, I took everything I could from Dr. Tenney. I consider his courses in Galatians, Bible Study Methods, and the Pastorals to be three of the most defining classes of my life. But they paled in comparison to the wisdom Dr. Tenney poured into me each week in his tiny Wheaton College office. We became close friends. I sought his wisdom many times over during those years. And he never once, *not once*, referred to me as Jimmy. I was honored to be known as Mr. Dodd. I will always think of Dr. Tenney as my friend, my teacher, my professor, and my mentor.

Dr. Tenney went home to be with Jesus on March 18, 1985, just three months before my wife and I would leave for Gordon-Conwell Seminary. Near the end of his life, he struggled to swallow water, so his doctor ordered him to get his necessary liquids from Cortland apples, the juiciest of apples. I went with my wife, Sally (we had married in 1983), to see Dr. Tenney during his last week on this earth. We took him a bag of Cortland apples. He was lying in his bed, barely able to speak. As we walked into the room, his eyes brightened, and he greeted me with the ever-familiar "Well, Mr. Dodd." To this day, whenever I am in a grocery store or market and I see a Cortland apple, I think of my mentor.

The Perspective of a Mentor

While statistics can vary, one consistent outcome of nearly every pastoral survey is that approximately four out of five pastors do not have a mentor. They do not have a spiritual leader to turn to in times of decision, challenge, or crisis. While many claim to have had a mentor at one time, most have lost touch over the years. Furthermore, the vast majority of pastors have not encouraged their congregations to seek out mentors. Again, four out of five pastors said there was no regular discipleship or mentoring program at their church. Yet God has given us the concept of a mentor! Mentors provide counsel, wisdom, and encouragement. And in dark times, mentors provide much-needed perspective. Sometimes, when we are in the midst of a battle, they provide a "high-altitude perspective."

On June 6, 1944, American, British, and Canadian forces numbering 156,000 landed on five beaches along a fifty-mile stretch of the heavily fortified coast of France's Normandy region. This was the beginning of the Battle of Normandy, which lasted until August 1944 and resulted in the Allies liberating western Europe from Nazi Germany's control. For all practical purposes, the Allied offensive, also known as D-Day, won World War II. While there were still battles to be fought throughout the next year, the victory was won on D-Day.

It's interesting to study D-Day from the viewpoint of those who participated in the battle. There were two distinct perspectives. For the most part, soldiers on the beach felt the Allied forces were going to lose the battle. However, the soldiers in the air saw the bigger picture, and from their perspective, they believed the Allied forces were going to win. Sometimes, when we are in the midst of a battle, we need a little perspective. We need a "high-altitude mentor" to tell us we are on the right path and what we perceive as impending disaster is actually sure victory. A mentor is an objective observer who provides perspective, encouragement, hope, and wisdom as we navigate through life.

Earlier I mentioned that a mentor could be a short-term, focused relationship. Recently, a pastor reached out to PastorServe asking for help in finding a mentor to walk him through his wife's impending death from cancer. We were able to find a number of pastors who had lost wives to cancer. Several of these pastors became mentors to this pastor, walking with him through one of the deepest valleys of his life, a valley each man had personally endured.

When all seems lost, a mentor can help a pastor to stay in touch with reality. At times, drinking deeply from a vision may cause pastors to suffer a certain loss of perspective and, subsequently, make inappropriate decisions. A mentor keeps a pastor sober without quenching the spirit.

A mentor brings a biblical worldview to the relationship. It's how we make sense of our life in this world. It's the framework through which we view all of life. What do you understand about the reality around you? Why are you on this earth? Is it to love and serve God and His bride, the local church? Is your purpose to seek pleasure and satisfaction at any cost? Your answer defines your worldview. A mentor understands that life is hard, leadership can be lonely, and you need to regularly drink deeply from the gospel. A mentor helps us to remember our bigger purpose in the grand scheme of things. In many ways, a mentor is a cheerleader. Pastors are pioneers, doing front-line ministry that is potentially harmful to their physical, emotional, and mental health. They need someone behind them cheering them on.

A Wise Word from a Mentor to Mentors and a Pastor to Pastors

John Stott is one of the most influential evangelical figures of the last century. Declining the invitation to become an Anglican bishop, Stott chose to pour his life into young evangelical leaders; he wrote more than fifty books, including his classics *Basic Christianity*, *The Cross of Christ*, and *Christian Mission in the Modern World*. Stott emphasized both the ministry of the Word and the ministry of deed.

As I have mentioned, one of the benefits of serving on the staff of the College Church in Wheaton was the evangelical giants who regularly passed through, filling our pulpit. It was not unusual to have J. I. Packer, James Boice, R. C. Sproul, Ralph Winter, and John Stott preach in the same calendar year.

One weekend, Stott was the guest preacher. He taught with a clarity I have heard very few times in my life. On Monday morning, Stott had a speaking engagement at Trinity Seminary, about two and a half hours from Wheaton in Chicago rush-hour traffic. Pastor Kent Hughes invited me to tag along and join him, Stott, Larry Fullerton, and Jerry Root on the trip to Trinity. I gladly agreed.

I will never forget those hours in the car with Stott. Kent, Larry, and Jerry were pumping him with questions about everything from theology to church growth. Stott's answers were both articulate and elegant (he spoke with a crisp British accent). I sat in the back seat feverishly taking notes on four-by-six cards, wanting to capture every pearl that fell from Stott's lips.

As we neared Trinity, Kent Hughes turned to me and said, "Well, Jimmy, you haven't said a word this entire trip. Is there a question you would like to ask Dr. Stott?"

Here it was. My big chance. After a brief hesitation, I said, "Dr. Stott, do you ever feel like just giving up on the Christian life? Do you ever want to just chuck the whole thing and find something else to give your life to?"

Shock and awe would best describe the faces of the Wheaton pastors in the car, although no one actually said, "Are you out of your mind?"

But Stott's answer literally changed my life. I have never forgotten the exact words he spoke to me that day: "Yes, Jimmy, I often feel like giving up on the Christian life. But when I feel this way, I always do the same thing. One, I catch up on my sleep. I find that when I catch up on my sleep, those feelings almost always dissipate. Two, I will do something fun to get away from the daily routine. After I rest and relax, I am ready to enter into another busy period of ministry."

How's that for a deep, theological answer! Get your sleep and have fun! Is that great, or what? Those words have burned in my heart for more than thirty years. It's words like these that a mentor can deliver. That weekend, Stott was a short-term mentor speaking to me in the area of boundaries, rest, and relaxation.

Jesus as Mentor

Without question, the greatest mentor in history was Jesus Christ. Mark 3:13–15 tells us Jesus chose twelve men to "be with him." He mentored by allowing His disciples to be with Him: they did life together side by side while Jesus modeled love, patience, friendship, generosity, and kindness. In my time of being mentored by Jerry Root, I lived with him, his wife, Claudia, and their young children. I saw Jerry in the good times and the hard times. He allowed me into the back stage of his life. I have tremendous respect for Jerry because of the fact that he allowed me to be with him. Find a mentor who will allow you into his or her life, both the front stage and the back stage, and you will have a revelatory experience.

Jesus was mentoring His disciples even when they weren't ready to accept His mentoring. When Jesus instructed Peter in what was coming, Peter felt the need to pull Him aside and rebuke Him (Matthew 16:22). Disciples don't always do everything the mentor recommends. Mentoring can be frustrating, even disheartening, when we see protégés go down paths we know will end in great difficulty. Find a mentor who is committed to your relationship, even when you fail to heed his advice.

Additionally, Jesus poured His life into His disciples so they would pour their lives into others. In 2 Timothy 2:2, Paul writes, "And what you have heard from me in the presence of many witnesses entrust to faithful men who will be able to teach others also." Jesus mentored men who would go on to mentor church fathers who would go on to mentor leaders who oversaw the spread of Christianity around the known world. Mentors don't see their protégés as buckets, but rather as conduits to mentor and teach other believers.

Finally, Jesus mentored His disciples through the most painful times. When the pressure is on, the potential and opportunity for learning escalate. In the Garden of Gethsemane, Jesus mentored His disciples. He taught on prayer, suffering, and perseverance, even in the midst of His darkest hour. Ultimately, Jesus is our great mentor. We can pastor, shepherd, and live in the greatest security with the greatest confidence awaiting the greatest hope. The hardest work of life has been accomplished—Jesus Christ upon the cross.

Questions for Reflection

Reality—Who are some of the mentors in your life right now? How often do you connect with them? How long have they known you? Why do you look up to them?

Who are you presently serving in the role of mentor?

Rewind and Review—Can you think of any biblical examples of people being mentors for others? What can you learn from their examples?

A mentor reminds us that the gracious love of Jesus is daily lavished on us. A mentor helps us to remember our bigger purpose in the grand scheme of things. In many ways, a mentor is a cheerleader. Which of these do you need most in your life right now? Why?

Is it hard for you to walk away from needs when you see them? What compels you to help others? If you are honest with yourself, to what degree does your serving others come from God's prompting versus your own need to be needed?

On a given day, are you driven more by your schedule or by the Holy Spirit? What would it look like to be led more by the Holy Spirit in your ministry? What might be some positive results? What would you need to do on a daily basis to be more open to the Holy Spirit's leadership in your life as a pastor?

What kinds of things do you tend to regret at the end of a long day of ministry? How do you deal with that regret?

Reflect—Jimmy mentioned several areas of your life that could use mentoring: preaching, marriage, conflict, writing, and so forth. Where could you use a mentor in your life right now? Why there?

Why does it feel so good to be needed? What are the dangers of a pastor who gets too much fulfillment from meeting the needs of others?

Remember—Jimmy wrote, "Ultimately, Jesus is our great mentor. We can pastor, shepherd, and live in the greatest security with the greatest confidence awaiting the greatest hope. The hardest work of life has been accomplished—Jesus Christ upon the cross." How does this truth give you hope?

Respond—Considering the advice of John Stott, which do you need most right now, a full night of sleep or a fun day with friends and family?

Is there someone who is currently not your mentor but you wish was? Why do you want that person to mentor you? What keeps you from asking him or her to mentor you? What would you need to do to pursue that person as a mentor?

Whom do you believe the Lord is calling you to mentor? Who could benefit from your wisdom, experience, and friendship?

Chapter 12

Every Pastor Needs a Friend

It's impossible to overstate the power of friendship. It's also difficult to overemphasize the importance of confession.

I was contacted by a good friend who emphasized the need to immediately connect. I told him I would have the time for an uninterrupted phone conversation the following week.

"You don't understand," he said. "I need to meet with you face to face, today."

A meeting that quickly would be nearly impossible, I told him, as I was flying to Denver early the next morning. He wasn't giving up that easily.

"Could we have breakfast tomorrow morning in Denver right by the airport? I can meet you any time that would be convenient for you."

I admired his persistence, and we agreed to meet the following morning. Rusty flew from his home in Seattle to Denver for one simple reason. Confession. The power of the conversation that morning significantly impacted my life.

When I walked into the restaurant, Rusty was already on his third cup of coffee. Shoulders slumped, head bowed, and eyes tired, he looked as if he was carrying the weight of the world. "Jimmy, I've been carrying secrets for my entire life, and I'm at a point where I can no longer bear their crushing weight. I desperately need to share my secrets with a friend."

His initial confession came slowly through a flood of tears. He explained that during his sophomore year of high school, he was one of the top two or three players on the school golf team. Chuck was a well-liked senior, the best player on the team, and the team's undisputed leader; he'd been playing golf since the age of five and had diligently worked to achieve his elevated level of golf proficiency. More than anything, Chuck wanted to win the city championship, which would be a natural step before moving on to play major college golf. During the city tournament, Rusty cheated, robbing Chuck of the championship he had rightly earned.

"Chuck was by far the best player on the course that day. He had worked so hard to be the city champion, and I stole that from him. For no real reason I cheated on my scorecard and robbed him of what would have been his athletic crowning achievement." Rusty went on to share story after story, each a secret that he had carried for many years, in some cases decades. We talked about the need to make things right. In the case of Chuck, it would mean tracking him down and personally apologizing for stealing a golf championship.

As we talked, I noticed that Rusty's eyes began to slowly brighten. His slumped shoulders began to gradually straighten. It was almost as if I was watching Christian reach the cross of Calvary and release his burden, as told in *The Pilgrim's Progress* by John Bunyan.

> Now I saw in my dream, that the highway up
> which Christian was to go, was fenced on either

side with a wall, and that wall was called Salvation
[Isaiah 26:1]. Up this way, therefore, did burdened
Christian run, but not without great difficulty,
because of the load on his back. He ran thus till
he came at a place somewhat ascending; and upon
that place stood a cross, and a little below, in the
bottom, a sepulchre. So I saw in my dream, that
just as Christian came up with the cross, his burden
loosed from off his shoulders, and fell from off his
back, and began to tumble, and so continued to do
till it came to the mouth of the sepulchre, where it
fell in, and I saw it no more.

Then was Christian glad and lightsome, and
said with a merry heart, "He hath given me rest by
his sorrow, and life by his death." Then he stood
still a while, to look and wonder; for it was very
surprising to him that the sight of the cross should
thus ease him of his burden. He looked, therefore, and looked again, even till the springs that
were in his head sent the waters down his cheeks
[Zechariah 12:10].

Rusty walked out of the restaurant a different man. While this
was only the first step in a long journey, it was the critical step that
demolished the shackles of secrecy and shame that had imprisoned
Rusty his entire life. That morning in Denver, he took bold steps
to narrow the gap between front stage perception and back stage
reality.

The Need for Friendship

Was I the only one who blubbered like a little girl during the 1995 Disney-Pixar classic *Toy Story* when the Randy Newman song "You've Got a Friend in Me" was first introduced? I can ask that question because I originally saw *Toy Story* with my then five-year-old daughter who asked me to "please cry more quietly because you're embarrassing me." The song has since become one of the classic friendship songs.

The power of friendship cannot be exaggerated. Who doesn't want to brave the storms of life alongside someone who promises to stick with you through rough roads, trouble, and life's challenges? Everyone needs a friend who commits to loving you forever.

God created people with an intrinsic need for friendship. We need one another to get through the labyrinth of life. Though never meant to take the place of everyday earthly friendship, the divine friendship we are offered in Jesus is the greatest gift ever given. Jesus affirms the value of friendship in John 15:13–15. Three times in this passage Jesus affirms that believers are His friends. The greatest extent to which anyone can go in order to demonstrate love is to sacrifice his or her life for a friend. Jesus shows the depth of His love for His friends by going to the cross.

The Johari Window

In addressing the fundamental need for friendship, PastorServe regularly uses the Johari Window. Developed by Joseph Luft and Harry

Ingham in the 1950s, the Johari Window revolves around information known by oneself and others.

JOHARI WINDOW

	WHAT I KNOW ABOUT ME	WHAT I DON'T KNOW ABOUT ME
WHAT YOU KNOW ABOUT ME	OPEN / PUBLIC	BLIND SPOT
WHAT YOU DON'T KNOW ABOUT ME	PRIVATE / SECRET	HIDDEN

Placed in a grid, the Johari Window reveals four areas: First, if the information is known to both of us, it is open, public information. Second, if the information is known only to me and not to you, it is private or in some cases a secret. Third, if information is known neither by you nor by me, it is unknown. Finally, information known by you but not by me is my blind spot. There are three areas of the window that are highlighted problem areas, each pointing to the critical need for friends.

The Power of Secrets

Secrets carry enormous power. Harboring secrets can destroy a life. In Rusty's case, by sharing his secrets with only one friend, a significant percentage of the crushing power was lifted. I have watched this story play out over and over again. By sharing secrets with just one person, a significant percentage of the power of guilt and shame is lifted. That is why we so desperately need to disclose our secrets to select trusted friends.

If you were around in the '50s and '60s, you remember the game show *I've Got a Secret*. Premiering in 1952, the show was a simple concept: a panel of celebrities would ask questions in an attempt to determine a contestant's "secret," something that was unusual, electrifying, or humorous. If it were only that easy!

It is necessary to make a distinction between private information and inappropriate secrets. There is a certain amount of information that appropriately remains private. I likely won't share my Social Security number with you. I won't disclose my bank account or Visa number to you (even though you tell me you need it in order to transfer an African fortune into my bank account). These are healthy secrets. On the opposite side, there are inappropriate secrets, such as those carried by Rusty. There are harmful secrets that twist our hearts and burden our souls. These are the secrets that cause us to stay awake at night for fear of being found out.

We encourage every pastor to have two or three friends with whom they have shared everything. Do you have a friend who knows *all* of your life history, including sexual history? When was the last time you had a conversation with a trusted friend that began with the words "I've never told anyone about this, but ..." Is there a risk in sharing everything? Of course! There are many stories of broken confidences and betrayal. And yet, the reward is worth the risk of disclosure. When the secret is shared, the shackles of secrecy are broken and the captive is free.

Blind Spots

At PastorServe, we regularly use the Johari Window to help pastors understand that everyone has blind spots—and we need friends in our lives to love us enough to reveal our blind spots.

I was blessed to lead a team of believers from an African American church to minister in Haiti. I consider the lead pastor of this church to be one of my closest friends. To give you a little background, I spend a significant amount of time with people who don't share my white skin color. I find that I know Jesus better in a multicultural environment. I love the fact that my own family is multicultural (Paige and Allie are Chinese). As a result, I feel comfortable around people who are from differing ethnic backgrounds—perhaps too comfortable.

As we traveled across Haiti in a bus, while joking with my pastor friend, I made several lighthearted comments (which, at the time, I personally thought were hilarious) about my love for Motown music (which I truly love). Later that night, my friend pulled me aside and lovingly, gently, said to me, "Jimmy, you know I love you. I know that you are very comfortable around African Americans. My church knows that you would do anything for us. But the people on this trip, they don't know you. I'm not sure why you can't see this, but for some reason you are missing that many of the people from my church think that your comments are being said to mock African Americans. They think that you are racist."

It was if someone had punched me right in the gut. I was speechless. The words stung deeply. And yet, my friend was right; I had missed this. I was blind to how my words were being interpreted by others. We all need select close friends who love us enough to point out our blind spots. I received the loving rebuke from my friend primarily because he was my friend. We all need people in our lives who are not impressed by us. We need friends with the courage to confront us (lovingly), calling us to a higher standard of following Jesus. We need Nathans in our lives.

Nathan and David

We know the story about David's moral failure with Bathsheba. A powerful king, David steals a married woman from one of his mighty men, Uriah the Hittite. In 2 Samuel 12:1–15, we are told that God responds to David's sin by sending the prophet Nathan to tell David a story about a rich man, a poor man, and the theft of a lamb. When initially confronted, David is furious. His response is over the top, far out of proportion with the crime. Lamb stealing was a crime but not a capital offense. David's conscience is coming alive. And then Nathan delivers the ultimate sermon application when he says to David, "You are the [guilty] man!" When David desperately needed to be confronted, God sent a friend.

Without Nathans in our lives, we are spiritually and emotionally stagnant, if not altogether dead. To be sure, not everyone has the right to declare himself or herself a Nathan. Nathans are brought into our lives by invitation only; they are not self-appointed. Every church has self-appointed Nathans. These are the people who feel as if they have a moral obligation to tell you everything that is wrong with your life. This is the man who corrects your children for running in the sanctuary after church and then informs you that God told him to enlighten you in the area of child rearing.

We need to deputize two or three of our closest friends to be our Nathans. Nathans are not sent to criticize and condemn, but to convert and care. Nathans love us enough to point out blind spots—the areas of sin that are killing us—and they love us enough to walk with us as we do the hard work of cutting out the cancerous sin.

There is a risk in being a Nathan. It's uncomfortable to approach a friend and say, "Are you aware that whenever your wife is around the staff, you tend to make jokes at her expense? She always laughs along with the crowd, but I can tell that it cuts her deeply." It's risky to pull a friend aside and tell him that what he thinks is nothing more than kindness to a waitress is taken by many as excessive flirting. David would have never seen the depth of his sin without his friend Nathan. We will never see the blind spots in our lives without friends who can speak with confidence that we will receive their words without getting too upset. I know pastors who have appointed men to be Nathans, but these friends wouldn't approach him for fear of being harshly reprimanded for telling the truth. Remember, "faithful are the wounds of a friend" (Proverbs 27:6).

The Power of Friendship

One of the most important gifts given to us by God to confront isolation is friendship. Friends are a vital part of an emotionally healthy life. Friendships nourish our souls as nothing else can. The Godhead is steeped in relationship. Friends are an earthly, visible reflection of the relationship between God the Father, God the Son, and God the Holy Spirit. We desperately need friends.

I find it intriguing that a trio of twentieth-century friends—
Jack, Ronald, and Chuck—created some of the greatest works of
literature of their time. Jack is better known as C. S. Lewis, Ronald is
known to the world as J. R. R. Tolkien, and Chuck is better known
as Charles Williams. The three were a part of a legendary gathering
of friends called the Inklings. All of the Inklings were British males
affiliated with Oxford University, most were veterans of World War
I (including both Lewis and Tolkien), all of them were creative writers and lovers of imaginative literature, and all were Christian. They
met on Thursday evenings in Lewis's and Tolkien's college rooms in
Oxford between 1933 and 1949 for readings and criticism of their
own work and general conversation. C. S. Lewis's brother Warren,
also a member of the Inklings, said the group "was neither a club nor
a literary society, though it partook of the nature of both. There were
no rules, officers, agendas, or formal elections."

Personally, I am an ardent admirer of Lewis, Tolkien, and
Williams. I first fell in love with the writings of Lewis as a young
child. Later I came to love Tolkien and Williams while studying
at Wheaton College, the home of the Marion E. Wade Center, a
research complex dedicated to the study of seven British writers,
four of whom were part of the Inklings. Wheaton College is also
the home to Jerry Root, one of the world's foremost authorities on
C. S. Lewis (and one of the men who discipled me during my time
at Wheaton). I learned more about the Inklings in the one year
I lived in Jerry's attic than I have throughout the rest of my life.
Maybe I became a bit obsessed. I asked my wife to marry me over a
two-day odyssey using The Chronicles of Narnia. But that's a story
for another time.

Some of PastorServe's most effective ministry tools are drawn from The Lord of the Rings trilogy, perhaps the greatest story of friendship ever told. If you want to see me in tears, read the section in The Lord of the Rings when, after the ring is destroyed at Mount Doom, Sam wakes up from his postadventure sleep, thankful to be alive. He turns to Gandalf and asks, "Is everything sad going to come untrue?" The question acknowledges that there is something very wrong with the world in which we live. We live in a world filled with pain, sadness, and darkness, all of which had just been experienced by Sam. Pastors live in a world cursed by sin. And our great hope, Tolkien reminds us, is that one day all will be made right in the light of Jesus. In Jesus, everything sad will come untrue.

The unexpected death of Charles Williams in 1945 had a profound impact on the friendship of Lewis and Tolkien. Contrary to much written about it, there is no evidence that Lewis was jealous of the special friendship shared between Williams and Tolkien. However, Lewis did assume that the passing of Williams would mean that he would get more of Tolkien; although, he found he came to know Tolkien less and less. Jerry Root first pointed me to C. S. Lewis's 1960 work *The Four Loves* in which he reflects on his friendship with Williams and Tolkien.

> Those who cannot conceive Friendship as a sub-
> stantive love but only as a disguise or elaboration
> of Eros betray the fact that they have never had a
> Friend. The rest of us know that though we can
> have erotic love and friendship for the same person
> yet in some ways nothing is less like a Friendship

than a love-affair. Lovers are always talking to
one another about their love; Friends hardly ever
about their Friendship. Lovers are normally face
to face, absorbed in each other; Friends, side by
side, absorbed in some common interest. Above all,
Eros (while it lasts) is necessarily between two only.
But two, far from being the necessary number for
Friendship, is not even the best. And the reason for
this is important....

In each of my friends there is something that
only some other friend can fully bring out. By
myself I am not large enough to call the whole man
into activity; I want other lights than my own to
show all his facets. Now that Charles is dead, I shall
never again see Ronald's [Tolkien's] reaction to a
specifically Caroline joke. Far from having more of
Ronald, having him "to myself" now that Charles
is away, I have less of Ronald.[1]

Lewis is making a profound point. We can only fully know one
another in the context of relational community. No one person can
draw out the entire personality of another. In a circle of friends, each
person shines a unique light onto the personality of another. It's not
possible to thrive as freestanding, isolated entities. And when we live
isolated lives, not allowing others to rub against our insecurities,
fears, and sins, we rob others of the opportunity to get to know us.

If that is true of a finite human being, how much more so of
God? We need a community to fully know the Lord. And the more

diverse the worshipping community—age, gender, and race—the better understanding you will have of God.

Later in *The Four Loves*, as we discovered in chapter 10, Lewis goes on to say,

> There is no safe investment. To love at all is to be vulnerable. Love anything, and your heart will certainly be wrung and possibly be broken. If you want to make sure of keeping it intact, you must give it to no one, not even an animal. Wrap it carefully round with hobbies and little luxuries; avoid all entanglements; lock it up safe in the casket or coffin of your selfishness. But in that casket— safe, dark, motionless, airless—it will change. It will not be broken; it will become unbreakable, impenetrable, irredeemable.[2]

Lewis is right when he states that there is no safe investment when it comes to friendship and love. There is always a risk. Why is it worth it to risk the possibility of untold pain? Because every pastor *needs* a friend.

Never Walk Alone

Rock Chalk Jayhawk … KU.

Many of America's sports authorities have called this the greatest cheer in college sports. I couldn't agree more. I passionately cheer for the Kansas Jayhawks. The "Rock Chalk" chant starts every basketball

game and rains down at the close of every home victory. I am regularly asked what "Rock Chalk" means, which leads me into a history
lesson about the limestone surrounding the KU campus and the KU
geology professor … But, again, I digress.

While I had long maintained that the "Rock Chalk" chant was
the greatest tradition in all of sports, I recently changed my mind.
It's the greatest in *college athletics*. But the greatest sports tradition
in the world is the singing of the song "You'll Never Walk Alone"
before the start of every Liverpool Football Club game at Anfield,
the historic soccer pitch (or field) located on the northeast side of
Liverpool, England.

You know the song. It has been recorded over a hundred times
by everyone from Elvis to Frank Sinatra to Pink Floyd to Johnny
Cash. Jerry Lewis closed his MDA telethon every year by singing the
song. "You'll Never Walk Alone" was written in 1945 by Rodgers and
Hammerstein for the musical *Carousel*—and for nearly twenty years,
the song was relatively unknown. When Gerry and the Peacemakers
recorded the song at Abbey Road Studios in Liverpool in 1963,
it soared to number one on the pop charts and was immediately
adopted by the Liverpool Football Club as the team anthem. Since
1963, the song has been sung by forty-five thousand Liverpool fans
before every home football game. The phrase "You'll Never Walk
Alone" was incorporated into the club crest and adorns the entrance
gate into Anfield.

The lyrics to the song are unspectacular. The song speaks to
walking through the storms of life. The wind and the rain of life will
toss you about, but you can walk on with hope in your heart, because
you'll never walk alone. Yet the message reaches deep into our hearts.

Life is hard. There are painful storms and agonizing rains that pound us. There are Black Riders waiting to inflict an incurable wound. But there is hope: there are others walking by your side. The message is one of hope, unity, courage, and above all, friendship.

Pastoring is lonely. Many pastors don't have friends with whom they can walk through the storms of ministry. And there is something deeper still. Why does this song strike such a profound chord? Because it reminds us of the good news of the gospel. Jesus Christ came to earth so we would never walk alone. Proverbs 18:24 reminds us that "there is a friend who sticks closer than a brother." Hebrews 13:5 promises us that Christ will never leave us. Indeed, we never walk alone.

Who Is in Your Car?

On September 5, 1989, a horrible car accident took place in the eastern United States. A car with several passengers was driving on a steep mountain highway when the driver lost control. The car careened off the road, over the sheer cliff, and plunged more than sixty feet into the gully below. While there were concussions, broken bones, and minor lacerations, remarkably, no one died. When I first heard the story on the news, I couldn't believe I had correctly heard the specifics. And once I learned the details, the story became that much more incredible.

The car was filled with fourteen passengers—eleven of them children. This was not a van or an SUV; this was a midsize car. The passengers had literally stuffed themselves into the car. This reminded me of my childhood when we would regularly shove, twist, and pack nine or ten into the back seat of my parents' Pontiac. When the drive-in movie theater charged per car and not per person, making yourself a human sardine was a small sacrifice.

When the car went off the cliff, though it spun in midair, by the grace of God the tires landed nearly flush. And although there was an incredible impact that caused serious injury, all fourteen survived. Medical personnel consulted with engineers to discuss the miracle, and together they concluded that because the car was full, the occupants literally acted as shock absorbers for one another. The impact of the crash was shared by all. Furthermore, they determined that if the car had eleven or fewer occupants, the odds were high that everyone would have been killed instantly.

The story caused me to consider who is in my car. Crashes are inevitable. Who are the faithful friends with me in my car? I can name a number of friends for whom I am immensely grateful. Woe to the one who crashes and finds that he is in his car alone. Commit to risking friendship. The benefits are eternal.

Questions for Reflection

Reality—Who was your best friend when you were growing up? What did you do together? What made him or her a good friend? Who are your closest friends right now? How often do you get to spend time with them?

As a pastor or church leader, would you say you tend more toward isolation or toward having many friends? What factors cause you to move toward isolation? What has helped you to take the risk of making friends?

Rewind and Review—We all have secrets. Some people keep those secrets hidden away for years. Why do you think it is so hard for people to share their deepest secrets with others? What is the cost to your soul when you do not share with someone the secrets that are burdening you?

Proverbs 27:6 says, "Faithful are the wounds of a friend; profuse are the kisses of an enemy." Can you remember a time when a friend pointed out one of your blind spots? How did you feel at the time? What long-term effect did this encounter have on your life?

Reflect—In what ways have you experienced Jesus as your friend in life? In what ways is it hard to experience Jesus as a friend?

C. S. Lewis learned that no one person can draw out the entire personality of another. Thinking of your closest friends, what aspects of your personality does each of them draw out?

When was the last time you felt Christ walking beside you through a hard time in your life? What was going on at that time? How did Christ make His presence known to you?

Remember—Can you think of a time when confessing a sin or sins to another person helped you feel set free from your burden? To what degree does your knowledge of the cross of Christ help you let go of the shame, burden, and guilt of your sins?

Hebrews 13:5 is just one of the many times we are promised that Christ will never leave us. Indeed, we never walk alone. What difference in your life does this truth make today?

Respond—Who are the faithful friends who are with you in your car? Take a moment and write down all of their names. Take time this week to text, email, or call them. Tell them how much you appreciate their friendship.

If your car is a little low on friends, what can you do to fill it up? Who are friends you know from earlier in life with whom you would like to reconnect? Who are people in your church you wish you were closer to? What other pastors or leaders are in your community whom you could pursue getting to know as friends?

Gospel Transformation

Taking the All-Important Next Steps

We are at the point where it is essential to talk about next steps. And any discussion of next steps always begins at the question of motivation. Why are you going to take next steps? What encouragement do you need to begin taking steps for the right reason in the right direction? And any discussion of motivation takes us back to the chains of religion and the freedom of the gospel.

It is only the gospel that can motivate us to deep life change and permanent inner transformation. External motivation, which is always centered in religion, cannot provide the long-term stimulus needed. Remember:

> Religion centers itself on behavior modification.
> The gospel brings deep, inner transformation.

> Religion says, "He who has the best front stage is the most spiritual."
> The gospel says, "He who is open about the back stage is the most real."

> Religion reforms people on the outside.
> The gospel transforms people on the inside.

Religion says, "I begrudgingly obey; therefore, I am accepted."

The gospel says, "I am accepted; therefore, I joyfully obey."

Religion needs a list to feel justified.

The gospel reminds us that we are justified because Jesus *is* the list.

Religion tells us that we are saved through obedience to Jesus.

The gospel declares that we are saved *by* the obedience *of* Jesus.

Religion says, "I obey in order to get things from God."

The gospel says, "I obey in order to delight in God."

Religion finds God useful.

The gospel finds God beautiful.

Religion makes people nice.

The gospel makes people new.

Religion motivates through insecurity and fear.

The gospel motivates through freedom and joy.

Religion drives us to hide in the darkness of fear and self-loathing.

The gospel frees us to come into the light of self-disclosure.

Religion says, "If people really knew me, they wouldn't like me."
The gospel says, "Fully known by God and fully loved by God."

Religion is death.
The gospel is life, peace, and freedom.

Section 3 is a call to implement the lessons of sections 1 and 2. It begins with an honest assessment: Am I on the right road? If not, what does repentance look like? It again asks the question, what steps will I take to escape isolation and come into relational community? It reminds us that our freedom is found only in Jesus. It reminds us that we have life because of the shed blood of Jesus. Above all, section 3 reminds us that the lessons of this book can bring about lasting transformation only if we are motivated by the gospel.

Chapter 13

Where Do We Go from Here?

I always enjoy the question that begins with the words "Where were you when ..." "Where were you when Kennedy was shot?" (Most of you were probably a distant, faint light in your parents' dreams.) "Where were you when Princess Diana was killed?" "Where were you when the Kansas Jayhawks won their fifth national basketball championship?" And one of my all-time favorites, "Where were you when the US Hockey Team defeated the Soviet Union in the 1980 Lake Placid Olympics?" I know exactly where I was. Although I have tried to forget, my memory just will not let this one go.

It was February 21, 1980. Wheaton College was on a break and I decided to head to Boston to visit my brother Kenny and his wife, Cathy, while they studied at Gordon-Conwell Seminary. My parents had plans to be in Boston at this same time, so it seemed like the ideal opportunity to make the trek. There were several other Wheaton students who were also planning to make the trip to Boston, so we decided travel together. We were able to borrow a station wagon (how great was the station wagon! Those were the days!), so we piled seven guys and one girl into the car and headed for Boston. Leaving Wheaton around 9:00 p.m., I took the first driving shift.

Going from Chicago to Boston is not complicated. Essentially, you take I-90 out of Chicago and keep going until you get to Boston.

Did I mention it's not complicated? I drove the tank dry and, around 11:00 p.m., turned the wheel over to my friend Craig (his real name, as I have no desire to protect him in this story!). Craig assured us that he was rested and could drive well into the night. We all went to sleep, and Craig began to drive.

Around 4:00 a.m. (now February 22), Craig woke everyone informing us that we needed gas and he was ready to be relieved. We all stumbled out of the car, and I remember walking past a map on which there was an arrow stating, "You are here." But something didn't quite register. I figured it was because I was exhausted and half-awake, so I gave the map a closer inspection. "Hey, Craig, come over here. Funny thing, but this map says we are in Kalkaska, in northern Michigan."

Craig explained that while there had been a confusing highway cloverleaf, he was 75 percent sure we were on I-90. But in fact we were on Highway 131, close to the Upper Peninsula and very near Canada. For a moment I thought I heard hockey sticks banging in the distance. We were five hours from I-90 and what seemed like a million miles from Boston.

The first problem was we didn't have a map (did I mention you take I-90 East to Boston?) and the gas station didn't sell maps. So we proceeded to steal the "You are here" map (a banner moment in Wheaton College history). Second, we faced a whopper decision. Should we take Highway 131 back to I-90 (which meant that we would have wasted close to ten hours) or take back roads, cut through central Michigan (Highway 127 to Highway 10 to I-75), and hope to make up some time? Our decision for the back roads was a poor one, we discovered after we'd gone too far to turn around.

The rest of the story is not worth telling. Let's just say that we arrived in Boston sometime in late March. Okay, that's a slight exaggeration. On Friday night, February 22, in our twenty-sixth hour of driving, as we encountered a blizzard in New York that we could have avoided had we skipped the Canadian detour, we learned that the United States hockey team had miraculously defeated the Soviet Union, 4-3.

The Map That Corrects

The little arrow on that map was a jolt of reality. "You are here." It could just as easily have read, "You are on the wrong road, idiots!" We were going the wrong direction and we needed to immediately make a radical change. There are many times in life when I need to pause and honestly evaluate, Where am I? What road am I traveling on? Am I traveling the right direction? What do I need to do to get back onto the right road? Is there a shortcut I am tempted to take that will result in short-term relief but long-term consequences?

My guess is that many readers have determined that they need some life changes. Many have prayed that this book would be used of the Lord to reveal areas in our lives that are crying out for immediate attention. Perhaps you have a wide Maturity Gap Index and you are committed to closing the gap by allowing people into the back stage of your life. Perhaps you have a boss and a friend, but you do not have a coach, trainer, mentor, or counselor and you see the need for each of the relationships to be filled.

I know from teaching this material to thousands of pastors over the past fifteen years that, for most, the first step is repentance. You sense a need to repent for believing the lies of Satan that have led you to live an isolated life. Repentance for living a dualistic back stage–front stage life. You realize you must repent for not allowing friends to point out your blind spots. There is a new awareness that you need to repent for not having one or two friends who know all of your secrets. Repentance is unquestionably always the best first step.

First Next Steps: Repentance

It was one of the more memorable conversations of my life. I was standing in the lobby of a Christian college with a dear friend who was suffering through one of the most painful experiences of his life. Approximately twenty years my senior, he was smart, wise, and weathered. He had been through many storms in life, and he had withstood them with patience and grace. And for some reason, tonight was the most difficult. He had recently learned that one of his daughters had suddenly and unexpectedly run away with a much older man. He was grieving the loss of innocence, the loss of relation-ship, and the loss of control. Because I had long respected the man as well as his parenting abilities, and despite the agony of the moment, I gently asked the question I was longing to ask. "In light of what has transpired today, if you could do it all over again, what would you do differently in life?"

He bowed his head, silent for several minutes, before he looked at me with tear-filled eyes and said, "If I had to do it all over again, I would repent more … in front of my children."

Repentance. It is often the first step in a forever journey.

A famous French theologian was asked as he lay on his deathbed, "What will you miss most about this life?" His answer? "Repentance."

Jack Miller, the founder of World Harvest Mission and a man I considered to be a mentor, had an incredible perspective on repentance. I knew that every time I saw Jack, he would make one statement and ask one question. The statement: "Cheer up, Jimmy; you are worse than you think. But you are more deeply loved by Jesus than you will ever comprehend." The question: "What are you repenting of right now?" That's a powerful question that every believer should ask himself or herself every day. What am I repenting of today?

Identifying Genuine Repentance

A young pastor, Mike, called me in the early evening. Through his tears, he told me that his wife had just informed him she was leaving, with no plans to return. He pleaded with me to immediately meet with the two of them. I reluctantly agreed. I had known Mike for close to five years. I knew him as a supremely gifted, intelligent, well-spoken master manipulator. I knew him as someone with a dangerously high Maturity Gap Index. I wasn't surprised that his wife was ready to permanently walk out the door.

As we spoke that evening, the wife calmly, unemotionally explained that she could no longer live with her husband's addiction to pornography and alcohol. She simply couldn't take another day of lies, excuses, and heartache. She was tired of the flirting with other women, his prolonged unexplained absences from the home, and his propensity to ignore his wife while maintaining a commitment to spend time with old college buddies. Furthermore, she was tired of Mike's addiction to work and his need to seek the approval of others. She had pleaded with him over and over again to seek help, but he had refused. She saw no other options. She wanted a divorce.

Mike got down on his knees and literally began to beg. "Please, sweetheart, please," he said over and over again. "I'll change. I am so sorry. I repent. I'll do whatever it takes." I sat by, silently watching the heartbreaking agony of a dissolving marriage. After nearly half an hour of begging, the wife relented. "All right," she said. "I'll give you one more chance. But if your repentance isn't sincere, we are done. *Done!*"

Mike immediately confessed his litany of sins to his board of elders. They acted with grace and did not immediately release him, instead placing him on probation while significantly reducing his pastoral duties. The elders committed to walk with Mike and his wife through the difficult months that lay ahead. The couple immediately started weekly counseling. Mike began attending AA meetings. He installed accountability software on his computer and smartphone and began attending a weekly sexual addiction group. He regularly met with a small group of elders as well as fellow staff.

His wife was cautiously optimistic. Mike frequently expressed repentance and gave glory to God for repairing his damaged marriage. Everyone who knew Mike marveled at his newfound commitment to sobriety, moral purity, and marriage fidelity. Following the three-month probation, Mike was restored to full pastoral responsibilities. The elders spoke openly of Mike's repentance and his rekindled commitment to his marriage and to Jesus. Unquestionably, Mike did change. For about six months.

After six months, Mike was right back in the same rut, only deeper. His wife, true to her word, filed for divorce and moved to Florida to be closer to her parents. Mike's pastoral ministry subsequently came to an end as his addictions erupted in every imaginable manner. What happened?

Expressed repentance and the hatred of the consequences of sin look exactly alike, for a time—and then the paths separate. Over and over again PastorServe has been called into a church crisis in which an overseeing board tells us, "Though the church is wounded, we are on the right path, because we know our pastor has repented of his sins." Our response: "You have no idea if your pastor has repented of his sins, and you won't for some time."

What motivated Mike to temporarily change? He hated the humiliation of losing his marriage, he feared losing his good name in the community, and the thought of losing his job at the church (and the accompanying salary) scared him to death. But his appetite for lust, alcohol, attention, and affirmation had only been temporarily suppressed because Mike never hated the sin; Mike hated the consequences of the sin. Was he sorry? Of course he was sorry. Hard-hitting consequences will produce profound sorrow in the hardest of hearts. But overpowering regret and godly repentance are two very different things.

Repentance and the Glory of Jesus

The greatest model for repentance can be found in Psalm 51, after David has been confronted by Nathan. David pens a psalm of repentance, truth, and trust. Some selected verses from David's heart cry:

> Have mercy on me, O God,
>> according to your steadfast love;
> according to your abundant mercy
>> blot out my transgressions.
> Wash me thoroughly from my iniquity,
>> and cleanse me from my sin!
>
> For I know my transgressions,
>> and my sin is ever before me.
> Against you, you only, have I sinned
>> and done what is evil in your sight,
> so that you may be justified in your words
>> and blameless in your judgment....
>
> Create in me a clean heart, O God,
>> and renew a right spirit within me.
> Cast me not away from your presence,
>> and take not your Holy Spirit from me.
> Restore to me the joy of your salvation,
>> and uphold me with a willing spirit....
>
> The sacrifices of God are a broken spirit;
>> a broken and contrite heart, O God, you will
>>> not despise. (Psalm 51:1–4,
>>> 10–12, 17)

The key to David's repentance can be found in verse 4 when he says, "Against you, you only, have I sinned." Wait a minute. What does he mean by "You only"? What about Uriah, all the men killed along with Uriah, and Bathsheba? Wasn't David's sin against everyone? How can he say that his sin was against God alone? That sounds like he is shirking responsibility! That can't be right. Keep in mind that David isn't writing a doctrinal thesis. He is writing a heartfelt prayer of repentance.

Let's put this in language applicable to you. If you are broken-hearted today over some persistent sin in your life, you say, "Against my wife I have sinned, against my children I have sinned, Lord, against Your church I have sinned, against Your law I have sinned—look at the mess I have made out of my life. I'm going to change! I *have* to change!" If those words express your heart, sadly, I can tell you, you will not change.

Stated another way, if your motivation is *I have to change or else* I am going to lose my wife, my children, or my job. I am going to lose my self-respect, my friends, and my good name in the community. That won't ultimately address your pain, because these are all consequences! Your motivation to repent has to be Jesus! Anything short of genuine godly repentance is counterfeit repentance. If your "repentance" is to bring immediate personal relief rather than lasting glory to God, you are mocking the true purpose of repentance.

You may be terribly sorry for the mess you created and you convince yourself that you will make a lasting change—but you are not repentant! So many believers are desperate for change, but honestly, they only want the consequences to go away. They hate the guilt. They hate the shame. They hate what the sin may do to their future. But deep down, they love the sin.

I hope and pray the Lord has used this book to speak to your heart. I applaud your desire to take next steps. I celebrate your vow to come out of isolation and live in community. I affirm your commitment to the six relationships and the radical difference they can make in the life of a pastor (or any believer). I'm excited about your commitment to narrow your Maturity Gap Index. I support your desire for godly accountability. I affirm your longing to find a pastoral band of brothers or sisters to do life with. But understand this: All of the above can be described as behavior modification if you are doing them to fight the consequences of your sin. If the ultimate motivation is anything other than the glory of Jesus, you will never experience lasting transformational change. You must learn to hate the sin for what it cost God (the blood of His Son, Jesus) and not the painful consequences it brings in your life. Begin by admitting that you have sinned against the Lord: *You, O Lord, You alone have I sinned against.* Only then can there be lasting change.

Be Careful with the Word "Repentance"

PastorServe is regularly asked to work with churches experiencing the fallout of pastoral moral failure. Occasionally, once the dust has cleared, we are asked to coach the pastor (and the church) through a plan of restoration. We very rarely, if ever, use the word *repentance* during the first year of pastoral restoration.

Why do we wait? Because while a pastor may show every conceivable outward mark of repentance, we simply don't know the heart. Only God knows the heart. Am I saying that if the prophet

Nathan had reached out to PastorServe and asked us to restore David to the office of King of Israel, and we had read Psalm 51, that we would have not openly classified David as repentant for a minimum of one year? Yes, that's exactly what I'm saying. And we receive heat from denominations frustrated that we don't wait longer.

At this point, it's necessary to briefly clarify what I mean by "restoration process." The restoration process is generally a minimum of three years (depending on the particular situation). In cases of restoration, PastorServe will always operate within denominational or network guidelines, never trying to work around existing ecclesiastical structures. There are some denominations that, following moral failure, do not allow for any form of pastoral restoration. Other denominations operate under a minimum seven-year waiting period to even begin a formal restoration process. If the church or pastor has no denominational affiliation, we will create the restoration plan. Regardless of the existing church structure, we have found there is no one-size-fits-all plan of restoration. Every situation is unique. A further necessary clarification: At times we are asked to restore a fallen pastor to the position of pastor; other times we are asked to work toward restoring the pastor to vocational Christian ministry (minus pastoral responsibilities). Occasionally we are asked to restore the pastor to meaningful Christian service.

Repentance versus Penance

To many in the American church, repentance means going out and trying harder. That's penance. And all too often, we confuse penance with repentance. While penance can be one aspect of an outward representation of an inward transformation, penance is in no way a sure sign of repentance. Penance comes to church and wants to leave with a list of the things to do that week to appease God's anger. Repentance understands that Jesus is the list. Penance encourages us to leave church thinking about what we need to do. Repentance encourages us to leave church thinking about what Jesus has done. Scripture makes clear that true repentance means we are gripped with the state of our sinfulness and the damage our sin brings primarily to the heart of Jesus. Penance wants to remove the consequences ASAP.

In John 8:1–11, Jesus confronted a woman caught in adultery.

> But Jesus went to the Mount of Olives. Early in the morning he came again to the temple. All the people came to him, and he sat down and taught them. The scribes and the Pharisees brought a woman who had been caught in adultery, and placing her in the midst they said to him, "Teacher, this woman has been caught in the act of adultery. Now in the Law Moses commanded us to stone such women. So what do you say?" This they said to test him, that they might have some charge to bring against him. Jesus bent down and wrote with his finger on the ground. And as they continued to ask him, he stood up and said to them, "Let him who is without sin among you be the first to throw a stone at her." And once more he bent down and wrote on the ground. But when they heard it, they went away one by one, beginning with the older ones, and Jesus was left

alone with the woman standing before him. Jesus
stood up and said to her, "Woman, where are they?
Has no one condemned you?" She said, "No one,
Lord." And Jesus said, "Neither do I condemn you;
go, and from now on sin no more."

Read verse 11 again. The final statement of Jesus is the key to
the story. After the woman reports that her accusers had been struck
silent, did Jesus say, "Forsake your sins and I will condemn you no
more"? No, that's religion. Did Jesus say, "From now on, be really
good and I'll give you another chance"? No, that's a fear of consequences. Jesus said, "Neither do I condemn you; [and as a result,] go,
and from now on sin no more." This is the gospel.

In Psalm 51, the power to repent is found in verse 1: "Have
mercy on me, O God, according to your steadfast love."

The power for repentance, transformation, and deep life change
is the Lord's steadfast, unfailing love. The power to change is not
moralism. Seventeenth-century Puritan pastor Thomas Watson
famously said, "Morality can drown a man as fast as vice. A vessel
may sink full of gold or full of dung."

While speaking at a church-planter breakfast, I heard Pastor Joe
Novenson share a truth with stirring words I have never forgotten.
Speaking of repentance, he said, "The Lord wants to use brokenness to conform us to His image. When God bears the knife, it is
a spiritual scalpel. He bears the knife not to slay me but to perform
surgery. God wants to do deep, lasting, permanent surgery on our
hearts today. Knowing that, when God bears the knife—kiss the
blade and pull it in."

First Next Steps: Believing God Can

Numerous pastors and ministry leaders are in the midst of profound brokenness. Unresolved conflict, financial trials, unforeseen health challenges, marriage difficulties, spiritual emptiness, workplace stress, and the fear of little to no hope for change all contribute to a cloud of hopelessness hanging over one's life. There are countless pastors in the depths of an apparent unresolvable crisis in desperate need of a "But God" moment. For some reading this book, the next step beyond repentance may be to simply believe that God is able. Believe that no matter how dark the night, God can bring the light of transformation.

"But God" moments arrive in those seasons in life when everything seems to be against us. These times are recognized by words such as these: *there is no way my pastorate can be saved; the conflict simply can't be resolved; the prognosis gives zero hope; the church will never recover; his ministry is over.* In these times, only God can reverse the situation. In the midst of indescribable fear, but God …

The Scriptures are filled with stories of "But God" moments.

Noah was convinced he would die on the ark. Yet in Genesis 8:1 we read, "*But God* remembered Noah and all the beasts and all the livestock that were with him in the ark. And God made a wind blow over the earth, and the waters subsided."

Joseph was sold into slavery by his brothers and essentially left for dead. When they learned he was not only alive but also now led Egypt, they assumed they would be put to death. But Genesis 50:20 recounts the words of Joseph to his brothers: "As for you, you meant evil against me, *but God* meant it for good, to bring it about that many people should be kept alive, as they are today."

In Psalm 73:26 we read, "My flesh and my heart may fail, *but God* is the strength of my heart and my portion forever."

Every follower of the Lord Jesus has personally experienced a "But God" moment. Romans 5:8 addresses every believer by stating, "*But God* shows his love for us in that while we were still sinners, Christ died for us."

Likewise, Ephesians 2:4–5 tells believers, "*But God*, being rich in mercy, because of the great love with which he loved us, even when we were dead in our trespasses, made us alive together with Christ—by grace you have been saved."

There are countless pastors in the depths of an apparent unresolvable crisis in desperate need of a "But God" moment.

First Next Steps: Committing to Escape Isolation

For the past several years, my favorite band has been Arcade Fire. When they won Album of the Year at the Grammy Awards, it suddenly became very important to me to tell people that I was an ardent fan when they were a struggling, unknown band.

Arcade Fire is deeply involved in Haiti. When they learned of my involvement in Haiti, they invited me, along with my daughter Megan, back stage after a concert to hang out with the band. I can say firsthand they are incredibly nice people who genuinely have a heart for the people of Haiti as well as a talent for making great music.

The one thing that solidified Arcade Fire as my favorite band was the 2006 song "Intervention." The first time I heard the song, I literally had tears in my eyes. It is not an uplifting song. Rather, it is an incredibly insightful song defining the painful realities of pastoral ministry. ("Working for the church while your family dies … Hear the soldier groan, 'We'll go at it alone.'") I immediately dubbed "Intervention" the PastorServe theme song. I encourage you to purchase the *Neon Bible* album to listen to the entire song. "Working for the church while your family dies" hits dreadfully close to home for scores of pastors. The feeling that you are laboring in a church alone is a reality for many pastors. Pastoring can be lonely, frightening, and destructive.

Statistics confirm the pain of pastoral ministry alluded to in "Intervention." An overwhelming majority of pastors feel as if they are "going it alone" with no true community. Again, an overwhelming majority will leave the pastoral ministry within the first five years, feeling as if they had their "head handed to them in a sling." A majority of pastors report that the pastoral ministry has had a negative effect on their families.

Speaking from one pastor to another, I encourage you to not live an "Intervention" life. I pray that your life is not defined by the words "Hear the soldier groan, 'We'll go at it alone.'" Rather, I pray that your life would be defined by "You'll Never Walk Alone." Don't believe the lies of Satan. God knows everything about you, and He loves you with an endless love. When you allow others into the back stage of your life, they will love you too.

Questions for Reflection

Reality—How do you respond when the map tells you "You are here" and it is not where you thought you were or where you are supposed to be?

Think back over the six different relationships that help a pastor thrive. Is there one relationship that immediately comes to mind as neglected? Is there a relationship you need to pursue immediately?

Rewind and Review—Is there a discrepancy between the back stage of your life and the front stage of your ministry? What in this book has the Lord used to reveal this inconsistency?

How can the acceptance of Christ's work on the cross release you from the need to protect or promote yourself?

Why do you think repentance and penance are so commonly confused in the Christian church? Why do we feel more comfortable believing that simply trying harder can make all the difference?

Reflect—Jack Miller made it a habit to ask people the same question every time he saw them. Most famously, he would ask, "What are you repenting of today?" So, what are you repenting of today?

Can you think of times when you have erroneously labeled a hatred of sin's consequences as repentance? How can you determine the difference between repentance and penance in the future? What does Psalm 51:4 mean when it says that David's sin, and every sin, is ultimately against the Lord?

Can you recall a "But God" moment in your life?

Remember—Psalm 51 reminds us that the Lord's mercy, unfailing love, and great compassion are eternal. How does understanding the love, mercy, and compassion of God help you to repent rather than merely be sorry for the consequences (real or potential)?

Respond—Is God's gospel message to you different than the message you speak to others? Do you believe that God can change lives? Yours? What needs to change in your teaching to more clearly reflect the truth of the gospel?

Do you believe you need others in your life, not only to serve the Lord, but even to live for Him? Is there someone you can talk with about your life and ministry? Is there someone with whom you can share honestly and openly? Is there someone who can listen to you and speak to you? Ask the Lord, who is rich in mercy, to provide a coach, mentor, friend, counselor, trainer, and even a boss—some of the people you need to survive and thrive in ministry.

Chapter 14

Gospel Implications

Undoubtedly, the Holocaust imposed by Nazi Germany is one of the darkest periods of world history. Several years ago I had the opportunity to visit the Dachau concentration camp with my wife, Sally. It was one of the most sobering days of our lives.

If you travel 249 miles to the north of Dachau, you will encounter Buchenwald concentration camp, a death hole constructed in 1937 that trailed only Auschwitz in the horrors it imposed. Despite having no gas chambers, tens of thousands died here from disease, malnutrition, beatings, medical experiments, and executions. The atrocities committed at Buchenwald are largely incomprehensible.

On April 11, 1945, Buchenwald was liberated by American soldiers from the 6th Armored Division, part of the Third Army. US troops stormed the gates of Buchenwald in the late afternoon to find the Nazis had fled only hours earlier. When the American soldiers entered the camp, they found twenty-one thousand starving men and boys tightly stuffed into bunks, piled from floor to ceiling, in barrack after barrack. (One of the young boys was sixteen-year-old Elie Wiesel, who would go on to win the 1986 Nobel Peace Prize for his deeply moving, insightful reflections on the horrors of the Holocaust.) The US troops declared to the captives (in English) that the camp had been liberated and they were now free. Yet not one Jew moved.

The American soldiers began waving their hands and pointing toward the door. They were free! The Nazi captors were gone! And yet, the Jews remained motionless in the barracks. It was later revealed that because those who had come to liberate the captive Jews were strangers in uniforms, they assumed that new faces only meant new oppression. The Jews disbelieved the freedom that was now a reality.

Army Chaplain Rabbi Herschel Schacter was one hour away when he heard the news of the Buchenwald liberation. He immediately commandeered a Jeep and sped toward Buchenwald. He became the first Jewish chaplain to enter the now-liberated concentration camp, but there was no sign of life. "Are there any Jews alive here?" Rabbi Schacter asked a young American lieutenant.

He was led to the Kleine Lager section of Buchenwald, where he observed Jews stacked from floor to ceiling on rough, splintered wooden planks in filthy barracks—who hadn't moved for more than an hour. Though free, they were paralyzed by fear. They lay motionless, gazing with unthinkable trepidation at the rabbi in his unfamiliar military uniform. Then something transformational took place. Rabbi Schacter spoke to them in Yiddish, the language of the Jews. "Shalom Aleichem, Yidden," Rabbi Schacter cried. "Ihr zint frei!"—"Peace to you, Jews. You are free!"

Gradually, the truth of freedom began to sink in. Rabbi Schacter began to run from barracks to barracks, repeating the words of liberating proclamation: "Peace to you, Jews. You are free!" He was joined by a handful of Jews who could walk as they, too, found delight in proclaiming the message of freedom.

Rabbi Schacter would stay in Buchenwald for months, ministering to the freed captives, leading services, and caring for the more than one thousand newly orphaned children. He would later arrange transportation for many of these children to France, a convoy that included the teenage Elie Wiesel.

Freedom in Jesus

Galatians 5:1 reminds us, "For freedom Christ has set us free; stand firm therefore, and do not submit again to a yoke of slavery." The liberation of Buchenwald reminds me of the glorious truth that Christians have been freed from the slavery of sin by the shed blood of Jesus Christ, who stormed the gates of the enemy and liberated His children. Through the application of gospel grace to our enslaved hearts, the Lord Jesus has brought us into the redeeming light of freedom. Paul makes freedom a predominant theme of his letters. He reminds the church that in Jesus they have been set free (Romans 8:1–2), which allows them to live in a perpetual state of freedom (Galatians 5:13) because where the Spirit of the Lord is, there is freedom (2 Corinthians 3:17).

And yet, countless believers remain in bondage to their sin, held captive by fear. For many, the reality of liberation has not resulted in life transformation. The truth of deliverance appears too good to be believed. Fear keeps shackles locked. Shame hides the key. Sadly, many pastors are also held captive by loneliness, secrets, shame, guilt, and fear. While many proclaim the message of liberation and freedom to their congregations, they themselves struggle to believe that the truth of deliverance from bondage can personally apply to them. Pastors, along with every believer, need a daily reminder that in His infinite mercy, Jesus Christ proclaims freedom. His message is bold, "Peace to you, believer; in Me, you are free!"

I have heard the phrase over and over again. "I know that Jesus forgives me, but I simply can't forgive myself." I want to ask them in the kindest, most pastoral voice possible, "Excuse me, but who in the heck do you think you are?" I mean, really! Who are you to place yourself above God? In reality, you are saying, "I know God forgives my sin, but in my rebellion, I refuse to accept that for which Jesus Christ shed His blood on the cross. I refuse to believe that my record of sin has been absorbed by Jesus. I don't believe that I am free."

Daily Set Free by Jesus

For many, the month of April is synonymous with the Masters, the crown jewel of golf's Grand Slam held annually in Augusta, Georgia. I am blessed to have a friend, Roger, who has invited me to attend the Masters as his guest on a number of occasions. I was privileged to be present at the 2005 Masters. That particular year, Tiger Woods won the tournament, highlighted by his incredible slow-rolling chip on 16, which will forever be remembered as one of the greatest golf shots of all time. But I will forever remember the 2005 Masters as the time I finally grasped the lengths that Jesus went to in order that I might be free.

On Thursday, April 7, 2005, Roger and I were sitting in the bleachers of the 16th hole, a 170-yard par 3 protected by a beautiful pond. Throughout the day, we had witnessed several breathtaking shots executed by the greatest players in the world (yes, I know—the greatest of those who have had the opportunity to learn how to play golf).

As the afternoon grew long, we watched as a seventy-three-year-old slowly approached the tee. Winner of three major championships,

Billy Casper had been encouraged by the Augusta members to consider not playing, lest he embarrass himself and the game of golf.
But Masters champions are forever exempted into the field and the
decision was Casper's alone. He hit his first shot—into the water.
The crowd groaned; Casper was the only player that day to hit a shot
into the water. But he was far, *far* from finished. Shoulders slumped,
he retreated to the drop zone and proceeded to hit his third shot
(first shot plus a penalty stroke), once again, into the pond. Casper's
fifth shot—water. The seventh shot—water. The ninth shot—water!
I couldn't believe I was personally watching this meltdown. On his
eleventh shot (5 strokes plus 5 penalty strokes), he finally put the
ball onto the green and three-putted for an embarrassing 14, the
single-worst hole in Masters history! For the day, the 1970 Masters
champion amassed a round of 106, 34 over par, the worst round in
the history of the Masters by a whopping 11 shots. Casper was 21
over on the front nine alone (another record).

But look up Masters history and search for Casper's dubious
records and you will find … nothing. There is no documentation.
No hint of anyone ever shooting over 100, let alone 106. How is this
possible? The answer is quite simple. There is no official record of
the worst round in Masters history because at the conclusion of the
day, the seventy-three-year-old was officially disqualified for failing
to sign his scorecard. When Casper refused to sign his scorecard, it
was as if the dreadful round of golf never happened. It was like he
wasn't even there.

Wouldn't it be great if life were like that? Having a really bad day
at work? At the end of the day, just don't sign your scorecard and it's
like it never transpired. Preach a flop of a sermon? Don't sign that

scorecard and no one will ever know. A great day with the kids? Sign that scorecard; today was a keeper! Moderate a great leadership team meeting? Sign that one! A $200 speeding ticket on the way home? No problem! It's as if it never happened!

I am reminded of two important truths. First, Jesus Christ signs my scorecard with His blood *every day*! All my sins and all my self-righteousness were paid for by Jesus Christ on the cross of Calvary. He does not hold my sins against me. Instead, He graciously grants me a fresh start every day (2 Corinthians 5:17). He encourages me to not dwell on past sins (Isaiah 43:18) but to look forward to His fresh grace (Ezekiel 36:26). Any record of my sins is cast into the deepest sea as God chooses to remember them no more (Psalm 32:1; Jeremiah 31:34). I am daily reminded that God loves me, God cares for me, and God has promised that He will never leave me (Lamentations 3:22–23).

Second, every pastor needs to hear this message—day after day, weekend after weekend. Pastors need to be reminded that the gospel is for *them* as well as their congregation! So many pastors believe the gospel for others but struggle to apply it to themselves. God's Holy Word is as true for pastors as it is for anyone in their church. Like their congregation, pastors must look to Jesus alone for their righteousness, their hope, and their sanctification, knowing that He alone signs their scorecard—every day.

Believing the Gospel

I connected by phone with a pastor of a church in Southern California. He had emailed asking if we could schedule a couple of hours to talk through his exceptionally grim situation. During the course of the call, he expressed that he felt as if the walls were closing in from every side, as he was experiencing deep struggles with his children, his marriage, his church, and his personal belief in the goodness of the Lord. He began by telling me about the heartbreaking situation with his daughter. She had made a series of terrible decisions and had run away to Los Angeles. Multiple times, the pastor told me, he had made the two-hour trip to some of the shadier neighborhoods of LA to look for his daughter. He shed tears as he told me of his love for his daughter and how her sin actually drew him closer to her as he desperately wanted to free her from the bondage of her sinful choices. It was clear that this pastor loved his daughter with an undying, undeterred, unstoppable love. Personally, I was deeply moved by his depth of love for his prodigal daughter.

The phone conversation then turned to serious challenges he was facing in his church, followed by a lengthy exchange about his difficult marriage. As we entered into the latter portion of our second intense hour of conversation, the pastor began to confess his own sin. His voice betrayed severe anguish as he recounted the sins he had committed. And then he said, "I am a pastor, and my life is a mess. I know that because of the depth of my sin, God wants nothing to do with a pitiful person like me. He is pushing me away because I am an embarrassment to Him."

I am generally not one to make statements that could potentially push pastors away (especially when we have never met face to face), but I felt a prompting in my spirit to speak hard words of gospel truth. "So," I said, "what I hear you saying is that you should be nominated for Father of the Year and that as a father, God sucks."

Trust me, "sucks" is not my go-to expression. But it seemed to be the right word!

My assertion was followed by a lengthy, uncomfortable silence. I feared he might hang up. I waited, promising myself I would not be the next one to speak.

"What did you say?" I knew he had heard me, but he was looking for time to process what I had just said. I repeated my statement. Finally, he blurted out, "What are you talking about?"

"Well, about two hours ago you told me the story about your daughter. You mentioned the irony of her sin actually causing you to love her more. You detailed the trips you have made to Los Angeles, pursuing your daughter with a father's undying love. You journeyed into squalid neighborhoods, questionable businesses, and back alleys, all in the loving pursuit of your prodigal daughter. You made clear that despite her sin, you would welcome her home in an instant as a full member of the family. And yet … when it's your sin, it has the exact opposite effect upon your Father. Rather than God pursuing the child He loves, your sin pushes God away. Therefore, I concluded, you should be nominated for Father of the Year and, conversely, God sucks as a father."

The phone went dead silent for close to a minute. (When you're talking on the phone, that's a long time!) Finally, I heard muffled sobs, and then I heard a grown man openly weeping. When, after several minutes, he regained his composure, through his tears he uttered, "I have never thought about that in my entire life."

When I hung up the phone, it was my turn to be overcome, as I found my heart flooded with conflicting emotions. While I was immensely grateful for the opportunity to share a small piece of the truth of the gospel with a brother who desperately needed to hear a word of grace, I was troubled that a pastor leading a congregation had never considered this foundational gospel truth. What was he preaching week after week? Was he telling his congregation that God's love fluctuated week to week depending on the level of our obedience or rebellion? This pastor's back stage behavior was mis-informing his front stage belief. The truth is that our heavenly Father relentlessly pursues His children with an unyielding, never-ending love. Our Father loves us with a love so deep that it takes Him into the back stage of our hardened hearts.

Each of the six relationships reminds us that, ultimately, we need Jesus. Jesus is our Fatherly Loving Boss (Proverbs 3:11–12). Jesus is our Gentle Trainer (2 Timothy 3:16). Jesus is our Inspired Coach (1 Corinthians 9:24–27). Jesus is the Wonderful Counselor (Isaiah 9:6). Jesus is our Eternal Mentor (Proverbs 9:9). And Jesus is our Forever Friend (John 15:15). Every human relationship is a faint reflection of what our heavenly Father has promised.

Sea Glass and the Pain of Growing in Jesus

I don't exactly know how a hobby starts, but I am now an official collector of sea glass.

Recently, I had the incredible privilege of speaking to pastors in Puerto Peñasco, Mexico, which is located at the northernmost tip of the Gulf of California. While the waves crash against the breaker wall during high tide, they are more than 175 yards from the wall during low tide. The massive expanse of beach during low tide creates a prime opportunity to find incredible shells *and sea glass*.

Sea glass is formed when pieces of broken glass from bottles, tableware, or even shipwrecks tumble through the ocean, colliding against rocks and other objects until the sharp edges are smooth and rounded. Because of the salt water, the glass takes on a dull, frosted appearance.

The thought of a once-sharp object tumbling and constantly colliding with other objects until the edges are rounded appeals to me. It reminds me of the Holy Spirit using trials, hardships, and painful difficulties to round the sharp edges on my personality. Throughout my life, the Lord has used stuttering, a crisis of personal faith, the death of both parents, and other seasons of intense pain to round off some of the rough edges of my personality (I say "some" because I am a work in progress). When we encounter painful periods in life, we can submit to the trial as an opportunity for the Lord to shape our personality or we can resist the refining work of the Lord.

Walking that Mexican beach each morning, I found dozens of pieces of sea glass. However, most pieces, while having lost their sharpness, lacked the perfectly smooth edges and frosted appearance. In other words, the glass needed to spend another couple of decades in the ocean to truly smooth its corners.

First Peter 1:7 tells us that these trials have come "so that the tested genuineness of your faith—more precious than gold that perishes though it is tested by fire—may be found to result in praise and glory and honor at the revelation of Jesus Christ." God graciously, kindly, mercifully, continually throws me back into life's stormy seas in order to shape my heart to more closely reflect the person of Jesus. I long to more gladly welcome trials as God's smoothing work in my sharp-edged life.

As I have mentioned, far too many pastors believe one of the primary lies of Satan: that exposing our sharp points is simply too much to risk. "If people really knew all the rough edges on my personality, they wouldn't like me." They guard against relationships that involve access into the messy back stage areas of their lives.

When we believe this lie, we play the happy life game. We approach every day in extreme loneliness. We put a smile on our face and make our way through life in isolation. We dare not risk sharing our life—we certainly don't bring our pain, brokenness, and insecurity into any relationship.

But years of serving pastors have taught me it's not possible to thrive as isolated entities. Sin loves isolation. It's not possible to survive without each other. Or without Jesus. My prayer is that pastors find the confidence to throw themselves back into the ocean of the Lord's mercy—to be shaped by the Holy Spirit and, above all, loved by God Himself.

A Picture of Gospel Grace

There is a billboard near my home that advertises a local senior retirement village with the slogan "Get what you deserve." Each time I pass the billboard, I thank God that I don't receive what I deserve. I am immensely grateful that rather than giving me what I so clearly deserve (punishment), He grants me what I in no way deserve (life in Jesus).

I'm troubled when I hear preachers tell their congregation that God owes them absolutely nothing, and yet, He has offered them the free gift of life in the Lord Jesus Christ. There is so much wrong with that statement, I hardly know where to begin.

First, it is unequivocally untrue that God owes us nothing. Romans 6:23 clearly tells us, along with an abundance of other scriptures, that the consequences of sin is death. Our sin is worthy of eternal punishment. What does God owe us? He owes us eternal damnation, eternal punishment, eternal separation. Those who believe God owes them nothing cannot have the faintest idea of the concept of grace. When God owes us nothing and we receive favor, the farthest we can go by logical definition is to describe God as good and kind.

Second, if we believe God owes us anything other than punishment, we see God as both cruel and evil (because He withholds where favor is deserved). The greatest we can believe about God is that He is just and fair, giving good gifts where they are deserved. This is what the majority of Western culture believes. God wants me to be happy (however I define happiness), and God wants me to enjoy His good gifts (however I define good). Therefore, if I live life in abundance (also known as the American Dream), God is a just, kind, and benevolent grandfather giving me what I so richly deserve.

Finally, if I understand sin to be the ultimate act of treason against the living King of Kings and Lord of Lords, and if I furthermore understand that my rebellion is worthy of immediate and certain death, then God is unescapably fair, just, merciful, and gracious. God can *only* be understood as gracious if we witness the eternal ransom being bought and paid by Jesus Christ as we stand before the heavenly Father as condemned sinners, worthy of eternal death. We can only see the light of grace while standing near the dark shadows of hell. And near the dark shadows of hell, indeed, in hell itself, is where we each deserve to be. Those who do not believe in hell do not believe in grace. If you do not believe in God's eternal punishment, strike the word *grace* from your vocabulary, as you have no right to utter the word.

	WE DESERVE FAVOR FROM GOD	WE DESERVE NOTHING FROM GOD	WE DESERVE PUNISHMENT FROM GOD
WE RECEIVE PUNISHMENT FROM GOD	God is cruel and evil, giving punishment when favor is deserved	God is cruel and evil, giving punishment when nothing is deserved	God is just and fair, giving punishment where punishment is fully deserved
WE RECEIVE NOTHING FROM GOD	God is cruel and evil, withholding His good gifts when favor is deserved	Fairness	Mercy
WE RECEIVE FAVOR FROM GOD	God is just and fair, giving good gifts to those who are so richly deserving	Goodness / kindness	Grace

Jesus Alone Sets Us Free

One gloomy commonality shared by a number of the Nazi concentration camps was a phrase visible for all to see as they entered through the front gates. Look up and there were the words "Arbeit Macht Frei," a German phrase meaning "Work makes you free." Ironically, the gates were made by prisoners with metalwork skills who were, in no sense of the word, free.

The slogan "Work makes you free" first appeared in the title of a 1873 novel by German author Lorenz Diefenbach in which he tells the story of gamblers, thieves, and conmen who eventually find the path to redemption and virtue through labor. The slogan was later adopted by the German Weimar Government as a way to extol the virtue of public works and to decry the scourge of unemployment. It was continued by the Nazi Party when it came to power in 1933.

The one camp gate that did not display the message of work through freedom was Buchenwald, whose gate displayed the phrase "Jedem das Seine," which essentially means "Everyone gets what he deserves."

There could not be two messages more devoid of grace and, subsequently, the gospel message of Jesus. Praise Jesus that I am not freed by my own work but that I am freed by the work of Jesus Christ on the cross of Calvary. Praise Jesus that I do not get what I deserve.

I have encouraged you to do hard work throughout this book. I have laid forth arguments for a boss, trainer, coach, counselor, mentor, and friend. I have asked you to live in community rather than isolation. I have made the case for the curtain of secrecy and shame—which separates the front stage from the back stage—to be removed. But make no mistake; doing all the things set forth in this book will not make you free. The message of this book is not "Work makes you free." The truth is, only Jesus can remove the curtain and only Jesus can redeem, justify, and lead us into a place of sovereign, unmitigated dependence on the Lord. This is true freedom.

Questions for Reflection

Reality—Ultimately, only Jesus entirely fills the role of each of the six key relationships. Share an example of a time when you experienced Jesus fulfilling each of these roles.

- Fatherly Loving Boss
- Gentle Trainer
- Inspired Coach
- Wonderful Counselor
- Eternal Mentor
- Forever Friend

In which of these roles does Jesus tend to manifest Himself to you most often? In which role is it difficult to let Jesus minister to you? Why is that?

Rewind and Review—The Jews in Buchenwald didn't immediately experience the freedom that was theirs. When was the first time you experienced true freedom through Jesus Christ? How old were you? What was going on in your life at the time? What means did God use to help you know about the freedom available to you in Jesus?

At this point in your life and ministry, what helps you to remember that you have been set free through Jesus Christ?

Read Galatians 5:13 and 2 Corinthians 3:17. In what ways have you personally experienced freedom in Christ in your life? What concepts in this book have helped set you free in a new way?

Reflect—The chapter talked about being held captive by loneliness, secrets, shame, guilt, and fear. Which of these five hold captive your heart most often?

Do you find that it is easier to preach the gospel to others than it is to apply it to your own life? Why is it so hard to apply to our own hearts what we so readily apply to others?

What has helped you to keep a firm belief and experience of the gospel in your own life?

Remember—Billy Casper's unsigned scorecard resulted in his horrible game of golf being unrecorded for history. Is there something you've been involved with recently that you wish you could completely remove from all record books? How does Psalm 103:11–12 impact your thinking?

Think of the pastor being overwhelmed by the reality of God's love for him as compared to his own love as a father for his daughter. When was the last time you had a deep, overwhelming sense of God's fatherly love toward you?

Respond—Having read this book, what are a few things you hope to immediately implement into your life from this point on?

Can you think of another pastor or ministry leader who would be helped from some of the principles you've learned in this book? If so, would you consider leading a small group discussion of this book with that pastor and possibly a few others?

Acknowledgments

A huge thank-you to Dan Rich, Ingrid Beck, Alex Field, and the wonderful team at David C Cook for believing in this project. Apart from your vision to serve pastors, there would be no PastorServe Series. Thank you for loving pastors and the local church, in the United States and around the world.

Thank you to my editing team, particularly Jamie Chavez, for their patience with a rookie author who was apparently absent in fifth grade the day they taught writing.

Thanks to Andrew Wolgemuth for being a great friend and agent. I could not have walked this road without your wisdom and guidance.

Thank you to the PastorServe team for encouraging me in the writing of this book. While my name is on the cover, I am well aware that each of you has contributed mightily to the contents of this book. I am grateful to Roy Bilyeu, Jim Wood, Charles Briscoe, Roberto Moreno, Dan Dermyer, Genetta Herrera, Jay Fowler, Wesley Horne, and Wade Brown for the joy you bring me each day as I am allowed to serve shoulder to shoulder with you. In particular, thank you to Jay for the enormous help with chapter questions.

Thank you to the PastorServe board for your support in this project, particularly Justin Moxley, Mark Eaton, and Dave Blue. Huge thanks to Bob Hodgdon, Scott Gulledge, Bruce Pfuetze, and

Doug Hall, the four business leaders who played an enormous role in birthing the ministry of PastorServe.

I'm grateful to Paul Moede, Becky White, and Rob Bentz for helping me revise early editions of the manuscript.

As I wrote, I was reminded of those who have poured their lives into me, serving in the roles of pastor, coach, counselor, and mentor. Thank you to my brother Kenny Dodd, George Wood, Sunday Wesche, Don Steadman, Dick Gorham, Jerry Root, Kent Hughes, John Henderson, Merrill Tenney, Paul Borthwick, Corb Heimburger, Matt Heard, Roger Sandberg, Terry Gyger, Jim Hatch, Harv Powers, and Rick Pierce. You have cared well for my soul.

I am grateful for my pastors at Redeemer Fellowship in Kansas City: Kevin Cawley, Kris McGee, Wes Crawford, Adam Breckenridge, and Matt Marasco. Thank you for pastoring me and my family well.

Thank you to counselors and friends Elizabeth George and Rick Pierce for your assistance on the counseling section. Thanks to Spencer Kerley for your lifetime friendship and your expertise relating to any medical references in the book.

A big thank-you to my dear friends and partners at Nehemiah 3. This journey has largely been made possible because of your generosity.

A heartfelt thank-you to Gary Ascanio, my most faithful prayer partner who likely has more to do with the publication of this book than anyone. Please don't stop praying Gary!

I am incredibly grateful to my parents for instilling within me a spirit of service and generosity that planted the seeds of PastorServe in my heart long ago. I'm sad you aren't able to see the completion of this book, but I trust you are smiling in heaven.

There are not adequate words to say thank you to my wife, Sally, for her incredible love, support, and encouragement over these past thirty-four years. I could not have asked for a better friend, partner, and spouse. This book is as much hers as it is mine.

Thank you to my family for their love and support. To Mark, Holly, and my granddaughter Ivy, Megan, Sarah, Paige, and Allie. You have provided me great joy and abundant laughter in the midst of life's journey.

Finally, I am supremely grateful to the Lord Jesus, my Great God, Savior, and King. Your love for a broken person like me causes me to stand in wonder before Your throne of grace. I pray this book glorifies Your name, advances Your kingdom agenda, and blesses the church and those whom You have called to lead. *Soli Deo gloria.*

Notes

Chapter 5: Paul's Thorn and Charlie's Angels

1. You'll find this attributed to Oswald Chambers all over the Internet, and in fact, I have used this quote for years. But neither my editor nor I were able to locate the original source material, and one of us remains unconvinced about its attribution to Chambers.

Chapter 9: Hey, Coach! Put Me In!

1. Ray Williams, "Why Every CEO Needs a Coach," *Psychology Today* (blog), August 13, 2012, accessed June 16, 2015, www.psychologytoday.com /blog/wired-success/201208/why-every-ceo-needs-coach.

2. "What Business Leaders and the Media Have to Say about the Power of Coaching," In Alignment, accessed June 4, 2015, thealignedcareer.com /quotes-about-coaching/.

Chapter 10: Counselor: Scrubbing the Wound

1. J. R. R. Tolkien, *The Return of the King* (New York: Del Rey, 1994), 290, 333.

2. Mother Teresa, *Come Be My Light: The Private Writings of the Saint of Calcutta*, ed. Brian Kolodiejchuk (New York: Doubleday, 2007), 187, 192–93.

3. C. S. Lewis, *The Four Loves* (Orlando: Harcourt Books, 1988), 121.

Chapter 12: Every Pastor Needs a Friend

1. C. S. Lewis, *The Four Loves* (Orlando: Harcourt Books, 1988), 61.

2. Lewis, *Four Loves*, 121.

About the Author

Jimmy Dodd is founder and president of PastorServe. A graduate of Wheaton College (BA) and Gordon-Conwell Theological Seminary (MDiv), he pastored in Chicago, Boston, Greenville (South Carolina), Kansas City, and Colorado Springs, where he served for ten years on the teaching team of Woodmen Valley Chapel. A well-known speaker, Jimmy has had the privilege of making more than 125 trips to train leaders in third world countries. In 2000, he helped launch Cross International, a ministry devoted to serving the poorest of the poor. Jimmy and his wife, Sally, have five children, one daughter-in-law, and one granddaughter. Two of their daughters were adopted from China. In his spare time, Jimmy can be found with his family, walking Murphy the dog, or at Allen Fieldhouse in Lawrence, Kansas, cheering on his beloved Jayhawks.

About PastorServe

In an effort to help the church reach its full redemptive potential, PastorServe works across denominational lines to support, encourage, train, equip, coach, and consult with pastors across the country. Founded in 1999, PastorServe has been recognized as one of the leading organizations helping pastors and churches navigate the challenges they face—during seasons of crisis and noncrisis. PastorServe would be honored to journey with you in safe and confidential ways.

You can learn more about PastorServe by visiting their website at www.pastorserve.org.

PastorServe encourages you to pray for your pastor. A daily text reminder can be received by texting the word *pastor* to 74574.

PastorServe ... Because Every Pastor Needs a Pastor

The PastorServe Series is dedicated to producing grace-centered, timeless books for pastors, ministry leaders, and church leadership ministering in a variety of settings around the world. These books expose and address critical issues in pastoral ministry with an emphasis on the relentless love of Jesus. The series focuses on both the front stage and the back stage of pastoral ministry in order to help readers bring their entire lives into alignment with the gospel of Jesus Christ.